GREEN
MORALITY

Mankind's Role in Environmental Responsibility

Edward Flattau

The Way Things Are Publications
Los Angeles

ABOUT THE AUTHOR

Edward Flattau has been the only nationally syndicated environmental newspaper columnist regularly publishing twice-weekly commentary since 1972. His prize-winning column first appeared in June of that year when he took over the assignment from the late former Interior Secretary Stewart Udall. Udall had started the column on the nation's first Earth Day in 1970 out of concern about the void of environmental commentary in American newspapers.

Flattau has written more than 3700 columns on pivotal environmentally related events and personalities from his Washington, D.C. base and around the country, as well as from Europe, Asia, Africa, and South America. His work has appeared regularly in as many as 120 daily newspapers over the years, and he is the recipient of ten national journalism awards.

Flattau was born in New York City and graduated in 1958 from Brown University, where he played basketball and was captain of the varsity tennis team. He attended Columbia Law School, and prior to writing the column worked as a political correspondent for United Press International in Albany, N.Y. and Washington, D.C.

Flattau is married and the father of two children. *Green Morality* is his fourth book.

ALSO BY EDWARD FLATTAU

Evolution of a Columnist: The 40-Year Journey of America's Senior Nationally Syndicated Journalist

Peering Through the Bushes

Tracking the Charlatans: An Environmental Columnist's Refutational Handbook for the Propaganda Wars

GREEN
MORALITY

1ST EDITION

Published by The Way Things Are Publications, Los Angeles.

Jacket design by Pacific Coast Creative, © 2011.
Jacket photography: © 2007 J. Sullivan/Getty Images.

Preface by William A. Butler.

Photograph credits appear on page 291.

ISBN-10: 0-9821419-2-0
ISBN-13: 978-0-9821419-2-2
LCCN: 2010926594
UPC: 9-780982-141922-8

Includes index, references, and illustrations.

Edited by Jennifer Havenner and Angela Hooper.
Index by Becky Hornyak.

http://www.edflattau.com
http://www.waythingsarepublications.com

The Way Things Are Publications
11664 National Blvd
#401
Los Angeles, CA 90064

Printed on acid free paper. Meets all ANSI standards for archival quality paper.

Columns by Edward Flattau are syndicated by:
Global Horizons
1330 New Hampshire Avenue NW
Suite 609
Washington, DC 20036

Dedicated to the late Albert Van Nostrand, former chairman of the English Department at Brown University, who was a cherished mentor to me both in my formative years and professional life.

PREFACE

—

PREFACE

—

FOR ALMOST 40 YEARS, Ed Flattau has written more than 3,700 syndicated newspaper columns on environmentally-related crises and personalities in the United States and abroad. From his viewpoint, well established solutions have been largely neglected. As a consequence, his frustration has boiled over in his new book, and the residue is very strong medicine.

Failure to heed clarion calls for environmental awareness and action on the part of world leaders has led him to see them as not only wrong, but also immoral in their failure to take the fate of future generations into account. Ever-growing scientific evidence of environmental perils is frequently downplayed or even ignored in official circles and among the general public. Strong charges, but a *cri de coeur* to the world to recognize its danger before it is too late.

Ignorance and alleged scientific uncertainty are no longer credible excuses for the failure of leadership on all levels to act on humanity's ultimate critical question: survival.

Ed is unsparing in criticizing leaders across political, economic, and even religious spectrums who have failed to recognize and act on evermore clear evidence as to environmental damage. Too frequently, opportunities have been squandered by leaders' focus on perceived short-term benefits of environmental inaction, which in reality produce terrible long-term costs. The torrent of his litany of supporting examples is devastating. His targets are as varied as the Vatican and former Vice President and Nobel Prize winner Al Gore. President Bush comes in for special criticism for his failure in eight years to exercise environmental leadership.

Ed has written a biting polemic, yet he retains his optimism that it is not too late for us to reverse course. He remains moderately hopeful and offers positive examples in the last few years to illustrate that at least some leaders are finally awakening to our environmental threats and are willing to act to prevent them, even at personal and professional cost.

This book is a diesel horn wake-up call to startle us out of our inertia and to recognize that quick and decisive action by world leaders on environmental problems is the only realistic approach. The longer we wait, the more costly will be mitigation, if feasible at all. Ed has only disdain for those who believe in salvation from mankind's neglect solely through future technological fixes. He disputes the claim that nature has the capacity to heal itself within an acceptable time frame from mankind's most grievous wounds. We have the necessary answers to act now, and lack only sufficient leaders courageous enough to educate the public on the moral as well as practical imperative of administering cures that may at first be painful. Not to do so demonstrates lack of respect for nature, and human hubris about our mastery of it. It also constitutes what Ed feels is an immoral betrayal of public trust by leaders in all walks of life, intent on telling the public all is well on their watch, and ignoring increasingly insistent warnings that icebergs lie ahead.

In addition to many examples of cowardice (and some of courage) in confronting the challenges posed by environmental degradation, Ed scrutinizes the degree of honesty on the part of government, the private sector, and individuals in articulating the extent of environmental problems and how to solve them. He also offers copious examples of persons of authority who either betray or uphold the special trust placed in them in making environmentally-related decisions. He reviews what he feels needs to be done to establish what he calls a sustainable relationship with the biosphere and expresses his belief that goal can be achieved in time to prevent irreversible decline, if we act now.

Some books are written as measured treatises, cautious in avoiding any obvious bias in discussing environmental problems, their severity, and their potential solutions. This is not such a book. It is a frontal assault, challenging readers to think and act. While it will no doubt infuriate some and reinforce the views of others, Ed's intent is neither. It is to speak to the oblivious and unconcerned public, and to galvanize them to demand active leadership on the questions he raises. He dares refutation of his conclusions based on 40 years of close attention to environmental trends. Much is made of the world's, and particularly America's, lack of real concern about present and future environmental threats to life as we know it.

This is not a bedtime book, but it is a critically important one.

William A. Butler
Adjunct Professor
Environmental Law
Georgetown University
Washington DC
January 2010

INTRODUCTION

—

MOST OF US WOULD CONSIDER environmental protection fundamental to survival and, by logical extension, a moral imperative. Yet all too often we behave with reckless abandon in our interactions with the environment, leaving many victims in our wake.

The dictionary defines morality as conformity to established sanctioned codes of conduct, or put another way, adherence to accepted societal notions of right and wrong. But morality can be relative, given the variability of cultural norms between and even within nations. Take overindulgence as an example. We tend to condemn it as sinful. Yet the amount of material wealth we accumulate is all too often perceived as the measure of our stature.

Besides making allowances for the sometimes arbitrary nature of morality, this writer will not dwell on misdeeds whose injury is limited to the perpetrator (unless the offender is society itself, in which case many innocent people are impacted). Nor will more than passing mention be given to questionable "eco" behavior prior to the advent of the modern environmental era in 1970. For the purposes of this book, the examination of morality will be confined to instances of human interaction with the environment where the effects—beneficial or detrimental—extend well beyond the originating parties.

Back to the notion of "conformity." If they are clever enough, people can superficially embrace moral values and get away with the deception for a very long time. A favorite ploy is to use righteous-sounding rhetoric to camouflage questionable objectives that almost always end up to the detriment of society.

Ignorance is not Bliss

An innocence stemming from unawareness may conceivably be a legitimate excuse for fouling the environment. But such an excuse nowadays should be closely scrutinized, given modern electronic communication of a wealth of information identifying problems and remedies. Even if the claim that the abuse was committed unwittingly has some credence, the plea of ignorance cannot be sustained for long when corrective measures are public knowledge. To put it charitably, ignorance is no excuse when there is no excuse for being ignorant. That being the case, failure of a modern-day wrongdoer to at least make an attempt at prompt restitution once environmental damage has been exposed creates a *prima facie* case of willful neglect.

Fishermen on the Hook

Are fishermen who—out of desperation to support their families—harvest a stressed commercial species to the verge of extinction guilty of willful neglect? One can understand the urgency they feel, but cannot condone their conscious eradication of a vital renewable resource. An obligation exists to preserve that resource for future generations. Still, when daily survival is an issue, the besieged fishermen cannot be expected to desist solely on the basis of society's interests and their own self-restraint. Whether we like it or not, it is human nature for the survival instinct to trump morality if the two should come into direct conflict. Fortunately, they tend to be symbiotic, other than in the direst of circumstances. The rule of law is really nothing more than the collective need for survival imbedded in an ethical framework defined by mutual respect and cooperation.

Fishermen should thus receive help from official circles through government subsidies and job training to tide them over while depleted marine species recover. Also required of authorities is a strictly enforced moratorium that speeds sea life's resurgence.

Unfortunately, governments often fail to fulfill their moral obligation to assist beleaguered fishermen. Officials' reluctance to spend national treasure to subsidize alternative employment for an industry in distress is sometimes attributable to lining their own pockets. It may also be politically more expedient in the short term to accede to panicked fishermen's nihilistic pleas and let future leaders shoulder the blame for the empty seas.

What is the result of ignoring the warning signs of depleted marine species' loss of regenerative capacity? A 2007 United Nations survey found that 52 percent of the world's commercial fisheries were fully exploited and another 25 percent were well on their way to being so. Out in the open ocean, beyond any one nation's jurisdiction, UN researchers reported that deep-sea trawlers, using massive nets for bottom fishing, were wiping out the stocks of Atlantic Cod, halibut, blue fin tuna, and sharks, along with non-target species. Government subsidies were often made available to these trawlers, which were operated by large, politically well-connected outfits (as opposed to the little guys). Eliminate these irresponsible subsidies of more than $20 billion annually, and the environmentally unsustainable practice of indiscriminant bottom fishing would diminish, allowing hard-pressed species to rebound.[1]

Technological Copout

Some people are aware they are wreaking havoc on the environment but convince themselves they will be bailed out by technology. They choose to ignore the fact that human beings have had little success in restoring natural systems to their original state. There isn't any absolution for them when common sense alone dictates that no "technological fix" is likely to rejuvenate degraded air, water, or land on a massive scale.

For example, try as we might, we have been unable to duplicate the original wetlands' rich biodiversity that has been lost in the course of human activity.[2] That's why creation of new wetlands to offset the deliberate destruction of indigenous ones is a Faustian bargain. It is not a complete write-off, but the end product is decidedly inferior, and that is why there should be a permanent moratorium on development of our nation's irreplaceable virgin wetlands, more than half of which have already been destroyed.

Porous Barriers

No amount of engineering and sand replenishment can do more than temporarily delay the tide-driven migration of barrier island beaches towards the mainland. Given their natural dynamic character, these aesthetically spectacular barrier islands should be places to visit, not sites to be permanently settled. Where there is no development on such islands, laws should be enacted to keep it that way. Where ill-advised development has been allowed to occur, homeowners should suffer the inevitable wrath of nature at their own expense. They should have known it was only a matter of time before their barrier islands' naked exposure to the sea would invite a punishing blow. It is grossly unfair to ask society to endlessly subsidize foolhardy individuals' repeated property losses as a result of a stubborn—and futile—defiance of the elements. If Mother Nature were allowed to run her course on the barriers without island residents' access to artificially cheap federal flood insurance and subsidized beach replenishment, even the most affluent inhabitants would eventually beat a retreat. And when they did, the unstable landmasses would resume their inexorable advance towards the mainland at a natural pace.[3] Should any government subsidies be made available, they should go to vulnerably situated beach dwellers willing to relocate inland rather than repeatedly rebuild their storm-shattered houses in the same place. As for vulnerable beaches that are the economic base of tourist communities, visitors and town people alike should be charged beach user fees to cover the bulk of the endless cost of sand replenishment. That is a far more equitable alternative than imposing the entire open-ended burden on taxpayers across the country, most of whom will never receive any of the benefits while having valuable revenues diverted from vital national social and environmental programs.

Chill Out

If environmental offenders don't invoke technology as a panacea for their malfeasance, chances are they will maintain that their destructive activities are grossly exaggerated and fleeting in impact. Be leery of such rationalizations, which are rarely accompanied by scientific verification, and are far more likely to stem from calculated expedience than genuine conviction.

Should the preceding dismissive explanations fail to exculpate them, polluters fall back on the notion that the environment is far more resilient to human perturbations than people realize. This claim is usually nothing more than a specious attempt at self-vindication. Humanity is quite capable of inflicting long-term environmental devastation and has an unenviable record of doing so. A dramatic case in point is the Middle East's ancient desert agriculture. Much of it was laid bare by unsustainable farming practices in biblical times and has yet to recover. Nature's resiliency clearly has its limits.

How do those who know quite well they are giving false assurances remain upbeat about their own future? At least some believe their wealth will shield them from any adverse environmental consequences. You'd think they'd be smart enough to realize that all the money in the world cannot shield them from the deterioration of Earth's life-support system. Then again, greed is such a powerful emotion that any fleeting misgivings are often repressed through denial of reality.

Slow Learners

Any lessons derived from environmental destruction committed decades ago often seem to have little effect in preventing a repeat of the same mistakes. Such failure is galling, given that the means for averting such mistakes were common knowledge way back then. Perhaps the lack of urgency can be attributed to the fact that environmental damage often increases in imperceptible increments.

When public inertia occurs in dealing with serious environmental concerns, two scenarios immediately come to mind. Either a political leader is courageous enough to step forward and risk career advancement by asking people to go out of their way to address problems not yet at a visibly crisis stage; or we let things slide until an environmental catastrophe jolts us belatedly into action—hopefully before the damage has become irreversible.

From an economic as well as a moral and an environmental standpoint, waiting for the other shoe to drop is unconscionable (and untenable), especially in the case of climate change. The Tufts University's Global Development and Environment Institute cited a projected $12-trillion-a-year hit to the world's economy from global warming and said that such a catastrophe could be avoided by taking conservation measures amounting to one-fourth that cost.[4] In another economic analysis, researchers estimated that failure to take sufficient remedial action against climate change would reduce global gross domestic product (GGDP) anywhere from five to 20 percent.[5] Conversely, if appropriate measures were implemented, GGDP would suffer only a one percent loss and greenhouse gas emissions would be substantially reduced.[6]

No Rest for the Weary

Even when we get things right and stave off ecological disaster as in the international treaty to close up the stratospheric ozone hole, we have been slow to acknowledge the necessity for eternal vigilance. Victory is always subject to reversal in environmental controversies, while defeat can be final for all practical purposes—witness my earlier reference to humans' inability to restore disturbed wetlands to their original biologically productive state.

How this Book is Organized

Considering that the issues dealt with in the book are complex, the same event can be, and sometimes is, used to illustrate different concepts. For example, the manmade destruction of coastal wetlands serves to demonstrate three important points: the lack of respect for nature; human hubris; and the betrayal of public trust by politicians in league with unscrupulous developers.

Regarding the book's structure, Section One addresses the respect, or lack thereof, that human beings display towards the world around them and each other when it comes to preserving environmental quality. Section Two is a reflection on whether nature is humane or malevolent. Section Three explores our capacity for compassion in interactions with other human beings as well as with lower life forms, and Section Four assays courage and cowardice in confronting the challenges posed by environmental degradation.

Section Five scrutinizes the degree of honesty on the part of government, the private sector, and individuals in articulating the extent of environmental problems and how to solve them. Section Six pertains to humility and hubris in our treatment of fellow humans and the surrounding environment. Section Seven examines persons in authority and/or possessing specific responsibilities who either uphold the special trust placed in them or betray it in the course of their environmentally related duties. In Section Eight, the discussion revolves around people rising to the environmental challenge with extraordinary resourcefulness and tenacity or, conversely, throwing in the towel in an exercise of willful neglect. Section Nine reviews what needs to be done to establish a harmonious, sustainable relationship with the biosphere, and whether that lofty goal can be achieved in time to prevent irreversible decline.

Edward Flattau
January 2010

SECTION ONE
—
RESPECT

CHAPTER ONE

—

TAMPERING WITH NATURE

A BASIC PREMISE of this book is that human beings have a moral obligation to preserve the Earth's biological life-support system, not just for each other, but also for future generations. Failure to maintain a harmonious relationship with natural systems will ultimately jeopardize the quality, and in some instances the quantity, of the air we breathe, the water we drink, and the crops we eat.

People were not cognizant of such profound challenges—and behavioral limitations—in our nation's pioneer days when a frontier mentality held sway. The United States' abundant natural resources seemed infinite, and when settlers stripped a plot of land of its natural wealth, they simply pulled up stakes and moved on to new pastures over the next rise.

A more sobering perception of our resource base began to emerge in the middle of the 20th century when agricultural overuse contributed to the massive erosion that led to the "Dust Bowl" in our western plains. Modern industrial activity was polluting our air and water. The realization slowly dawned that our natural wealth was finite and could be squandered if not utilized in sustainable fashion. An "environmentality" was born.

This new reality inspired philosophers such as the renowned British economist E.F. Schumacher, to challenge traditional thinking. In the 1970s, he stressed in his book, *Small is Beautiful*, that we were not entities distinct from the natural world but integral components of it. From his perspective, it was crucial to synchronize our actions with the ebbs and flows of nature if we wished to avoid self-destructive behavior.

How does morality play into that equation? Living in harmony with nature automatically infuses human existence with moral purpose, for nature's essential function is to perpetuate life, and by osmosis, its noble cause becomes ours as well.

Besides the obvious obligation to preserve a livable world for future generations, there is another basic answer: morality for morality's sake. An exposition of that principle can be found in the *Encyclopedia of Earth*, which includes a passage that reads, "Humans and non-humans proliferate in a shared moral system wherein environmental issues are first and foremost ethical concerns; and nature has intrinsic as well as extrinsic values."

Yet we don't always follow this wise counsel. When emergency legislation to protect healthy wild horses from being slaughtered *en masse* was brought to the floor of Congress in July of 2009, some Republican lawmakers attempted to frame the issue as a choice between equine and human survival.

"Instead of spending millions to restore American mustangs," declared Rep. Doc Hastings, R-Wash., "let's restore American jobs and put the horsepower back into our economy."

In response to Hastings, Rep. Nick Rahall, D-W.Va., restored some sanity to the debate. "We can address unemployment and other aspects of the economy without sacrificing the nation's wild horses," he said.

Lord help us if we can't. Our future quality of life depends on co-existence with the world around us. Designating wholesale slaughter of wild horses (or any other species for that matter) as a *quid pro quo* for jumpstarting our economy is a transaction we cannot afford in either a moral or practical sense. Thankfully, a majority of Congress ultimately agreed.

A Delicate Balance

Interacting with nature without disrupting her fundamental equilibrium is easier said than done. Modification of our surroundings to further our interests may be initiated with the best of intentions, but if it strays beyond the boundaries set by natural processes, the consequences can be devastating. For instance, razing stands of timber to create farmland can work only as long as rows of trees are retained as wind breaks to prevent soil erosion.

Other tried and true examples of success include reforestation of flattened timberland, which almost always produces major dividends through such benefits as improved air quality and biodiversity. Indeed, fruitful attempts at resurrecting some degraded aspect of the environment are optimal exercises in sustainability. A classic example: restocking a body of water with a native species of fish that had been wiped out by human harvest.

The vulnerable Asian country of Bangladesh is seeking to modify Mother Nature on a massive scale by shaping her to work more on its behalf. Silt carried from the Himalayas by seasonal floods is being diverted to build up the coastal nation's sediment-starved, low-lying flatlands to protect against climate-change-induced rising sea level.[1]

One of the purest forms of harmonization with nature is manifested in structures designed to take advantage of the light and heat of the sun, a technique that contemporary architects have labeled "passive solar." Yet passive solar is not a modern phenomenon. Positioning structures to

Bangladesh—Harnessing the flood

Nauru: Beauty before the (human) storm.

exploit the angle of the sun was commonplace and common sense among our forefathers, who had no recourse to electric heating, air-conditioning, and specially insulated windows. There was no environmental movement back then; necessity was the mother of invention.

Today, necessity is making a comeback. Passive solar is being revived with verve thanks to the global warming menace, escalating energy prices, and a morally responsible vision of the future. German architects, for example, have designed tightly insulated solar-heated houses that fully function without a furnace and have attracted attention in the markets of other nations, including our own.

When Things Go Awry

The short and turbulent life of Caprice, an Alabama barrier island, provides a graphic warning to coastal dwellers rash enough to thumb their noses at nature. Caprice was formed in 1917 by a tide-driven convergence of sand bars in the Gulf of Mexico, and it succumbed to those same currents a mere 15 years later. In the interim, people were foolhardy (and greedy) enough to erect a casino and other tourist facilities on the fragile sand spit. By 1932, Caprice was virtually gone because of tidal erosion, and in the ensuing years, it completely slid beneath the waves, dragging some expensive real estate with it.[2]

The plight of Nauru, a tiny and little-known South Pacific island nation, is an equally dramatic example of mind-numbingly poor judgment in managing the surrounding environment. Only 21 square kilometers, with a population of 12,000, Nauru had the second highest per capita income in the world in the 1970s. Its wealth stemmed from the discovery of rich phosphate deposits that were extracted indiscriminately for export until most of the island resembled an open mine pit. What little tourism existed steadily vanished along with the phosphate. Nauru went bankrupt, its port became deserted, and electricity was suspended for a good part of the day. The nation barely survived as a detention center for asylum seekers from Afghanistan and Iraq hoping to relocate to Australia.[3] Here was an instance where human beings managed to parlay material self-indulgence into material ruin—an unconscionable dereliction of collective responsibility.

On a larger environmental stage, the Caribbean island nation of Haiti offers a grim preview of what awaits the rest of the world if it continues to neglect natural-resource conservation. Haiti has seen its population explode and strip the land virtually bare of tree cover (only 3 percent remains) in order to harvest charcoal for cooking and heating. The hillsides of this mountainous island nation have been exhaustively farmed and then abandoned. Deprived of crops and/or original vegetation to hold the topsoil in place, the thin layer of dirt has been washed into the sea by tropical torrential rains. Today, much of Haiti resembles a moonscape and

Haiti: Misery on top of misery.

is highly susceptible to catastrophic flooding. Poverty and malnutrition are endemic; the implementation of sufficient reforestation and other sustainable strategies to turn things around remains a daunting task. The futile, historically corrupt Haitian government has betrayed its people by tolerating, and in some cases participating in, unsustainable practices that have brought the nation to its proverbial (and some would argue literal) knees.[4] If that dismal state of affairs weren't disheartening enough, Haiti was struck on January 12, 2010 by a catastrophic 7.0 earthquake that virtually leveled the capital of Port-au-Prince, killing hundreds of thousands of people and leaving the country's bare bones-to-begin-with infrastructure in shambles. For the foreseeable future, the long-suffering nation will literally have to lift itself out of its own ashes.

Coastal Mischief

In our own country, the government has also been complicit in shoreline mismanagement, albeit as yet without the dramatic environmental deterioration that plagues Haiti. As was previously noted, many coastal dwellers residing in areas particularly vulnerable to major storms have routinely received subsidies from Washington for the repeated restoration of demolished buildings and eroded beaches. Apart from encouraging reckless behavior, the federal government's ill-advised largesse in funding a losing battle against the elements has diverted sorely needed resources from some vital domestic social programs.

If that weren't deplorable enough, some coastal beneficiaries of taxpayers' open-ended generosity have had the gall to bar public access to beachfronts restored with "trespassers'" dollars.

Should any government subsidies at all be made available, they ought to go to beach dwellers willing to relocate from sensitive, flood-prone coastal areas to more secure sites further inland. Especially vulnerable beaches should be destinations for recreational day-trippers, not sites of permanent residences.

Another abuse of the coastal environment involves the conversion of many of our beaches into thoroughfares for dune buggies and even conventional vehicles. That aesthetic desecration, in which beaches end up looking like glorified parking lots, is just one aspect of the despoliation. Dunes that stabilize the beach to keep it from disappearing altogether, as well as marine organisms living in the inter-tidal zone, have been crushed under the wheels of errant vehicles. Even a snoozing sunbather has on occasion been a casualty.

Construction of jetties, breakwaters, and sea walls to curb beach erosion interrupt the natural dispersal patterns of incoming tidal sediment. The artificial barriers obstruct normal sand buildup and divert the fill away from adjacent beaches, resulting in a classic case of "Robbing Peter to pay

Paul." If you are going to fiddle with tidal inflows, you better have a well thought-out plan that mitigates negative impacts, and you better have cleared the operation with your neighbors all along the coast.

To save our shorelines and leave them in better shape than we found them, we need to pay greater heed to the National Academy of Sciences. It recently produced a study making a strong case for the restoration (and preservation) of coastal marshes and dunes that provide natural, mitigating defenses against severe storm surge.

Wetlands perform other vital functions besides flood control. At the top of the list are water purification, water storage, and the creation of ideal habitats for fish hatcheries. If morality were defined in terms of dollars and cents, how guilty would one be who paved over an acre of original wetlands estimated to be worth—depending on location—anywhere from $25,000 to $150,000 or even more? The value of the world's wetlands is pegged at nearly $15 trillion, yet the United States has allowed half of its original supply of this regenerative ecological treasure trove to be drained, dredged, and drilled for developmental purposes.[5] In the process, Americans have compromised the resource needs of future generations—and quite possibly the requirements of their own.

There has been no more egregious act of mindless coastal desecration in modern times than the destruction of mangrove forests along the coasts of Indonesia, Sri Lanka, and Myanmar. Eradicated to clear the way for tourism, shrimp farms, and other commercial development, these tropical maritime trees had served as a barrier capable of abating the fury of nature. Without this line of protection, the 2007 tsunami that scored a direct hit on Indian Ocean nations and the 2008 cyclone that struck Myanmar both took a far heavier toll in lives and property than would otherwise have occurred. The Asian governments were blinded to environmental reality by mercenary enticements.

Not Getting it Straight

Channelization is the Army Corps of Engineers' *modus operandi* for straightening out the natural meanderings of rivers and streams to expedite navigation and create more adjacent farmland. It may seem like a good idea at first glance, but significant drawbacks soon emerge. Transforming a stream into an artificial channel makes the current run faster and the water rise higher, which in turn intensifies flooding and sedimentation downstream in periods of heavy downpours. The fast-moving flow destabilizes riverbanks, precipitating erosion. Flooding is exacerbated by channelization's destruction of riparian wetlands that serve as natural sponges, absorbing excess rainfall. Diminished wildlife habitat and increased pesticide runoff also result from wetland loss.

A dramatic example of belated recognition of channelization's drawbacks has been the federal and state decision to order the U.S. Army Corps of Engineers to restore the natural curvature of Florida's Kissimmee River. The Kissimmee feeds Lake Okeechobee, which in turn funnels crucial water supplies to the Everglades National Park.

Despite recognition of the drawbacks of its original work on the Kissimmee River, the Corps has continued channelization on similar projects. Why the intractability? Such steps have been taken at the insistence of congressional allies of politically influential shipping and agro-business magnates far more concerned about short-term profits than long-term, adverse environmental impacts.

Ignorance is No Excuse

Unwittingly damaging the environment may warrant some tolerance if there is a reasonable explanation for pleading ignorance. For example, it may well be that the first wave of cattle ranchers and migrant farmers to clear wide swathes of the Amazonian jungle had no inkling of how biologically rich yet fragile the tropical rainforest was, and were unaware of how poor the soil was underneath the timber they were razing.[6] Nor is it likely they were well versed on the important, climate-regulatory functions of the greenhouse-gas-absorbing jungle they were leveling.

But there is always a statute of limitations on acceptance of ignorance as a legitimate excuse, and it grows ever shorter. Brazilian authorities now responsible for overseeing the irreplaceable natural assets of the world's mightiest rainforest know the Amazon's vital role in the ecological scheme of things full well. Hence, they have no excuse for allowing the environmental carnage that has persisted at the hands of ecologically insensitive entrepreneurs.

It should be noted that Brazil has no monopoly on shoddy forest management. Despite protests from the environmental community, commercial clearcutting (stripping an area clean of every sizable standing tree) in some of our own national forests has accelerated soil erosion and led to pollution of nearby streams. Bills have been introduced in Congress to ban clearcutting altogether in our national forests, but so far, without success. To boost timber sales, the Forest Service in a breathtaking premeditated dereliction of duty continues to create large, treeless tracts that may have difficulty recovering their thick mantle of greenery. Even if they manage to do so, they will end up being less biologically diverse.

In Africa, grasslands have been transformed into deserts at an alarming rate due to overgrazing. If human beings could step back and give nature half a chance, this severe land degradation could be avoided. That was graphically demonstrated by an experiment in a fringe area of the Sahara known as the Sahel, which stretches from Mauritania to Chad. A large stretch of grassland had been reduced to desert by overgrazing of cattle belonging to nomadic tribes. Part of the area was subsequently fenced off to keep cattle out, and within months, grass began to grow back despite the absence of significant rainfall. It became apparent that with a more disciplined grazing schedule, a viable environment could be maintained for livestock—even in that arid region.

Inexcusable recklessness in managing natural resources is not limited to the land. One third of the world's annual ocean-fish catch consists of small "forage" species and is totally unregulated, leading to a squandering of the resource. By over-fishing these species (e.g. anchovies, sardines, menhaden), mankind—in an orgy of unjustifiable ignorance—is depleting the food base for larger fish and disrupting the marine ecosystem. Compounding the desecration, these forage fish are being ground up for animal feed instead of being consumed directly—and more economically—by human beings on a sustainable basis. The result: another flagrant display of wasteful neglect in a world where famine is no stranger and humanity bears the responsibility for bequeathing an environmentally viable planet to future generations.[7]

Inferior Copycats

Trying to successfully remake the complex structure of nature according to our own whims is usually beyond our abilities. It should thus come as no surprise that deliberately introducing exotic wildlife species into the natural environment has tended to backfire. In the absence of natural enemies, many of these alien animals and plants have multiplied uncontrollably and proceeded to crowd out indigenous species and disrupt the ecosystem in general. South Florida is filled with such plants as well as with exotic pets that have escaped or been purposely released into the Everglades by their disenchanted owners. We now have pythons over 12 feet long slithering throughout the semi-tropical Florida paradise where there were none before.

Our elimination of virtually all large, native predators in the lower 48 United States and Hawaii has permitted their prey to propagate unchecked, often throwing ecosystems out of whack. A classic, late-19th-century case involved the eradication of the wolf in the lower 48, primarily at the behest of sport hunters seeking to eliminate competition. An ungulate population explosion ensued, causing problems ranging from loss of vegetation due to overgrazing to an epidemic of Lyme disease (because of the surplus of the deer carrying the tick that causes the illness). Lyme disease can be extremely serious if not promptly treated and is a malady once virtually unknown. (The ticks were far less concentrated in colonial times.) It is now a distinct threat throughout much of the year in the newly disease carrier-dense forests of the Eastern United States.[8]

A misguided predator policy has been carried over into the 21st

"Do fence me in."

century in the state of Alaska by no less than the first woman ever to be on the national Republican ticket. Governor Sarah Palin designated as one of her pet projects the wholesale aerial hunting of wolves, a practice so widely repudiated that a federal law exists to ban its use. Palin was able to proceed because of a loophole that exempted any state using aircraft hunting as a management tool for maintaining a healthy wildlife population—that is, at levels where neither extinction nor out of control proliferation were at issue.

But Palin's utilization of aerial hunting was not for conservation purposes. It was to give "sportsmen" a chance to collect some wolf pelts while experiencing a cheap thrill in what amounted to a simulated, high-tech shooting gallery. The wolves desperately scrambling to escape the hovering aircraft had little, if any, chance to survive, and the reduction in their population threatened to upset the ecological balance in a number of regions in Alaska. Of course, former Republican vice presidential nominee Palin insisted that the wolves were being killed to keep them from wiping out the moose that were the primary target of Alaskan hunters. It was a bogus rap against the wolves, as Alaskan wildlife biologists were quick to attest. They stressed that the moose population declined not because of wolves but because of changing weather patterns, food availability, and other variables of the natural cycle. It should be added that, if left undisturbed, nature eventually creates parity between predator and prey. When the moose population shrinks because of natural causes, the number of wolves fluctuates downward from attrition due to the dwindling food supply.

It is the preservation of biodiversity, not revenue from hunting licenses, on which the future quality of life depends, a distinction seemingly lost on Palin. Religious teachings dictate against inhumane treatment of man or beast. At least in the latter case, Governor Palin, a supposedly devout Christian, seemed impervious to such entreaties.

To reiterate, the complex relationships—and balance—within nature are so intricate and multi-layered that on their face, they are impossible for us to grasp. A classic example was a project in Kenya in which acacia trees were fenced off to protect them from the appetites of marauding elephants and giraffes. It turns out that when these animals were not around, the acacias produced less nectar, which discouraged protective ants from colonizing the trees. That opened the door for wood-boring beetles to invade and reduce the acacias to withered stumps.[9]

Leave Well Enough Alone

Society should be cognizant by now of its obligation to preserve indigenous species, including to a limited extent even those looked upon with disfavor. (Admittedly, it is hard to rationalize sparing potentially

Grey Wolf: The Hunter Becomes the Hunted

disease-conveying rodents, despite their fulfilling a waste-disposal function through their scavenging activities.) They all make important, if not readily detectable, contributions to the complex chain of life. Even mosquitoes, the bane of our hot-weather existence, are an important food source for a host of creatures in the wild. This is not to suggest we cease battling the noxious, sometimes-disease-carrying insect, which is so ubiquitous that no matter how successful our local efforts at eradication, it is in no danger of vanishing from the planet. (We need not emulate the benevolence of the conservation-minded Japanese monks who slept on the ground outside their monastery so their flesh could provide food for the pesky insects.)

Opportunities to make benign modifications of nature do exist. The key is to proceed with caution so we can quickly stop and reverse field if it suddenly becomes apparent that we are about to exceed the inherent limitations that a natural system imposes upon us.

Nature's pace is certainly deliberate. Well-known biologist William T. Odum once observed that as habitat becomes more crowded, resources must through necessity be shared. It is then that the inhabitants of an ecosystem typically evolve from confrontation to some form of accommodation. It just doesn't happen overnight.[10]

Spiritual Kick

MANY PEOPLE EXPERIENCE spiritual euphoria from their interactions with the environment. Such sentiments often stem from the conviction that the natural world is a manifestation of God's work and that humanity therefore has a sacred obligation to preserve a viable environment for posterity. Affirmation of this point of view can be found in all major religions. For example, *Psalm 24.7* in the *Book of Genesis* reads: "The earth is the Lord's and the fullness thereof. The fullness and everything it contains."

Most modern theologians—and for that matter anyone with environmental sensitivity—agree that to achieve a sustainable quality of life with all the basic comforts, the human race must maintain a harmonious relationship with the natural world and each other. Not surprisingly then, spirituality is often a driving force behind the advocacy and practice of this relationship.

Paul Gorman, executive of the National Religious Partnership for the Environment, alluded to this role of religiosity when he declared: "God's mandate of human stewardship dictates that we must give our support when sufficient consensus exists of a likelihood of a significant [environmental] threat to the most vulnerable population. That makes it morally prudent to take precautions, and it is a religious, not political determination."[1]

Rocks Have Souls?

As previously mentioned, the prevailing theological view of nature imputes intrinsic value to non-human objects, be they animal, plant, or mineral, and thus obligates us to treat them with care, even reverence whenever possible. Typical of modern-day religion is the position recently articulated by Cardinal Renato Raffaele Martino, head of the Pontifical Council of Justice and Peace. "The mastery of man over Creation," declared the cardinal, "must not be despotic or senseless. Man must cultivate and safeguard God's Creation."

But religion has not always held the high moral ground with

regard to environmental protection. There have always been those who believe that the worth of anything only derives from how useful it is to mankind. It is a hypothesis that conveniently justifies guilt-free plundering, and it was often a guiding behavioral principle on the American frontier. This myopic, anthropocentric sentiment still lingers in isolated pockets of our society, including certain ultra-orthodox elements among Christian fundamentalists. They regard nature as existing solely to be exploited to the fullest, with little thought given to the harsh consequences of total resource depletion. In fact, many of these folks view resource depletion as a necessary precondition to experiencing a spiritual state of ecstasy they call "Rapture"!

A notorious exponent of this school of thought was James Watt, Interior Secretary under President. Ronald Reagan. A born-again Christian, Watt subscribed to the biblical interpretation in which the Earth had to undergo an apocalypse to bring about the return of Jesus Christ, who would then take all God-fearing individuals with him back to Heaven. Although responsible for the conservation of federal lands, Secretary Watt had the temerity to declare publicly that "We don't have to protect the environment, the Second Coming [of Christ] is at hand."[2] Given that earthly destruction is a precondition to the Second Coming, Watt had few qualms about stripping public lands of their natural riches, and he proceeded to do just that until cut short when a strong public backlash moved Congress to intervene.

The real miracle associated with Watt was that he lasted as long as he did in office. Eventually, President Reagan could not ignore the widespread public condemnation. When Watt openly made a verbal gaffe in which he slandered minorities and the physically handicapped, a legion of critics pounced, and Reagan was forced to regretfully accept the Secretary's "resignation."

Why Save the Oddity?

Despite the well-deserved condemnation of Watt's jaundiced manipulations, the question persists as to why we should strive to preserve rare species that have minimal, if any, contact with human beings. The answer encompasses not only the moral obligation to protect all God's creatures but also a practical, scientific rationale. From a secular perspective, biodiversity is a rich repository of chemical compounds with wondrous properties, some of which may hold answers to the mysteries of life. The most unlikely animal or improbable plant could be the source of a chemical substance with miraculous curative powers. Indeed, approximately 70 percent of all new drugs introduced into the United States between 1982 and 2007 were derived directly from nature rather than medical laboratories. That includes about half of the anti-cancer medicines that have been discovered since the 1940s.[3]

Among the most recognizable drugs extracted from plants are aspirin, morphine, and alkaloid compounds taken from the rosy periwinkle and widely used in chemotherapy. Chinese scientists found that the roots of Ferula assa-foetida, a common plant with foul-smelling sap, contain natural antiviral chemical compounds that show promise against swine flu pandemics[4].

On the animal side, an example is the saliva of leeches, which has been demonstrated to be an effective anti-coagulant agent as well as a reducer of inflammation.

What about the future? There are literally millions of species—mostly invertebrates and many undoubtedly quite rare—that have yet to be examined. But the promise of undiscovered benefits does not reside solely in obscure flora and fauna. Some of the more familiar life forms, whose numbers are under severe pressure, also possess great potential to add to our medical arsenal. Polar bears, for example, could conceivably provide ways to prevent and reverse osteoporosis (the breaking down of bones in the aging process), kidney disease, and diabetes. Scientists hope to unlock the secrets of the bear's lengthy periods of hibernation, when virtually every part of the animal's body shuts down, only to have it emerge remarkably unscathed. The numbers of the once-ubiquitous horseshoe crab are dwindling under human pressure, a worrisome trend considering that its blood contains a molecule that has shown promise in preventing the spread of certain cancers and in reducing the severity of rheumatoid arthritis.[5]

As those examples demonstrate, we have a moral imperative to preserve the Earth's biodiversity to the best of our abilities so as not to foreclose the potential it holds for future generations as well as our own. Whether out of ignorance or willful neglect, humanity has not been doing a very good job.

Out of Sight, Not Out of Mind
From a spiritual perspective, nature is so finely interconnected that one has a hard time believing it is not the work of a Divine Force. Perhaps this is why so many people instinctively cherish wilderness, even when they have never directly experienced its most spectacular manifestations and have little prospect of doing so. It certainly seems to explain why many Americans strongly oppose any development of the Arctic National Wildlife Refuge, even though they lack any realistic expectation of ever witnessing that remote majestic panorama first-hand.

CHAPTER THREE

—

ABUSE OF FELLOW HUMANS

Do Unto Others

W HEN ENVIRONMENTAL DAMAGE can be substantially repaired, if not averted altogether, it is immoral to pass up the opportunity. Former President George W. Bush provided some of the most graphic examples of this wrongful behavior by a person in power, and they will be cited frequently in the book. He is linked to a treasure trove of malfeasance because purposeful neglect often epitomized his administration, despite his lofty moral pronouncements and the material means to make good on his reassuring promises.

Consider that among the world's 22 wealthiest nations, we were dead last in the percentage of gross national income allocated for foreign aid to improve the quality of life in the world's most impoverished countries. The Scandinavian states made Mr. Bush, with his vaunted boasts of American generosity, look like a piker in the realm of philanthropy.

That is not to say other developed countries should get off scot-free in the environmental blame game; everyone is at fault to some extent. According to an analysis conducted by the British newspaper, the *Manchester Guardian*, developing nations between 2002 and 2009 received less than 10 percent of the $18 billion that wealthy countries had promised to donate for the purpose of coping with global warming.[1] Meanwhile, researchers at the University of California, Berkeley recently produced a report in which they concluded that the world's wealthiest nations were wreaking enormous environmental havoc on their poorer counterparts. It was disclosed in the study that greenhouse gas emissions from high levels of consumption in wealthy countries had inflicted $2.3 trillion in environmental damage on the developing world between 1961 and 2000. Conversely, greenhouse gas emissions discharged by the poorer nations caused the industrial states $740 billion in environmental damage. The disparity illustrated the stark inequity between the haves and the have-nots, and the need for international cooperation to close the gap (although it should be noted that an economically resurgent China has displaced the United States as the world's leading greenhouse gas emitter).

On the domestic front, President Bush granted coal companies permission to rip asunder West Virginia mountaintops for mother lodes and dump the rubble into freshwater streams in the valleys below. More than 400 mountains in Appalachia were flattened in this manner, fouling 750 miles of once-pristine streams with contaminated spoil. Small villages at the base of these mountains were threatened with disaster, especially from the loss of clean water. Groups of local citizens filed lawsuits, and if they should ultimately lose in court (in the absence of a reversal of Bush policy by future administrations), one would have to conclude that justice really is blind. How else could one interpret a ruling that would doom communities by sanctioning destruction of a clean and essential renewable resource for the sake of a nonrenewable and single-use polluting one?

President Bush's effort to accommodate corporate America at the expense of public health and the environment was hardly limited to Appalachian coal extraction. His administration's proposal to reduce pollution from coal-fired power plants turned out to be weaker than existing law. He sought to relax curbs on pollution from industrial laundries, one of which just happened to be owned by a major Bush fundraiser. The White House attempted to roll back the standard for regulating Perchlorate, a toxic rocket-fuel contaminant detected at worrisome levels in the drinking water of 35 states.

What about our government's policy of permitting the export of pesticides deemed too hazardous for our own use? Sure, we required American chemical companies to notify foreign powers of our restrictions on the products being shipped. But the warnings rarely made it past indifferent overseas officials to those actually at risk—the exposed foreign workers in the fields.

Our government's lax oversight of American companies' export operations extended to the shipment to developing countries of discarded vehicles and equipment that were polluting and often energy inefficient.[2] Everyone would have been better served if the materials had stayed put and been recycled into more environmentally friendly products, but that was not where the profit lay. (A German research firm estimated that businesses in the United States ship $150 billion worth of secondhand, outdated equipment annually). Instead of loading up developing countries with "lemons," we should be helping them acquire clean, modern technologies so as not to repeat our mistakes. Failure to engage in this positive activity is not only questionable moral behavior, the overseas pollution will eventually come back to haunt us by way of air and water.

What of the occasions when materials outlawed abroad for safety reasons have been permitted to enter our markets?[3] Wood products containing carcinogenic formaldehyde are banned in many other countries but welcomed here. This is a situation in which caveat emptor does not, and should not, apply—our capitalist economy notwithstanding.

How should we judge major American companies that have moved facilities to developing countries specifically to escape stringent environmental regulations at home? "Do unto others as you would have others do unto you" has profound economic as well as ethical significance in today's world. At some point, either from public pressure or a pollution crisis, the host developing countries will lose their patience at being environmentally exploited. Whether their solution will be as drastic as nationalization or expulsion of their American corporate *émigrés* remains to be seen. Either way, it won't be comfortable for expatriate entrepreneurs. They might even have to bring their businesses (and job opportunities) home to the United States.

"Caveat emptor" is the operative terminology in our free-market system. By contrast, such "backward" countries as China seem far less carefree about consumers' welfare, at least as far as formaldehyde is concerned. In that Asian nation, public health takes precedence over the sales volume of the business community *vis-à-vis* that toxic substance. Meanwhile, back on our shores, the increasing evidence that formaldehyde is a potential carcinogen has belatedly begun to have an effect. Environmental and fair housing organizations petitioned the Environmental Protection Agency (EPA) to toughen regulation of the chemical substance because of unhealthy levels in post-Katrina emergency trailer housing on the Gulf Coast.[4]

The European Union and a host of other countries have adopted a "better safe than sorry" policy in the face of uncertainty regarding the lethality of chemical toxic substances used in finished products.[5] In comparison, we have invoked "uncertainty" as the reason not to regulate, often leaving it up to companies as to whether toxic ingredients should be phased out of product lines. It seemed that our government would rather gamble with human life than subject industry to more stringent regulation, a strategy much to the liking of many corporate chieftains, but hopefully reversed permanently in the post-Bush era.

Government Without Morality

Is it ethical for government regulators to reject as uneconomical the additional business expense of protecting the elderly, chronically ill, and other highly vulnerable elements of society from industrial pollution? What of government's approval of industry's cold-blooded request to delay proactive environmental regulations because the incriminating evidence, though significant, was not absolutely definitive?

Shouldn't the Bush administration have been condemned for not taking corrective action against occupational hazards in the workplace until after an injury had occurred? AFL-CIO Director of Safety and Health Margaret Seminario certainly thought so. At an April 2007 Senate hearing, she denounced the decision by Bush's Occupational Safety and Health Administration (OSHA) to substitute voluntary industry compliance for mandatory protective workplace standards with stiff penalties.[6] It was a policy that at best could be described as "too little, too late."

During Bush's presidency, OSHA was severely under funded, understaffed, and uninspired in enforcing existing laws. Why couldn't his administration have followed the counsel of people such as John Carr, secretary of the U.S. Catholic Conference, who perceived a broader significance to pollution cleanup than just the health benefits? "Air quality standards are not about particulates," Carr declared, "but about morality." Unfortunately, the Bush administration and the corporate world were all too often of one mind in how they perceived pollution threats to the American people. The bottom line became the end of the line for many victims of environmental degradation.

Justifying the Means

The supreme irony of the stridently pro-business Bush administration was its embrace of the fundamental Marxist tenet that the end justifies the means. Bush seized on such an "alien" philosophy as an excuse for his camouflage of a controversial, feeble environmental agenda (and just about every other questionable policy) that he sought to foist on the electorate.

Sure, a little white lie now and then does no harm and may even be necessary for a politician to keep a worthwhile, albeit unpopular cause alive until the general public sees the light. But the systemic pattern of deception in which Bush engaged to promote some policies and conceal others indicated that he feared a candid relationship with the American people. And his fears were well founded. Subordination of the public interest to corporate aspirations has never been a big vote-getter in either the short or long term.

Thus, we had Bush embellishing his environmental programs with euphemistic labels to obscure an underlying pro-business orientation. His "Clear Skies" initiative allowed industry to emit more air pollution than did existing law. His "Healthy Forests" plan gave timber companies license to expand their operations on public lands by cutting down previously protected stands of biologically invaluable old-growth trees—which also just happen to absorb large amounts of the greenhouse gases associated with global warming.

The president termed his proposal for drilling on the pristine, 1.5-million-acre-coastal plain of the Arctic National Wildlife Refuge "environmentally responsible" since it supposedly applied to a mere 2,000 acres. No mention was made of the more than 200 miles of connecting roads and pipelines that would be required to crisscross the refuge and would defile our country's last, great ecologically intact wilderness system.

I've Got a Secret

Secrecy shrouded much of the Bush administration's environmental decision making. For example, Vice President Cheney refused to reveal the deliberations he had with oil executives regarding the formulation of the White House's proposed national energy policy. Considering that such a policy would have a profound impact on all Americans, the public was surely entitled to know the rationale behind the plan and whether all interested parties received equitable treatment. Reasonable as that may sound, the administration remained steadfast in its plutocratic contempt for the general public and used the president's executive privilege to cover its sorry tracks. It was a ploy the U.S. Supreme Court sadly refused to overturn at the behest of an environmentalists' petition. Instead, the justices sent the issue back to the D.C. Circuit Court of Appeals for review. Unfortunately, that court dismissed the lawsuit in May 2005. It was left up to the media to obtain the names of the energy lobbyist participants and the gist of the secret discussions through news leaks received in drips and drabs. Here was a situation in which the press demonstrated its indispensability, for government without transparency is not democracy.

Private Is as Public Isn't

You would never have known it from the budget-busting federal deficit that President Bush foisted on the nation, but he subscribed to the Conservative mantra postulated by Ronald Reagan, namely that "the federal government is part of the problem rather than solution." Accordingly, Bush considered the private sector to be inherently superior to the public one in providing the bulk of society's most essential services. An inescapable truth appeared to have eluded him and many other conservatives. Neither private companies nor individuals have the resources or overview to fill a central national government's role in keeping a multifaceted society on an environmentally and economically sustainable track.

President Bush and his minions were aware they could never directly sell the nation on the expansive privatization in which they devoutly believed. But they were convinced that they knew what was best for America, and that over time, their ideological agenda would win begrudging acceptance from a belatedly appreciative electorate. Meanwhile, Bush attempted to move toward his privatization goal through unobtrusive (some would say devious) maneuvers. Wherever possible, administration officials facilitated the private takeover of public lands, whether through inconspicuous property exchanges, expanded leases, or low-profile concessionaire contracts.

There were of course boundaries that even Bush and like-minded individuals dared not cross. Any proposal to shift ownership, or even supervision, of such a revered national crown jewel as the Grand Canyon National Park to a private entity would have ignited a mass rebellion among members of Congress as well as the public at large. Just the same, it was unsettling to think that if hard-core conservative ideologues could have gotten away with privatizing this unparalleled monument of nature, they would have jumped at the chance.

The Perfection Smokescreen

Making the perfect the enemy of the good as the basis for rejecting an environmental policy option usually signifies malicious intent. That is because requiring perfection as a prerequisite for approval of an environmental regulation (or just about anything else for that matter) is normally a deliberate attempt to bring about failure. Environmental problems are usually too complex for any single solution to cover all bases.

Hence the failure of an environmental regulation to totally eradicate a problem should not be grounds for repudiation. Laws should be judged by the degree of success they achieve. In that vein, regulatory proposals ought to be rated by how effectively they apply the "precautionary principle," which is the philosophical underpinning of environmental activism. A straightforward definition of the principle is "better safe than sorry." Invoking it is a no-brainer when the weight of evidence suggests a serious environmental problem is at hand and cost-effective remedies are available that make sense in their own right. Nothing is therefore lost, even if the original environmental threat turns out to have been overblown. It is a win-win deal in which conclusive proof is not a precondition to prudent action, and uncertainty not an insurmountable barrier to regulation.

Yet opponents of more stringent environmental proposals will often play the ambiguity card to the hilt. They will point to incomplete knowledge of a particular threat as reason for delay. If enough unanswered questions are raised, they know full well that momentum for immediate regulatory action may weaken, even in the face of a significant body of incriminating evidence.

It doesn't have to be that way. The perfect can be the friend of the good. Our landmark Clean Air and Clean Water statutes set as an ideal goal the zero discharge of pollutants. Drafters of the bill conceded that a zero discharge might be extremely difficult (although not impossible) to achieve. But they obviously had the same mindset as the famed British poet Robert Browning when he wrote that "a man's reach should exceed his grasp or what's a heaven for." Accordingly, they set the bar at its peak level to press those regulated by the statute to perform to the very best of their ability.

Los Angeles—West Coast miasma

The Imperfect Climate

Employing the perfect to discredit the good has been utilized with particular effectiveness to impede the progress of global warming initiatives. Industry executives and a tiny corps of scientists they co-opted have invoked two variations of the "perfect" theme in opposition to emission reductions. First, they have stressed the uncertainty surrounding climate change to argue that any decisive action would be premature and might impose heavy, unnecessary pollution-abatement costs.

Should that argument fail and society accept the existence of a bona fide global warming threat, the naysayers seek to kindle public resignation to the accelerated temperature rise. They assert that climate change is so complicated that human efforts to alter the process are futile. The only alternative is to adapt to—rather than try to mitigate—climate change, thereby opting for a Band Aid instead of a cure. It's an option that, just by coincidence, imposes fewer overhead costs on the business community.

Solid arguments counter the global warming skeptics. Although humanity cannot stabilize global temperatures in the near future, the momentum can be slowed if we become more energized activists. Adaptation has a role, but when government officials and business interests try to exploit it to postpone decisive cutbacks in greenhouse gas emissions, a line must be drawn. Let's be clear. Adaptation should be considered only the overture. Mitigation is the main act.

The Inuit village of Kuujjuaq, in Northern Quebec is a dramatic example of why adaptation is merely a temporary reprieve. Because of climate change, the village inhabitants, who are best known for the ice structures (igloos) they build during the winter months, were forced to install air conditioners in their summer homes to survive unprecedented temperatures approaching 90 degrees Fahrenheit. Given that development, who could say what future winters would bring? A way of life was vanishing with no guarantees that a happier alternative was in the offing.

The Alaskan coastal village of Kivalina was in even more dire straits. It had been compelled to move inland because of melting sea ice that had eroded the barrier island on which it stood. The relocation cost more than $100 million. What will happen if more melting forces the Inuits into a further retreat?

Their plight is an extreme example of the disruption caused by climate change. The degree to which the Inuits' experiences presage our own fate is unclear. Most likely, any correlation will probably be determined by the global community's effectiveness in reducing emissions in the ensuing decades. We obviously have a moral obligation to prevent further deterioration of the lives of these people, who were among the first to experience hardship from an energy policy gone awry.

Alaskan barrier island village—At the mercy of nature

The More, The Merrier

President Bush's pronouncement that shopping binges were the ideal expression of national defiance to the terrorists attack on the World Trade Center was misguided on several counts. Instead of urging the public to hunker down for a struggle against international terrorism by making sacrifices—financial and otherwise—for our troops, the president implored us to wallow in avarice (to prove our economy could handily survive a hit). That is what many Americans happily chose to do, sinking further into debt in the process. But that was not all. Just like the president, they failed to make a connection between their shopping-spree exploitation of the Earth's natural resources (much of which was imported) and the very terrorism they were being asked to fight. It did not register that Third World inhabitants' widespread lack of adequate food, water, shelter, and sanitation facilities was a catalyst for a significant portion of the social unrest that spawned terrorists.

When Americans experienced any pangs of conscience over their privileged material status, they quickly rationalized away their doubts by embracing the "trickle-down" theory. Under such thinking, American prosperity stimulated international trade that had a positive ripple effect on the economies of less fortunate countries.[7]

Sadly, the "trickle-down" theory that enables low-income wage earners to gain from the affluent class's conspicuous consumption has not worked very well internationally. Lifting impoverished nations up by their bootstraps requires far more than a trade relationship. Direct financial assistance is necessary. And here was where Bush's clarion call for increased spending—so resonant when it came to arming our military to the teeth or acquiring merchandise for our personal enrichment—was reduced to a murmur. As was previously mentioned, we ranked 22nd among the prosperous industrialized countries in the percentage of gross national product allocated to foreign aid, despite being the world's wealthiest nation. Our government's effort to mask its parsimony was unconvincing. In its indefensible defense, Washington pointed out that when our private charitable contributions were combined with our foreign aid, we stood among the world's leading donors. Unfortunately, private charitable gifts are generally one-shot, short-term propositions. They do not provide the continuity that effective government assistance programs supply and recipient developing nations need.

Oblivious to those countries' plights, Bush glossed over the excessive demands that our high per capita consumption was putting on the Earth's natural-resource base. Lamentably, we did not have a leader who possessed a better grasp of reality, a reality incompatible in the long term with any culture obsessed with extravagance. To prosper throughout the 21st century, our nation will need not only leaders but also a general public to recognize and adopt the practical constraints dictated by this reality.

Babies Galore

In a world of limited resources, perhaps we shall one day become sensitized to the discordance of reveling in the advent of multiple births. If you think about it, it doesn't make much sense to lionize such feats of propagation. Large families—especially in industrialized countries—are prone, simply by virtue of their size, to impose an unsustainable drain on the planet's natural-resource base. Yet our media, particularly television newscasters, don't have a clue. They have invariably used their nightly broadcasts to gleefully celebrate any childbirths in excess of triplets, with the laudatory tone usually rising in proportion to the number of newborn delivered.[8]

No one is suggesting that we demonize multiple births. One simply hopes that the media would come to the realization that from an environmentally sustainable perspective, a family with three or more kids is no cause for rejoicing. Indeed, such sizable broods run at cross purposes to the goal of population stabilization, attainment of which is essential to assure a decent quality of life for future generations.

Two English doctors writing in the British Medical Journal had the right idea. They proposed that the medical profession encourage patients to limit family size to two siblings on the grounds that it would be the most significant contribution a couple could make to combat climate change. Smaller families would generate fewer greenhouse gases, the doctors declared, and limiting the number of children should be brought "into the arena of environmental (bio) ethics, analogous to avoiding patio heaters and high-carbon cars."[9]

Stabilization of population will indeed require the global birth rate to settle at a replacement level, i.e. an average of two children per couple. That message should be conveyed in a positive way without a hint of coercion. If multiple births must be a news item, the story should be presented in matter-of-fact fashion, noting the difficult financial challenges the parents will face. Broadcasters should periodically remind their audience that it takes more than quarter of a million dollars to provide the bare essentials in raising a child in the United States, a sobering revelation that might evoke reservations—even among those couples most determined to have a passel of kids.

Although parents should never be forced against their will to limit their family size to two siblings (at least in our democracy), stiff financial incentives and disincentives as well as environmental education would go a long way towards instilling moderation. One might be surprised at the demographic impact if our government limited the child income tax credit to two kids per family instead of making it open-ended.

Back in 1982 in testimony before Congress, Richard Benedict, then the State Department Coordinator for Population, declared: "Given the potential implications of population growth for the future of human life on this planet, I believe an insistence on the 'right' to multiply indiscriminately represents a misplaced morality... It seems fair, in a world of growing scarcities and strains on biological systems, to require those who have more children to bear a heavier share of the cost of services to those children."

There was a man ahead of his time, who reasoned that while an appeal to protect the planet's future might not dissuade those determined to produce a large family, a revised tax structure likely would. It will take a while before people en masse acquire enough environmental awareness to limit their family size as a matter of conscience.

The Culture of Waste

Americans' obsessive consumptive patterns take on an air of debauchery when juxtaposed with the widespread deprivation experienced in a world that is ever more interdependent. Planned obsolescence has been instrumental in earning us the reputation of being a "throwaway society." It's an especially reprehensible when so much of humanity is wanting and the planet's resources are being depleted faster than they can be replaced.

Then there is agriculture. With famine and malnutrition all too commonplace, it is especially criminal to waste food. Yet that is what we do on a shameful scale, according to a 2008 study conducted under the auspices of the United Nations.[10] Researchers found that, in the United States, approximately 30 percent of the food produced annually and worth $48.3 billion is tossed into the garbage. Up to one quarter of all fresh fruits and vegetables is lost between the field and dinner table. And we are not alone. According to United Nations researchers, almost a third of all food bought annually in Britain is never consumed.[11]

The contrast between our per capita consumption of natural resources and that of inhabitants of developing countries is especially stark. For example, we generate roughly five times as much solid waste per capita as inhabitants of Third World nations.[12]

Americans' massive consumption monopolizes valuable resources (especially raw materials) that are in short supply in many parts of the world. Moreover, our unsustainable demand for both renewable and nonrenewable commodities is seriously diminishing our own ecological systems as well as others. By using three times the world's per capita average of fresh water, we are draining our ground water supplies more rapidly than nature can replenish them.

The fact that our per capita rate of energy consumption is twice that of Western Europeans—despite their comparable living standards—is another graphic example of our wasteful habits. Because we are splurging with nonrenewable imported oil for which we currently have no viable substitute on the scale required, it is an excess that threatens to eventually put us in a crisis mode.

There are some explanations for this disparity between us and our transatlantic brethren. Shortages experienced by the Europeans during and immediately after World War Two instilled a conservation-oriented mentality that persists to this day. Greater population density and a more modest natural-resource base have made energy costlier in Europe and instilled a higher propensity for thrift (and the use of renewables). One does not have to look far to observe that conservation is much more integrated into their daily life. How many American hallways are equipped with lighting timed to operate only when someone is actually present? Name an American city where small, fuel-stingy Smartcars are a frequent sight.

The Counter Culture Against Waste

One can persuasively assert that as the world's only superpower, we have an obligation to create an environmentally sustainable economy that not only assures a bright future for our children but sets an example for other nations. Otherwise, we risk running our society into the ground and quite likely setting off a negative chain reaction throughout the rest of the world.

Some scientists estimate it would take five Earths to provide sufficient resources for everyone on the planet to indulge in our current rate of consumption. To describe the profound challenge to our society another way, if all six billion people on Earth were to share the world's resources equally, Americans would have to reduce consumption by 80 percent.[13] This is not to suggest we need totally scrap our current way of life, but clearly, significant structural revision and more efficient use of resources are in order.

What would the appropriate recalibration of our society look like? In a general sense, it would involve shifting the emphasis from quantitative to qualitative values. "Keeping up with the Joneses" would be phased out unless the competition switched from material acquisition to intellectual accomplishment. Goods would be manufactured for durability and eventual recycling, mimicking the basic modus operandi of nature. Status would be measured more by mental acuity than the size of bank statements. Gratification would come more from the formation of enduring personal relationships than the accumulation of physical possessions. Conservation in general would take precedence over consumption.

Many studies indicate that this shift in cultural values would benefit not only the environment but also our collective frame of mind.[14] In societies where the rate of consumption is the primary means of acquiring self-esteem, researchers have found that the more material goods one obtains, the more one usually seeks in a frustrating Sisyphean quest. When the true source of happiness is closely scrutinized, it turns out that satisfaction stems more from solid family ties, a reliable social network, and jobs and leisure activities that hold one's interest, put a premium on self-reliance, and provide a sense of fulfillment.

In the short term, is there any way to quickly jump-start the transition to sustainability? Harsh economic reality and the menace of global warming have displayed promise as catalysts in this regard. The skyrocketing cost of gasoline has enhanced the value of conservation and, virtually overnight, modified American driving habits and vehicle preferences, all to the environment's benefit. If the trend persists, the inevitable outcome will be reduced energy consumption, less pollution, expedited production of clean alternative fuels, and an accelerated move towards clustered development and away from sprawl.

A majority of Americans have acknowledged the threat from global warming, and many appear willing to help curb greenhouse gas emissions, even if it means higher utility bills, an occurrence that would invariably promote greater resort to conservation.[15]

What about the global warming skeptics who use the prospect of remedial measures vastly increasing utility rates as reason to go slow on combating climate change? We need political leaders with the moral backbone to challenge the obstructionists and rally the public to take action. One way a savvy leader could overcome resistance would be to familiarize Americans with a well-documented economic analysis of the far greater fiscal burden they would ultimately bear if nothing were done to diminish emissions.[16] Researchers extrapolate that failure to significantly mitigate the environmental impacts of global warming will by 2100 result in a loss of nearly $1.9 trillion annually, a sum equal to 1.8 percent of our gross domestic product. And that does not include the enormous costs associated with adverse human health effects from the likely increase in hurricane activity, heat waves, drought, tropical disease, and ozone-laden smog.

Conversely, a 2009 study by UN economists concluded that if a "mere" one percent of global wealth (approximately $750 billion) were invested in five key sectors, an environmentally sustainable, robust world economy would result. The five sectors were: energy efficiency, renewable energy, environmentally friendly transportation, natural resource preservation, and sustainable agriculture.[17]

Another group of economists reviewed the research on the cost of achieving the drastic carbon emissions reduction that scientists now say is essential to curb global warming, and guess what? The economists found that the goal could be attained for an annual sum of $600 million to

$1.8 billion, roughly one to three percent of yearly global gross domestic product. In the big picture that amounts to chicken feed, especially when compared with the cost to civilization if no substantial action is taken.[18]

Guilty Until Proved Innocent

FOR AUTHORITIES TO SIEZE the moral high ground in drafting environmental regulations, the health of the general public and surrounding ecosystems must take precedence over the business community's profit. The burden of proof should fall on the manufacturer to demonstrate that a product is reasonably safe, not on the consumer to show the product is unequivocally hazardous.

Why, you might ask, shouldn't the manufacturer be presumed innocent until proven guilty? Isn't that the American way? Sorry, products are not people! Prospective pollution victims, not potential polluters, should receive the benefit of the doubt, since relief from illness cannot match prevention of illness in terms of physical, psychological and economic benefits.[1]

Speaking of prevention, it is embodied in the previously mentioned Precautionary Principle, the philosophical foundation of progressive environmentalism. To repeat, the essence of the principle is that if the weight of evidence points to a significant threat, any cost-effective remedial measures should be taken, despite the absence of an open and shut case against suspected impending danger. Given the disastrous consequences if the worst fears are realized, anything less than a "better safe than sorry" approach would be morally indefensible.

Nevertheless, in the absence of immediate visible harm, it is human nature to exhibit complacency. That is why politicians typically balk at taking preemptive action against a prospective environmental hazard, even though they risk condemnation if it materializes on their watch. And that is why, until recently, Americans have been apathetic about the inaction of their leadership in aggressively facing up to the problems posed by climate change.

Prevention Better than the Cure

It should be noted that prevention provides ethical as well as monetary rewards. Curing a patient is an admirable achievement. But that sense of accomplishment and moral rectitude pales when compared to the satisfaction of keeping a vulnerable individual from getting sick in the first place.

Solely relying on balancing costs against benefits to determine public health policy raises the threat of us ending up as slaves rather than masters of statistics. It is essential to recognize that cost-benefit analysis is a tool, not an end in itself. Rare is the case when ethical, social, and political considerations fail to play a significant role alongside monetary ones in setting antipollution standards.

A classic example is regulation to protect the health of the most risk-prone elements of our society, such as the elderly and very young. The extra measure of protection involved may require businesses to fork out sizable additional pollution-abatement expenditures for a relatively small number of potential beneficiaries. Those in industry who balk at the idea are evidently unimpressed that we are talking about the survival of fellow human beings. If the extra fiscal burden worries the corporate honchos, you'd think they could defray at least part of the expenditure by levying a surcharge on their customers. That would be a better alternative than being complicit in the de facto, deliberate write-off of human life.

Money Isn't Everything

Benefits of regulation are often hard to quantify statistically when compared to costs. We can usually document the latter with hard and fast numbers for all to see. But the former are often defined as bad things that would happen if precautions were not taken, and thus have a nebulous quality. Industry has all too frequently used that ambiguity as an excuse for staving off the imposition of more stringent environmental protection rules. Uncertainty is parlayed into procrastination.

Fortunately, lack of a hard and fast case as a rationale for inaction is rapidly losing steam as scientists develop techniques to quantify more explicitly the monetary value of a healthy population and environment. The scientists' work is enabling environmentalists to fend off traditional opposition to antipollution regulation and destruction of valuable natural resources by responding in the bean counters' own language.

In 1990, EPA researchers calculated that Americans received approximately $20 in health benefits (i.e. reduction in illness and premature death) for every dollar spent to control air pollution.[2]

To our detriment, we have unwittingly sacrificed the quality of our health to subsidize the true costs of fossil fuel use throughout the years. According to the National Research Council (NRC), adverse impacts to human health from such use amounted to an estimated $120 billion in 2005, yet these external costs were not reflected in the price of fuel.[3]

Along those same lines, NRC researchers estimated that emissions from power plants and automobiles caused air pollution that resulted in

20,000 premature deaths annually.[4]

As for assigning a price to precious natural resources, the global economy's sharp decline in the fall of 2008 increased their value even more in the marketplace. Computations were made to determine the cash value of many unspoiled natural areas, the most unique of which were arguably priceless. As has been noted, researchers attached hefty price tags to nondescript virgin wetlands by tabulating values not readily visible to the untutored eye: flood control, groundwater storage, water purification, waste assimilation, and fish nesting benefits. Back in 1974, Dr. Eugene Odum, internationally renowned director of the University of Georgia's Institute of Ecology, came up with an annual average figure of $50,000 worth of services provided per wetland acre. In 1992, researchers from the University of California's Berkley School of Public Policy arrived at a more conservative valuation of $22,000 a year.

Scientists in another study found that the annual monetary value of healthy marine ecosystems due to sustainable fishing and recreational activities far exceeded yearly revenues from potentially polluting nonrenewable oil and gas extraction off shore.[5] Preserving tropical forests through sustainable use (e.g. closely monitored rubber extraction) have been calculated to reap far more pecuniary benefits than stripping the tracts clean of timber.

Not a moment too soon, an increasing number of countries (though hardly a majority) are beginning to acknowledge these eco-fiscal realities and incorporate the value of their natural resources into their economic models, thereby bolstering protections against environmental degradation.[6]

The quantitative value of natural resources has not just been measured in terms of dollars. In October of 2009, United Nations researchers released a "Blue Carbon" report in which it was calculated that the greenhouse gas absorptive capacity of marine plant life (e.g. mangroves, salt marshes) was crucial to bringing global warming under control.[7] Such vegetation was soaking up CO_2 in an amount equal to nearly half of the world's transportation systems' emissions. Yet these natural systems, which sequester carbon for free and on a far greater scale than any human invention, are being destroyed by civilization's encroachment at a rate of up to seven percent annually, raising the threat of their total elimination.

Although supposedly fiscally astute, some politicians still have not grasped the essential fact: failing to protect natural resources will clearly cost far more in the long run than maintaining ecological health, just as ignoring global warming will impose a far heavier financial burden than doing something about it. Instead, such "statesmen" have bowed to political expedience and, at the behest of well-connected corporate polluters (and campaign contributors), defaulted on a vested responsibility to preserve a biologically viable world. Their intransigence has been an embarrassment, considering that even traditional dollars-and-cents oriented economists have finally recognized that inaction on climate change is a "penny-wise, pound-foolish" policy.[8]

Corporate Welfare

Another morally questionable governmental practice has been the use of taxpayers' dollars to subsidize well-heeled, politically influential industrial interests. Look at Washington's below-cost timber sales of national forest wood to corporate entities and the giveaway grazing fees charged to ranchers using federally owned rangelands. Not only were the American people being denied a fair return on the use of their property, but the virtual handouts also encouraged over-harvesting of invaluable old-growth timber as well as livestock encroachment on public lands set aside primarily for conservation.[9] Between 1992 and 1997, the U.S. Forest Service saddled American taxpayers with a $2 billion loss from timber sales in which the revenues did not cover the expense of administering the transactions.[10]

Keeping it Private

A conservative, ideologically driven bias against big government was the driving force behind the Bush administration's doctrinaire allegiance to privatization of as many public assets as possible. Yet the private sector's preoccupation with turning a profit can easily put its management style at odds with the preservation of the environment.

Cape Cod provides a graphic illustration of why the private sector cannot be trusted to preserve pristine areas conducive to development. The creation of a national seashore in the midst of the spectacularly beautiful Massachusetts peninsula is its saving grace. Without such a permanent oasis, the Cape would almost certainly be swamped with tacky development, which defaces too much of its expanse as it is.

If making money didn't possess the potential to undermine entrepreneurs' responsible custodianship of federal lands, such a custodianship might be acceptable. But when financial expectations fall short, private interests in a controlling managerial position are likely to sacrifice resource preservation in favor of development to heighten (at least temporarily) publicly owned land's commercial value.

There is the also the critical issue of privatizing drinking water. In keeping with his ideological orientation, President Bush preferred that privately owned companies rather than governmental authorities controlled the liquid's distribution in the Third World. But water is not a commodity in the traditional sense. It is a *necessity* of life, to be supplied at all costs to every man, woman, and child. Would private water companies be comfortable continuing service to impoverished customers who could not

Cape Cod—Sprawl in paradise

afford to pay their bills?[11]

It is true that some government bureaucracies are too incompetent and/or corrupt to distribute clean, affordable water efficiently, creating room for participation of a reliable private entity (although finding a reliable one is sometimes easier said than done). Furthermore, even capable, honest officials may need the help of the private sector, and effective programs are being run jointly throughout the world. But we should remember that when survival is at stake, a government—by virtue of its official authority—can be held to account, if not by its own people, then by humanitarian pressure from the international community. In contrast, no such inherent leverage exists, moral or practical, to compel a private water-distribution company to provide services in the absence of payment. This ethical distinction between the public and private sectors seemed to elude President Bush and other conservative ideologues.

One of the most morally discordant demands emanating from the private sector is that landowners be paid not to violate the Endangered Species Act. It is asserted that they should be compensated for any governmental restrictions on their use of their property because of the presence of an endangered species, even when such restrictions are issued to protect the interests of society as a whole. Setting aside for the moment the obligation to balance individual rights and collective rights, if compensation were required for every regulatory restraint on the use of private property, the government would soon go broke, and anarchy would prevail.

Sell-outs

Government officials are susceptible to pressure from corporate interests, if for no other reason than industry money plays a major role in financing election campaigns. Their sell-outs of the general public are often buried in complex legislation and thus invisible to the untutored eye, but not all questionable official actions take place in the shadows. How about when a president appoints an individual whose previous job was to defend industry against the very agency he or she has been assigned to lead? It is a classic case of "the fox guarding the henhouse." A typical example of this egregious conflict of interest was President Bush's selection of coal-industry executive Richard Stickler to head the Mine Safety and Health Administration. This was the same Richard Stickler who from 1989 to 1996 managed a coalmine with an injury rate double the national average. It was a record that did not build confidence that the appointee would experience any epiphany upon taking office.

Then there was Bush's nomination of Michael Baroody to head the Consumer Product Safety Commission. Baroody was a lobbyist for the National Association of Manufacturers, in which capacity he campaigned against the very consumer protection regulations he would be expected to enforce.[12]

These appointments reflected a pattern of corporate cronyism that would erode any administration's regulatory credibility and raise serious concerns about a president's moral compass. Bush essentially adopted the strategy implemented in the 1980s by President Reagan: individuals were named as division heads of government agencies with which they had clashed in private life and that they were now expected to neutralize (instead of vitalize) whenever possible.

Rationalizing Harm

You might wonder how individuals who deliberately degrade the environment can live with themselves. Shouldn't they feel guilty about putting their families and friends—as well as future generations of each—at risk? An earlier section of the book describes several different rationales commonly employed to ease the pangs of conscience. Some environmental despoilers convince themselves that technological genius can repair any damage they have wrought. Others suppress concern by maintaining that any negative impacts are grossly exaggerated, and that, in any event, pollution is a natural byproduct of nature and not to be feared. Indeed, natural variation is the palliative song and dance we hear from some global warming skeptics.[13]

Then there are those who simply don't give a damn about the destruction they inflict. They are only concerned about realizing immediate monetary gain; let tomorrow take care of itself. By that time, they figure, they will have enough money to insulate themselves from any harmful environmental consequences—a delusional pipe dream that, if tolerated by society on a widespread basis, would ultimately leave everybody in the lurch.

The "technological fix" rationale for allowing environmental destruction is a familiar cop-out, and one of potentially disastrous proportions if exploited by an official entrusted with the welfare of the people who put him in office. Technology can be an important part of the solution but rarely a panacea. Mentally accomplished as human beings are, they have found no technology that can restore massively degraded air, land, and water to their original state. And it is highly unlikely they ever will.

—

CHAPTER FIVE

MORAL ABSOLUTISM

My Way or the Highway

Moral absolutism is often the product of an individual's egocentricity grounded in slavish adherence to ideology—religious or otherwise. Practical realities are secondary, and the opposite of the intended ethical outcome all too frequently occurs.

Yes, the basic concepts of good and evil are recognized by all humanity, but how these concepts are interpreted and applied in different cultures can vary. For example, it is universally accepted that it is wrong to punish an innocent person, yet the definition of "innocent" can differ in various societies. Although women don't have to wear a veil in the United States (and can attract stares if they do), in some countries failure to cover their face is a crime. Aggressively promoting voluntary sterilization is repugnant to our society. But in Nepal, population had been rapidly outstripping a meager natural-resource base, a worrisome state of affairs when more than 80 percent of the people depended on subsistence agriculture. The zealous voluntary sterilization program that was installed there seemed consistent with conditions on the ground at the time, and was arguably necessary for the country to remain self-sufficient and perhaps to survive as a viable sovereign state.[1]

Moral absolutists tend to view life through an all-or-nothing prism. President George W. Bush exhibited this inflexible, simplistic mindset with its enormous potential for causing harm and generating ill will. His inelastic posture and parochial vision were losing propositions in the field of international diplomacy. Classifying others as either allies or enemies with nothing in between was a surefire way to end up virtually friendless. Enduring human relationships are built around compromise. Hence, don't take comfort from those who always slavishly agree with you regardless of the circumstances. Given human nature, it is an unnatural condition and the odds are that some day it will end badly.

Furthermore, Bush's failure to acknowledge our mistakes (and strive to correct them) when we denounced the same shortcomings in others created a double standard that antagonized friend and foe alike.

There are those who regard moral absolutism as a righteous stance against oppression. Consider people who treat private property

rights as a license to do whatever they please on their land and view any
limits imposed by society as a persecutory encroachment on personal
freedom. They overlook that anarchy is a scourge even in a freewheeling
democracy—and is prone to elicit violence against the environment, not to
mention fellow human beings.

President Bush's ideological fervor against abortion led him to
withhold family planning funds from the United Nations Population and
Development Agency (UNPDA) because that organization channeled
money to nations where abortion was legal (as it is in the United States).
Consequently, many foreign family planning programs charged with
providing the necessary counseling and contraception to avoid unintended
pregnancies were shortchanged. The number of abortions actually increased
in the Third World, and abortion-related deaths soared to record-breaking
levels, hardly a triumph for the "pro-life" crowd.[2] Free of any ideological
shackles, President Barack Obama reversed this misguided policy as one
of his first acts in office, emulating President Bill Clinton, who did the very
same thing with George H.W. Bush.

The Bush family was certainly not the only purveyor of "morally
driven" policies with troubling ethical ramifications. Back in 1989, the
Vatican publicly labeled family planning "contraceptive imperialism."
Indeed, the Catholic Church has long looked askance at artificial
contraception, classifying it as a "mortal sin" (despite the vast majority of
its parishioners around the world rejecting that holy admonition).[3] It is easy
to understand laymen's defiance in the wake of Pope John Paul the Second
opposing the use of contraceptives even when one of the partners in a
marriage was diagnosed with AIDS. It would seem that in this situation, the
"mortal sin" would be not to allow contraceptive use as protection against
a highly lethal disease.

Pope Benedict expanded the reach of this parochial policy by
urging Italian Catholic pharmacists to refuse—on "moral grounds"—to sell
"morning-after" birth control pills. No matter that such a refusal would
violate existing Italian law, and just as profoundly, amount to a merciless
dismissal of many women's concerns and complex human relationships.[4]

George W. Bush—Business trumps nature

CHAPTER SIX

—

MILITARIZATION

War and Morality

IS WAR INHERENTLY IMMORAL? Not, I suppose, if it is an exercise waged in legitimate self-defense. But when nations' military spending runs far in excess of what is required to repel aggression, the drastic diversion of funds from vital public health and environmental protection programs is nothing less than sinful.

Think that indictment is too strong? Think again! Back in 2003, global military expenditures were $900 billion annually, an example of overkill if ever there were one. Just 12 percent of that sum would have halved global poverty and hunger by the year 2015 and fulfilled much of humanity's health and education requirements. That amount also would have been enough to provide safe drinking water for everyone on the planet (and quite possibly reduced tensions leading to violent outbursts in the first place).

Not sufficiently troubled? A paltry $500 million would have sufficed to eradicate malaria, which kills approximately 2.7 million people annually across the world.[1]

In impoverished developing countries, where military spending is grotesquely disproportionate, as it is just about everywhere else, there is an average of 20 soldiers to every doctor for a healthcare-deprived population.

Our own government spends enough to decimate our enemies many times over. In fact, the United States' yearly military expenditure in 2007, $500 billion, equaled nearly half of the world's "defense" budget, and exceeded the combined sum spent on weapons by the next 14 countries in the armaments pecking order. To demonstrate how out of whack our priorities were, consider that of every dollar in federal income taxes that Americans paid in 2006, the military received 40 cents compared to one hundredth of a penny for expanding renewable energy and conservation and three fourths of a penny for diplomacy and economic development.[2] After four years, the misbegotten Iraq War had cost us $450 billion, an amount sufficient to fund and educate all the world's poor for five and a half years.[3] By 2010, total U.S. military spending in Iraq and Afghanistan amounted to more than one trillion dollars, dwarfing expenditures for a myriad of domestic needs.[4]

Specific shocking disparities were uncovered by the Washington-based Institute for Policy Studies in late January 2008. The Institute released a budgetary analysis showing that the Bush administration had spent $88 on military security for every dollar devoted to combating global warming. The imbalance didn't stop there. We recently laid out $9.5 billion annually to provide small arms weaponry to other countries compared to the $212 million we contributed to their efforts to cope with climate change. These were dramatic cases of a "penny-wise, pound-foolish" policy, considering that climate instability in the long term poses a far greater threat to our national security than does a conventional shooting war.

Why a far greater threat? The United Nation's Intergovernmental Panel on Climate Change (IPPC) projected that unabated global warming would transform some densely inhabited areas into extremely inhospitable places. Such devastation would trigger a flood of environmental refugees, whose influx would possess enormous potential to stir social unrest wherever they chose to relocate.

According to an analysis by the British peace organization International Alert, 46 nations inhabited by 2.7 billion people are already at high risk of being politically destabilized because of global warming's adverse effects on their natural-resource base. Food and water shortages resulting from prolonged drought would exacerbate tensions and drive people in these nations to migrate to places where their presence would likely overload the resource-carrying capacity and alienate the locals. To curb the flight of their citizens, poorer countries need to adapt to climate change through revision of their land use and energy mix as well as through modernization of infrastructure and an upgrade in social services. Their lacking the resources to do so creates both a moral imperative and practical incentive (in the name of national security) for wealthy industrial states to extend a helping hand.[5]

Resource shortages apart from direct global warming impacts also create tensions that can, and have, erupted into armed conflict. In fact, the United Nations issued a report that concluded that 40 percent of modern civil wars stemmed from disputes over access to natural resources. According to the UN, at least 16 regional conflicts between 1990 and 2008, primarily in Africa, were sparked by competing claims to water, arable land, minerals, or other types of raw materials.[6]

Christian Aid, an organization affiliated with British and Irish churches, recently issued a report that held the United States responsible for a third of the annual global cleanup bill based on the output of American greenhouse gas emissions.[7] Yet it is a liability we have been reluctant to acknowledge. At this stage, it looks as though a global environmental crisis, rather than a moral epiphany, will motivate us to atone. Parenthetically—and ironically—one notes that by being the world's largest single greenhouse-gas-emitting organization, the U.S. military has become its own worst enemy, given the increased security risks attributed to global warming.

Prominent environmental analyst Lester Brown, president of Earth Watch, has succinctly put our defense expenditures in proper perspective. He calculated that by shifting approximately one third of our military appropriations to domestic needs, we could create an economically and environmentally sustainable economy and still have a larger military budget than Russia, China, and our NATO allies combined.[8]

Other nations have major adjustments to make as well. Their disjointed priorities forced the United Nations in 2006 to spend 228 times as much on its military operations as on its peacekeeping activities.[9]

Environmental Warfare

Although there are times when the conduct of war has a moral underpinning, no moral justification exists, even in the heat of battle, for laying waste to the enemy's ecological support system on which civilian populations depend for survival. Even in a "righteous" war, the objective is to vanquish enemy combatants, not engage in genocide.

That is why environmental warfare is especially heinous. It can quickly deteriorate into a scorched Earth crusade that punishes the innocent, both alive and unborn. Obviously, thermonuclear war would qualify in cosmic terms. On a lesser scale, so would the deliberate razing of a productive natural forest irretrievably lost to desert encroachment. Saddam Hussein's destruction of the Iraqi wetlands, once home to hundreds of thousands of marsh Arabs, certainly could be cited for motivation, if not effect. Since Hussein's removal from the scene, a recovery effort financed by Italy and Japan has been in progress. But only 50 percent of the swamp has been restored, and the project has been plagued by drought and the diversion of river water upstream by neighboring countries. Although no foregone conclusion, completion is targeted for 2010, and if and when the marshland is truly revived, the United Nations intends to designate the entire area a World Heritage Site to be preserved for posterity.[10]

The late Saddam Hussein can also be condemned for igniting the Kuwaiti oil fields, which fouled Persian Gulf coastal waters that bear the scars to this day.

Exposure to the use of defoliant Agent Orange in the Vietnam War had painful, long-term consequences. In seeking to eliminate the enemy's jungle cover, our military ended up being responsible for severely adverse health effects among both Vietnamese citizens and American soldiers who came in contact with the highly lethal herbicide. Definite links have been scientifically established between exposure to the highly toxic chemical compound and the incidence of soft tissue sarcoma, non-Hodgkin's

Pre-Saddam Iraqi marsh, paradise lost.

lymphoma, Hodgkin's disease, and chronic lymphocytic leukemia.[11]

With the confirmation of severe injurious impacts of Agent Orange, there was no longer an excuse to equivocate over redress. Any failure on our government's part to compensate victims for related illnesses was morally untenable; yet there was resistance, with Pentagon attorneys challenging the causality between the herbicide exposure and a number of diseases cited by claimants. Government officials stonewalled for more than a decade before conceding in 2003 that a range of diseases suffered by veterans stemmed from contact with Agent Orange. But the bureaucrats wanted to pay benefits from that year only rather than from the much earlier time when the 498 afflicted troops filed their claims.[12] The attempt to save tax dollars at the expense of Americans who were injured in the course of risking their lives for their country evinced shocking moral insensitivity.

Fortunately, the tide turned in the aggrieved parties' favor. Courts ultimately ordered the Department of Veteran Affairs to pay retroactive benefits to former Agent Orange-exposed servicemen. The number of diseases qualifying for compensation gradually expanded, with ischemic heart disease, leukemia, and Parkinson's added as latecomers to the list.

The Environment's Calming Effect

Environmental concerns can stave off violent conflict as well as provoke it. Trans-boundary environmental problems that threaten regional survival and can only be resolved through collaboration have produced détente even between societies that have been at each other's throats throughout much of their history.

None other than the lowly barn owl recently provided a microcosm of such a pragmatic reconciliation. The bird served as a chemical-free solution to a rat infestation that threatened crops on both sides of the Israeli-Jordanian border. Jordanian farmers discovered that their Israeli counterparts were successfully using the common barn owl to keep the rodent population in check. A low-profile meeting was arranged, resulting in the launch of a collaborative effort that transcended centuries of enmity. With the help of owl sharing, prejudice and suspicion were at least temporarily put on hold. Old enemies may not have become bosom buddies overnight, but some mutual respect and even trust took hold.

There are examples on a larger scale where the need for unity in tackling potentially catastrophic trans-boundary environmental problems led avowed foes to cooperate.[13] Indeed, for decades, the Mediterranean has brought together Israel and her enemies bordering the sea to combat severe pollution threats. The Democratic Republic of the Congo, Rwanda, and Uganda have cooperated in preservation of the rare mountain gorilla that inhabits their adjacent territories and is a major source of tourism

The last supper?

revenue. In 2008, these not the best of African neighbors agreed to a ten-year conservation plan for the 700 or so surviving animals.[14] The United States severed direct diplomatic relations with Cuba shortly after the dictator Fidel Castro seized power in 1959. But the two countries have long cooperated on data gathering and disaster preparedness strategy in the face of Atlantic hurricanes projected to strike both their landmasses.[15]

Perhaps the most publicized, expedient-driven détente among feuding sovereign states has been the Nuclear Arms Treaty. The document was signed by 180 nations and has been ratified so far by 140. You can be sure that not all of these countries are bosom buddies.

CHAPTER SEVEN

—

RESPECT FOR THE LAW

Government–Savior or Rogue?
EPA–Mediator or Advocate?

WHEN PRESIDENT GEORGE W. BUSH appointed New Jersey
Governor Christine Todd Whitman to head the Environmental Protection
Agency (EPA), she declared that the department's mission was to employ a
"balanced approach" in resolving environmental controversies. In saying
that, she demonstrated a lack of understanding of her agency's role. Within
the federal government, the EPA was supposed to be the people's advocate
for combating pollution and other forms of ecological degradation, just as
the Commerce Department championed the business community and the
Agriculture Department defended farmers' concerns.

Yet the EPA at times has been intimidated by corporate America's
political clout. Instead of fulfilling its moral as well as legally mandated
obligation to safeguard public health and environmental quality above
all else, the agency has often reverted to stressing "balance" in carrying
out its duties. Unfortunately, that tends to be an EPA code word for
making concessions before negotiations have even begun. You don't
hear representatives of the Commerce or Agriculture Departments
open deliberations by talking about balance in seeking benefits for their
respective constituencies. They start by asking for the whole ball of wax
and work from there.

Since EPA administrators serve at the pleasure of the president,
they are likely to be beholden to the office and act accordingly, even when
White House demands run counter to the agency's mission. Forgotten then
is the EPA's underlying directive, in which the President of the United States
ideally is considered more of a constituent than a boss.

With no past president, regardless of party affiliation, eager to
alienate corporate campaign contributors, it is clear why the EPA has been
far more deferential to business interests than legislative drafters originally
intended. Bush's last EPA administrator, Stephen Johnson, was among the
worst in kowtowing to industry at the behest of the White House. Witness
his declaration concerning a particularly nasty form of air pollution.
He announced that the annual standard to protect the public against
chronic, long-term exposure to primarily industrially generated particulate

matter would not be strengthened due to "insufficient evidence." Johnson stated this emphatically, even as 20 out of 22 members of the scientific advisory board counseling EPA on the matter recommended tightening the regulation.[1] That recommendation stuck in the craw of the laissez-faire-minded Bush, and he made his feelings known to a compliant Johnson in no uncertain terms.

Perhaps most egregious among Johnson's actions was his refusal to grant a waiver to California and 11 other states so that they could enact automobile tailpipe-emission standards stricter than the federal ones. Johnson said he did not think conditions warranted a waiver (even though his top advisors within the agency told him the opposite). His stonewalling reflected Bush's detachment towards the global warming threat, despite a persuasive body of scientific evidence, and made a mockery of the president's professed philosophical commitment to "states' rights."

Even so-called "big government" proponents believe federal standards should only set a floor and not a ceiling for regulation, leaving the latter up to the respective states. It would thus seem that centrists are much stronger advocates of states' rights than Bush and other conservative champions of the concept purport to be.

"Insufficient evidence" is an EPA catchword often used to justify federal inaction against pollution threats and to thereby ingratiate the agency with corporate polluters. The very elastic phrase was rolled out recently to explain a delay in strengthening the regulation of toxic formaldehyde fumes from wood products, even as California sought to tighten the rules.[2]

EPA should not ignore economic factors in promulgating environmental regulations. But if Congress's original intent were given its full due, the agency would not be putting corporate monetary interests on a par with protection of public health and our biological life-support system. Instead, the agency would be assigning the highest priority to environmental concerns and only from that frame of reference, begin to negotiate on commercial sticking points. That would be consistent with our major environmental statutes, which explicitly instruct EPA to take economics into account only in approving various forms of compliance with antipollution standards, not in setting them.

In all fairness, the EPA has taken some strong stands during its relatively short life span, but just not often enough. As a result, it has been the target of numerous lawsuits by environmental groups over the years.

Respecting the Law

Some pollution occurs naturally, but it is pollution to which the environment has acclimated over eons. The same cannot be said for the new kid on the block, human-induced pollution, which includes contaminated smoke from tobacco products. Smokers argue that because cigarettes are legal merchandise, banning tobacco use in public places violates their individual rights. But their argument has withered under the ever- increasing weight of evidence incriminating secondary cigarette smoke as a health hazard to nonsmokers within range of the fumes. Exposure has been linked not only to cancer and heart disease but to depression as well.[3] Indeed, after examining the latest studies, Dr. Richard H. Carmona, the U.S. Surgeon General from 2002 to 2006, felt confident enough to declare: "There is no risk-free level of exposure to secondhand smoke."

Nonetheless, as long as the sale of cigarettes remains legal, smokers have the option of putting themselves at risk by pursuing their noxious habit in private.[4] Where smoking is legal, the government is left with no obligation—regulatory or moral—other than to require that each cigarette pack display a warning label delineating the considerable health risks associated with tobacco use.

It is a different story when people are involuntarily exposed in public places to hazards not of their own making, such as secondhand smoke or highly toxic industrial pollution. Then, the government has the responsibility to intervene with prohibitions to protect individuals who have little other recourse.

Involuntary exposure is also the rationale for labeling genetically altered food. Although such products have not been proved dangerous, enough uncertainty exists for ingredients to be identified so that consumers can make an educated choice whether to partake.

Law-abiding Bribery

We have noted the right wing's brazen attempt to circumvent the intent, if not the letter, of the law by demanding that landowners be paid for not violating the Endangered Species Act. Invoking private property rights, the conservatives insist on compensation for the loss of the use of their acreage as a result of restrictions imposed to protect a rare species on their grounds. Such ideologues seem oblivious to the maxim that "no man is an island," and to the democratic manifesto that calls for a balance between individual and collective rights. If the premise of being compensated for obeying the law ever gained acceptance, it has been noted that there would be insufficient funds to enforce the laws, and the ideal of the "greater good" would give way to anarchy.

Let's just say that private property rights are not absolute, especially when pitted against society's responsibility for preservation of irreplaceable natural resources (be they endangered species, native wetlands, or the like). Taken in the aggregate, such resources are vital to the survival of the human race.

Out of Sight, Out of Mind
Fortunately, our legal system—primarily through zoning
regulations—has usually held firm against ill-advised property rights
challenges. But there are situations where permissible evasion of
environmental laws has occurred with disturbing frequency. To reduce
overhead costs and maximize profits, a number of American companies
have relocated to countries in which environmental regulations are either
not enforced or nonexistent. Time will run out on this unprincipled strategy
as the nations at the receiving end, however impoverished, come to realize
how much environmental damage has resulted from their permissiveness.
When this happens, governments of wealthy countries will likely support
their less affluent cousins' epiphany. They will do so not only because of
the anticipation that domestic companies will return from foreign shores,
but almost certainly because of the recognition that pollution can leapfrog
national boundaries and thus should ideally be controlled on American soil.

Proximity is Everything
A location near a toxic waste dump is an obvious negative,
but there are instances where people attempt to turn proximity to an
environmentally sensitive site to their advantage. Some parties who live
adjacent to our national parks or other publicly owned recreational land
maintain that their location entitles them to preferential treatment. They
demand greater control over the management of the territory's resources
than the rest of the nation's citizenry, even though the latter hold equal title
to the land. While proximity invariably makes for more convenient access,
it does not confer special ownership privileges. Everyone is supposed to be
subject to the same restrictions and permit processes, regardless of where
they reside. To allow otherwise would encourage locals to cultivate the
perception—and reality—that they are above the law.

Conflicts of Interest
Some of our national leaders have taken unconscionable liberties
in their conduct of environmental policy. Especially in the Reagan and
George W. Bush years, as noted previously, individuals have been appointed
to regulatory posts from the ranks of those whose corporate employers
were prime targets of the regulation, a prima facie conflict of interest and
a flagrant display of cronyism. Much of this shameful practice stemmed
from the thinly veiled contempt that conservatives held for the government
they headed and the regulatory agencies' encroachment on free market
capitalism. Their mantra was that the market could sort out abuse and
inequities more effectively than some government bureaucrats. To no one's
surprise, it then followed that these conservatives' favoritism toward their

corporate constituency ran rampant; and the environment suffered as regulations were sporadically enforced or dispensed with altogether. Just one more egregious example: what could be more unethical—or logically absurd—than to have government family planning programs headed by an individual who opposes distribution of contraceptives and other birth control information? Yet that is precisely what President Bush did when he named Eric Keroack Health and Human Services Deputy Secretary for Population Affairs.[5]

Sins of Omission

President Reagan was not enthralled by federal environmental regulation, but rather than roll it back directly and take criticism for a highly visible unpopular move, he resorted to stealth tactics. Whenever possible, he simply delegated enforcement of federal regulations to states that shared his naïve lack of enthusiasm for imposing restraints on industry and were sure to adopt a relatively passive stance.[6]

The George W. Bush administration sometimes took a different tack. It engaged in calculated neglect by maintaining that the EPA had no authority under the Clean Air Act to regulate carbon dioxide. The president's reversal of his campaign pledge to rein in CO2 emissions was a sop to his industry buddies who objected to footing the extra cost of reducing greenhouse gas emissions. It was such an outrageous flouting of the law that even the conservative majority on the U.S. Supreme Court could not stomach the move. The justices ordered EPA to regulate carbon dioxide unless the agency could give a darn good reason not to do so— which it could not, even though the Bush regime never ceased trying. The Bush administration's shenanigans served as a reminder that Congress and the courts must be ever vigilant in guarding against a president's arbitrary attempt to undermine a law not to his (or her) liking.

SECTION TWO

—

HUMANE OR MALEVOLENT?

CHAPTER EIGHT

—

IS NATURE MALEVOLENT?

Is NATURE MERCILESS? A hunter defending his avocation in a letter to *The New York Times* years ago definitely thought so. "Nature is neither gentle, kind nor balanced," he wrote. "Predators frequently prey on their own young or favor the babes of other species, often kill more than they need for sustenance, and often kill inefficiently, even consuming their prey while it is still alive. Wild animals seldom die of old age. Failing efficient management (i.e., hunting and trapping) by human beings, overpopulated animals succumb to starvation or diseases like rabies or sarcoptic mange, hideous and protracted deaths."

All of the conditions that the hunter referenced in his letter do occur in the wild; and it's true that, in a sense, nature metes out a harsh brand of justice through survival of the fittest. Viewed in a broader context, however, the letter writer evoked a harsher image than nature merited. Many philosophers and scientists consider nature amoral rather than immoral. A case can even be made that there is an element of benevolence in the way nature takes care of its own in the midst of surroundings full of pitfalls.

Apart from the fact that joys (however ephemeral) as well as tribulations are inherent in life, there is evidence that the natural order has built-in mechanisms to temper if not offset (at least temporarily) the sharp edge of existence. Obviously, wild animals cannot purchase an aspirin or retreat to a doctor's office for a pain-killing injection. Yet they are not without recourse. For example, research on deer suggests that when these animals die from starvation, their systems start shutting down, mitigating their suffering in the process. It is an extension of their normal behavior in food-scarce mid–winter, when their metabolism slows dramatically so that they need far less nourishment.

Renowned Supreme Court Justice Oliver Wendell Holmes once quipped: "There are three natural anesthetics—sleep, fainting, and death." With all due respect to Justice Holmes, he was guilty of some glaring omissions. Nature just might be more merciful than he gave it credit for. Our brains secrete chemical compounds, known as endorphins, which help to control pain. We also get a boost from our brains releasing serotonin and dopamine that assist in maintaining our immune systems. Human

endocrine systems produce natural hormonal anesthetics in response
to injury. Nature provides us with antibodies to combat disease and
coagulants to staunch wounds. Extreme cold has a painkilling effect.
The natural world also places at our disposal numerous balms, palliatives,
and anti-toxins that can be extracted from plants and other animals.
Studies suggest that all living organisms possess some sort of chemical
compound that benefits them and may be of use to other species–for
example, to reduce or prevent pain.

Even the "survival of the fittest" theory that human beings have
long regarded as the cold-blooded foundation of the natural order has
mitigating aspects. Wildlife that succumbs to predation, disease, and famine
usually is the most enfeebled to begin with. Though creatures' will to live
rarely disappears while breath is still being drawn, resistance fades rapidly
in such a diminished state. It is then that nature normally steps in and
reduces the subject to a painless, comatose state. The hunter's contentions
notwithstanding, such a closure seems much "'kinder" in the grand scheme
of things than a scenario in which a healthy animal is cut down in the
prime of life by a bullet or an arrow.

Biologists tend to take a more holistic view of the survival of the
fittest. They view this law of nature not so much as a matter of "kill or be
killed" but as a necessary building block in perpetuating life. Predation
is not only a merciful end to a suffering, infirm animal, but also essential
to keeping the natural system in demographic balance so that a healthy
regenerative process is not disrupted.

Nature is just as assertive in the prime of life as in illness and
dying. Every species is equipped with some feature that serves it in good
stead in keeping it alive, provided it is healthy. Predators are endowed with
finely honed weapons of attack. To maintain some sort of balance, their
prospective victims are endowed with a formidable means of defense—
camouflage, great speed, chemical repellent, and the like.

Benign interaction with nature seems capable of providing ample
reward. Studies have shown that proximity with green space enhances both
physical and mental health. Better air quality and exercise opportunities
are certainly factors behind this phenomenon, but so are uncluttered green
space's stress-reducing surroundings. Most importantly, if we stay within
nature's parameters and allow its rhythms to set the pace, chances are
the respect we show will be returned in kind, resulting in the optimum
longevity and quality of life for which one could hope.

SECTION THREE

—

COMPASSION

CHAPTER NINE

—

ALL THINGS EQUAL

Environmental Elitism

IN ITS EARLY STAGES, the environmental movement was dominated by relatively affluent individuals who gave "green" activism a bad name in working-class neighborhoods. Those well-to-do activists acquired their unenviable reputation by doing little to refute the impression that, in the words of some critics, "they cared more about butterflies than human beings." They bore the image of individuals willing to shut down a factory and throw people out of work because the site could be better used for songbird habitat.

Such an elitist image played right into the hands of those seeking to deprive the fledgling national environmental movement of political clout. And in the first few years after the initial Earth Day celebration in 1970, that strategy worked. Corporate polluters shrewdly turned the elitist stereotype into an effective propaganda tool that isolated environmental activists from their natural allies—labor unions, minorities, and the economically disadvantaged in general.[1]

The environmental "elitists" were not indifferent to their fellow humans. Their attitude stemmed primarily from naiveté and narrow focus rather than callousness. They tended to occupy a station in life in which they had minimal contact with those lower on the economic ladder. This fostered an "out of sight, out of mind" mentality that lent itself to a preoccupation with threats to the natural world and insensitivity to the industrial pollution plaguing their less fortunate brethren.

Many of the fledgling environmental organizations defined their mission as saving wilderness (and nothing else) from being overrun by civilization. Among the prominent politicians who typified the movement mindset in its early days (the 1970s) was the late Nelson Rockefeller, one time vice president and governor of New York. He was an ardent champion of nature preservation, but he left much of his enthusiasm for environmental reforms at the forest's edge.

As governor, Rockefeller took it upon himself to make certain that Adirondack State Park, the largest unspoiled wilderness left in the northeastern United States, was preserved for posterity. Yet this same Rockefeller would only upgrade air-pollution-abatement systems of oil-burning incinerators in buildings he owned when forced to do so by the courts.

As the 1970s progressed, the "elite" realized they needed massive public support to thwart corporate desecration of wilderness areas, and that environmental degradation had a human face to it. Meanwhile, it began to dawn on low-income segments of the population that they were the primary victims of industrial pollution; after all, toxic dumps and fume-spewing factories were invariably placed in or near their neighborhoods. Labor unions, minorities, and organizations representing the downtrodden, who once regarded environmental activists as snobs indifferent to job loss and creation, reversed field. Rifts were healed and coalitions formed to present a united front against corporate polluters. Cooperation was further reinforced by the prospect of "green" job creation for economically depressed areas and reflected in such joint climate change lobbying ventures like the one carried out by the National Association for the Advancement of Colored People and the National Wildlife Federation.[2]

Yes, there were a few holdouts to this sort of collaboration. The Association of Black Mayors continued to be seduced by industry's divisive, specious rhetoric that pollution was the price of job creation. Fortunately, the overwhelming majority of Americans from all social strata reached the point where they identified themselves as environmentalists to some degree, even if they weren't card carrying Sierra Club members.

This newfound public concern, combined with activists' creative lobbying, spurred Congress to distinguish the decade of the 70s' by enacting the nation's landmark environmental laws.

Kindness to Animals

DOLPHINS

Adrift with reprieve out of reach
By washing up upon a beach,
When suddenly dolphin fins appear,
A curiosity stoked by fear.

Did they hear my cry for help?
They did not answer with a yelp.
And yet attracted to my spoor
That marked my struggle towards the shore.

Encircled by a mammal ring
Impregnable to anything.
I felt myself immune to threat,
And truly in those creatures' debt.

No shark would dare to venture near,
Nor even linger in the rear.
As guided by a boisterous band,
I floated towards the nearest land.

How was I found in that vast sea,
So that the school could rescue me?
An act of God, a quirk of fate?
To wrest me from a desperate strait.[3]

Certain species seem to have a better record than many humans when it comes to familial relationships. Take the practice of monogamy. Wolves, Canadian geese, and some species of monkeys, rodents, and antelopes are among the creatures that mate for life, which is more than approximately half of the Americans who take wedding vows manage to do.

Many senior citizens in our society are shunted into old people's homes by relatives weary of caretaking responsibilities. By contrast, some members of the animal kingdom—elephants and lions being cases in point—protect their elders to a greater degree than many of us do. Elderly lions are not involuntarily sent out to pasture. They hang out with the pride and share the food, even if they can no longer hunt. As for elephants, the herd usually takes care of grandma to her dying day.

The maternal instinct in many lower life forms is every bit as powerful as it is in human beings. Indeed, certain species in the wild never voluntarily abandon their offspring. Try to step in and separate a healthy polar bear cub or baby elephant from their respective mothers and you are asking for a struggle to the death. Contrast that with accounts that periodically crop up in our newspapers and local newscasts pertaining to children being abandoned by their parents. Apes tend to linger and seem to mourn over the bodies of fallen comrades. Not all of us do the same with our dead.

Does this mean animals have souls and consciously feel affection, compassion, and grief as we do? Author Eugene Linden, who has written four books on animal intelligence, notes that it is very difficult to prove definitively that a creature has self-awareness and feels empathy toward others of its kind. And yet he cites experiments in which dolphins, elephants, and great apes appear to recognize themselves in the mirror—in effect displaying a sense of their own individual identities, a prerequisite for possessing human attributes.[4]

From a moral perspective, that is all beside the point. Whether animals have anthropomorphic feelings or are dumb, robotic beasts driven

Dolphin—Enslaved in captivity

solely by blind reflex should have no bearing on our obligation to treat them in benevolent fashion. Our cognitive superiority and moral code, paired with an appreciation for the interconnectedness of the biosphere, should instill a responsibility to preserve the natural world as best we can. Unless a life form poses a direct threat to our personal safety, we should treat it as humanely as possible.

With that thought in mind, we humans should not put an animal in a position where it is a direct threat to our safety. That is another way of saying people have no business making pets of wild animals. It is inhumane to try to domesticate species that have adapted over millenniums to a totally different environment. The environment is one where human beings are intruders, and thus, instinctively regarded as threats. It is a perception that can lead to even supposedly tamed wildlife exploding in a sudden primordial outburst of violence against their unsuspecting owners.

We also need to display more sensitivity in the use of animals in laboratory experiments where suffering occurs. The usual excuse given is that there are no substitutes for using live animals as guinea pigs. It is an excuse that is no longer valid in most cases. Nowadays, artificial simulation through such techniques as computer modeling and chemical testing can be employed to conduct the most risky experiments (although laboratory rats and mice still seem to be frequently indispensable in a number of fields of research).

As was previously noted, filmmakers have employed modern advances in cinematography, especially through computerization, to reduce the inhumane use of live animals. Occasional transgressions still occur in the course of production, but they are rare.

Wildlife is sometimes made a scapegoat for the shortcomings of human beings. Whales and dolphins have occasionally been slaughtered for supposedly depriving human beings of a fair share of the oceanic harvest. This butchery is not justifiable retaliation but a cover for acts of avarice associated with over-fishing or the illegal slaying of cetaceans for meat and body parts. The falsely accused "nuisance" cetaceans occupy a well-established ecological niche, and nature regulates their numbers through the availability of their food source. That leaves a generous surplus for human consumption—provided fishermen conduct their operations on a sustainable basis.

Compassion has been singularly lacking in modern-day Alaska, where hunters pick off wolves from helicopters in what is supposed to pass for sport hunting. This is nothing more than an orchestrated massacre in which the hapless victims are eliminated so that pusillanimous human hunters have no competition in bagging elk. As was previously pointed out, one of the unintended consequences of a shortage of wolves is the uncontrolled proliferation of elk that proceed to overgraze and decimate native vegetation.

Bad Sport

Sport hunting is distasteful not only because the competition tends to be so one-sided. In addition, it usually strikes down animals in their prime, just the opposite of natural selection, which is determined by the survival of the fittest and thus perpetuates a line of the healthiest specimens. It's one thing to gun down an animal for subsistence purposes, in self-defense, or in order to cull a species that has overrun its habitat, but blowing away wildlife for the sheer sake of sport is nothing more than ritualistic killing designed to titillate our primal instinct. Did it ever occur to the hunters that they could experience a similar, if not more satisfying sensation, through use of a camera rather than a rifle? Indeed, it is more of a challenge to maneuver near enough to take a dramatic close-up photograph of a hard-to-approach wild animal than to nail the creature with a telescopic, high-powered rifle from a hundred yards away.

Telltale Violence

Hunting often amounts to senseless slaughter, but at least it occurs within a prescribed framework. Some individuals, however, are prone to acts of random violence against animals, and these people are most likely in need of medical attention. Why? Physical maltreatment of animals often is symptomatic of similar aberrant behavior towards fellow human beings.[5] According to an FBI analysis, most imprisoned serial killers killed or tortured animals in their youth.

Appalling as that behavior is, it is dwarfed in magnitude by the systematic poaching of species into extinction. Is "killing the goose that lay the golden egg" a subconscious death wish on the part of the perpetrators? Or do greed and/or desperation prompt them to care only for the moment? Often it is a combination of the two.

Most profoundly of all, when people have no compunction about purposely eradicating a species from the face of the Earth, it challenges the idea that cognitive superiority elevates human beings above other life forms.

Heartless Ideology

Whether out of ignorance or design, there are those so intent on being politically correct that they are blind to the human suffering caused by their dogmatic stance. Witness the conservatives who worry that too much government assistance to the needy at home and abroad will undermine self-reliance—a rationalization that is little more than a self-serving cop-out to save money rather than lives. Their concerns about the corrupting effects of government subsidies miraculously vanish when public funds are lavished upon corporate beneficiaries. If these recipient companies should happen to be polluters, we have the general public ending up financing their tormenters. Morality turned inside out!

Compartmentalized Do-gooders

Then there are the merciless practitioners of compartmentalized good conscience. You will find antiabortion activists very protective of the fetus but losing interest once the birth has occurred. For them, a government safety net of social services for children born into poverty is at best an afterthought and at worst an unacceptable fiscal burden for taxpayers. I can think of no more painful example of this hypocritical behavior than the actions of the South Dakota legislature, which in 2006 voted to outlaw abortion, even in cases of incest or rape. While the lawmakers were expressing their heartfelt reverence for preservation of life, South Dakota was recording the 19th-worst record for infant mortality among all the states. In fact, the Washington-based Children's Defense Fund extrapolated from federal data that in South Dakota, an infant under the age of one was dying every five days. To top that off, the state ranked 16th worst in percentage of children who were poor, the sixth stingiest in dollars spent per pupil on education, and in the bottom ten in providing family planning counseling and contraceptive services to the public.[6]

Ideological Tyranny

No one is forcing those in our society who oppose the use of abortion and artificial contraceptives to partake of such practices. No one is holding a gun to their heads to engage in premarital sex if they believe an individual should remain celibate until marriage.

For certain types of fundamentalist conservatives, however, it's not enough that individuals are free to refrain from these activities if they so wish. In a pure exercise of ideological tyranny, those who disapprove of such legal activities demand that their behavioral code apply to everyone else, willing or not. That tyranny could have disastrous consequences if its adherents ever succeeded in institutionalizing their behavioral guidelines. Their views lack the flexibility needed to handle the complexity of human nature and everyday life. They still consider their way to be the sole formula for achieving "the greater good," regardless of the cost in human suffering and sacrifice of free choice. Not surprisingly, following their dictates increases the odds of reproductive health-related tragedies.

Take the case of the 11-year-old Columbian girl who was raped by her stepfather and had the ensuing pregnancy aborted. Reverence for life—all life—is crucial in preserving the world for future generations, but that reverence can be perverted.

As Exhibit A, I give you Cardinal Alfonso Lopez Trujillo, president of the Vatican's Pontifical Council for the Family. Cardinal Trujillo announced that the Catholic Church would excommunicate all medical personal and family members associated with the decision to abort the 11-year-old's pregnancy. There was appropriate reverence for life in this tale, but it was for the future of a deeply scarred child-mother, not the spawn of a sickening criminal act.

The most recent data show that outlawing abortion does not decrease the number of those traumatic procedures. On the contrary, researchers have found that the rate of abortions is roughly the same in nations where the procedure is banned as it is in the states where it is legal. What does happen when it is criminalized is that many women are driven underground to obtain abortions that put their own lives in jeopardy because they are carried out in unsafe conditions by poorly trained individuals.[7]

Fortunately, the absolutists have attracted relatively few converts to their one-dimensional view of a multidimensional world, and it is easy to see why. They oppose abortion even when delivery of the fetus could be fatal to the mother—if not physically, then psychologically. The same onerous inflexibility applies when the fetus is so hopelessly damaged that it would be little more than a vegetable if allowed to come to term (and should that birth occur, the voices of most champions of the unborn would almost certainly fall silent during the ensuing chain of painful events).

Disdain to Abstain

Ultra-right wingers advocate the teaching of abstinence in sex education courses without any mention of artificial contraception, which they consider a corrupting and ineffective intervention. Numerous studies show that students subjected solely to this restrictive curriculum are likely to be unprepared when their potent teenage hormones assert themselves.[8] Sexual expression is a natural impulse, and implying, if not directly denouncing it as a sin except in the case of marital coitus is too rigid a discipline for most psyches. At its core, sexuality is an emotion, and emotions are notoriously difficult to modulate and even harder to suppress. Certainly, there must be ground rules for striking a balance between sexual expression and unrestrained sexual behavior physically harmful to others. But bottling up normal sexual drives results in unhealthy pent-up frustration that can easily morph into perverse defiance (and in extreme cases, destructive violation) of accepted societal norms. This is why no one should be surprised that the region of the United States (i.e. the Bible Belt in the deep South) with the most puritanical stance towards sexuality has the highest rates of divorce, teen pregnancy, and sexually transmitted diseases.[9] The area is filled with uneducated youngsters who are prime candidates for the aforementioned scourges as well as sexually repressed neuroses and emotional breakdowns.

This abstinence-only ideology can be even more lethal in some African countries decimated by AIDS.[10] As a precondition for receiving financial assistance, the Bush administration required that one third of the annual $6 billion we donated to AIDS prevention had to be spent on abstinence-only programs in nations where adultery was woven into the daily cultural fabric. With abstinence programs diverting money from our government's condom distribution, those African nations had to prioritize and concentrate on supplying contraceptives to high-risk groups such as prostitutes and single men when protection was desperately needed throughout the entire population.

Thus, George W. Bush's failure to cast aside his ideological blinders and acknowledge the reality of certain cultures cost lives that need not have been lost. (After a trip to Africa, even First Lady Laura Bush found the lack of emphasis on artificial contraception morally indefensible.[11])

For the aforementioned reasons, abstinence-only sex education programs simply cannot stand the test of time. Thus, it is only a matter of time before funding of such programs in this county is discontinued and the money shifted to the support of a more comprehensive sex education curriculum throughout our school system.

More Myopia

The same narrow-minded conservative school of thought condemned the use of embryonic stem cells in medical research as infanticide. It made no difference that fertility clinics routinely discarded these unused embryos into the trash.[12]

And what of Bush administration officials who withheld sorely needed aid to Brazil's impoverished masses because of the presence of legalized prostitution in that country? Hypocrisy trumped compassion, considering that prostitution is a legal cottage industry in Nye County, Nevada. In addition, it is a fixture in most developed nations throughout the world. Governments have found that licensing civilization's oldest and most durable profession through regulation of prostitutes' health has helped purge criminal elements and cut down on sexually transmitted diseases.

Gender Discrimination

Women are often cruelly exploited in illegal prostitution rings. But in much of the developing world, they are a prime target for maltreatment and inferior status simply by virtue of their gender. Such bias has had major adverse environmental ramifications. The truncated education of girls has resulted in female illiteracy rates falling off the charts in some Third World nations. A typical statistic: of 72 million kids of primary school age not in school in the developing world, 57 percent were girls.[13]

Females in those countries are essentially confined to the home to have babies, prepare meals, work in the fields, and in some instances perform physically demanding manual labor on community brick-and-mortar infrastructure. Environmental protection suffers mightily because history has shown that women typically have a more nurturing nature than men and tend to be more sensitive to environmental concerns if given the educational opportunity to realize their potential. Poverty is reduced with more educational opportunity.

Education produces another important benefit. If women have access to equal schooling opportunities, lower birth rates almost always follow, along with population stabilization. The latter is a prerequisite for rescuing humanity from eventually overwhelming the Earth's ecological carrying capacity.[14]

And the sustainable use of Earth's riches is not the only global benefit that gender equity and population stabilization bring to the table. According to a 2009 United Nations report, reduced population produces fewer greenhouse gas emissions, thereby slowing the pace of global warming. Moreover, if the many women working in the fields in developing countries are better educated, they will exert a greater influence in shifting to environmentally sustainable, minimally polluting agriculture.[15]

Euthanasia through Statistics

Women are not the only individuals threatened with third-class citizenship. If the Bush administration had its way, elderly Americans would have faced a similar fate, with even grimmer ramifications. Using a cost-benefit formula to set antipollution standards, the White House concluded that the expense to industry of providing the extra protection senior citizens needed would not have saved enough lives to make the allocation "worthwhile." One could get more bang for the buck from weaker standards that would be sufficient to safeguard the health of sturdier younger generations who had more years ahead of them. (In the process, such a devaluation of seniors' lives would reduce industry's cleanup bill and bolster its balance sheet.) For the Bush people, money was the be-all and end-all, as attested by their strong inclination to treat life in purely dollars-and-cents terms. It was a mindset that reinforced their reputation as individuals who "knew the cost of everything and the value of nothing."[16]

And yet that dollar-oriented administration could conveniently neglect to peer through its cost-benefit kaleidoscope when the visual was not in keeping with its agenda. How else could the Bush supporters in good conscience have spent $40 million on a night of inaugural balls while some 29,000 youngsters under five throughout the world were dying every day of preventable disease? Even though a drop in the bucket, couldn't the sum have been put to better use in supporting programs that would have aided some of the 640 million kids living in extreme poverty and the more than 120 million unable to attend school? Why not have scaled back the lavish inaugural festivities to a single, token gala and diverted the bulk of the privately donated money to improving overall conditions in developing countries or some downtrodden areas on our own soil? At that time, one in three kids in the Third World had no toilet at home, one in five lacked access to potable water, and one in seven had no health care whatsoever. Although the ceremonial lure of lavish inauguration festivities seems well entrenched, one hopes that future presidents will consider modifying the celebration and using it primarily as a vehicle for raising money to reduce global poverty.[17]

SECTION FOUR

—

COURAGE

CHAPTER TEN

—

POLITICAL COURAGE AND COWARDICE

Fearing to Lead

ON FEBRUARY 29, 1980, in the East Wing of the White House, President Jimmy Carter told a private audience of several hundred environmentalists that "it's time for a society of consumers to become a society of conservers. This tremendous change is inevitable in our country, and it's only just begun."

Carter never dared repeat these frank words to the nation while he was in office. Indeed, a more modest public call to arms by Carter on behalf of greater alternative energy use eight months earlier had aroused such furor that he refrained from issuing any bold admonitions to the general populace for the duration of his term.

It was hard to blame him for not being more forthcoming since his bid for re-election was drawing near. And yet, if he'd only had the courage to repeatedly speak his mind and start a national dialogue… who knows? Maybe we would have been better prepared to respond to the formidable challenges posed by climate change, resource depletion, and demand for energy at the start of the 21st century. That would have been a legacy to be proud of even if he lost, as he did anyway, despite his overly cautious approach.

Could Carter's timorous silence be considered "immoral," or simply characterized as "pragmatic cowardice?" Morality factors into the equation when elected officials—in response to voters' demands for immediate gratification—forsake their own consciences (and the public's long-term best interests) in order to further their own careers. Based on those ground rules, Carter qualified as ethically compromised when he left office.

There is no denying that our system of government encourages such shortsighted expediency. Every few years, our elected officials must stand before a general public who for the most part fixate on short-term objectives. Few politicians are gutsy enough to promote the longer view, especially when it pertains to environmental problems that may intensify in barely perceptible increments. Even leaders considered most sympathetic to environmental reform are likely to back away from bold action when start-up remedial measures would be vigorously opposed in the absence of an obvious, imminent threat.

Yet our leaders were elected not only to provide us with instantaneous gratification but also to take responsibility for minimizing the environmental risks to future generations. Who else in an official capacity and with the requisite authority could act preemptively on behalf of the helpless unborn?

It was thus frustrating to hear Carter in private warn about the inevitable need to change from a society of consumers to one of conservers, but dare not display such unvarnished candor in public. (Only after being defeated for re-election did he feel free enough to openly share his prescient vision with the American people, a personal epiphany not unlike that of Al Gore.)

Former Colorado Governor Dick Lamm got the traditional code of conduct down pat when he cited Al Smith's observation that "a politician must not be so far ahead of the band that he can't hear the music." In Lamm's view, grassroots environmentalists should take the lead in precipitating change.

Lamm had it only half right. A strong-minded national leader would still be needed. Grassroots activists can be somewhat of a catalyst, but they simply do not have the cohesion, legal authority, and wherewithal to bring the public to heel. They would end up spinning their wheels without a head of state and Congress receptive to (and unafraid of) publicly promoting their cause.

It should be noted that totalitarian regimes with their ironclad rule are capable of bringing about environmental improvement much more expeditiously than a democracy can. For example, the Chinese government achieved a remarkable degree of cleanup of Beijing's filthy air virtually overnight because no one dared challenge the immediate imposition of Draconian measures.[1] Time-consuming debate on possible unintended consequences of the reforms was dispensed with under authoritarian rule. An argument can be made that when urgent action is required because of a rapidly approaching ecological point of no return, autocratic governance is better suited for the challenge. Democracies actually embrace this authoritarian approach in de facto fashion by providing their leaders with temporary emergency powers when it is universally accepted that a crisis is at hand.[2]

But if the public does not regard the threat sufficient to justify authoritarian control, the voter-sensitive democratic leader may shy away from adopting that course. Even in an impending crisis, it takes courage for the head of state in a democracy to act preemptively and behave as a benevolent despot. Hanging over the leader's head is the sobering realization that the dictatorial powers are only of short-lived duration and he (or she) must answer to the electorate if things don't end well.

A Renewable Dare

What about tapping clean, renewable energy as a superior alternative to tearing up the land in search of highly polluting fossil fuels? George W. Bush offered politically correct token support to renewable energy research. But more indicative of his true intentions was when in the next breath he stressed that the technology was still largely in the developmental stage and could not be counted on to significantly replace fossil fuel for a long time to come. To the delight of his drill-happy oil industry cronies, Bush wasn't much interested in the conclusions of studies to the contrary by such respected organizations as the Brookhaven National Research Institute.

Indeed, you would be hard pressed to find any world leader willing to make a serious effort to reverse the chewing up of the Earth and polluting of the air and water in pursuit of coal, gas and oil. It takes gumption to make a full-scale run at revolutionizing energy policy so that it ensures a sustainable high quality of life for generations to come. So far, Germany, the Scandinavian countries, Japan, and China have come the closest, with progressive (albeit still modest) government subsidized programs to harvest wind and solar energy. And with the departure of Bush, a young American president named Barack Obama gave strong indications he might join the club in a big way. To do so, he would have to embrace the kind of thinking that Bush eschewed and was articulated by three solar energy experts in a 2007 issue of Scientific American. Ken Zweibel, James Mason, and Vasilis Fthenakis used detailed documentation to make a convincing argument that solar power could supply at least half of our nation's energy by mid-century and possessed even further long-term potential.

Yes, some obstacles to their vision exist, but are they insurmountable? The trio conceded that for solar power to provide 69 percent of our nation's electricity by the year 2050, federal subsidies would have to total $400 billion over the next 40 years. That price tag would send most politicians scurrying for cover (unless the money was being allocated for weaponry or bailing out Wall Street brokerage houses).

The authors knew their plan would also draw criticism for requiring as much as 46,000 square miles of land to be covered by solar power installations. In defense, they cited a supportive study originating from the National Renewable Energy Laboratory in Golden, Colorado. The conclusion of the study was that there was more than enough vacant land in the American Southwest to accommodate extensive solar energy facilities without encroaching on environmentally sensitive areas and population centers.

Zweibel and his colleagues also addressed other major challenges to their grand design. Although conversion of a mere 2.5 percent of the solar energy striking the Southwest annually would provide a supply equal to the nation's total energy consumption in 2006, what about storing the power for times when the sun was not shining? How would the United States finance the enormous subsidies required? The answers offered by the authors: compressed-air storage and a carbon tax, respectively. Other techniques under development for storing solar energy include using molten salt that possesses the potential to preserve the sun's heat for up to six hours after sunset.[3] Also being perfected are benign recyclable substitutes for the toxic chemicals used in the manufacture of solar panels.[4]

As President Bush knew, or should have known, a number of proposed renewable-energy initiatives had enough substance to warrant substantial government support. But because he lacked the mettle to transcend his ideological and political lineage, the American people on his watch fell further behind in meeting the fearsome challenges of an ever more crowded, ecologically stressed world.

To solve the energy problem, nations need leaders of vision and fortitude as well as conscience, leaders who are upfront about the billions in subsidies required to bring to fruition the massive commercial application of solar and other renewable energy sources. Even then, that won't be enough without these officials possessing the political skills to persuade the public to accept the new direction, emphasizing that the substantial cost will produce bigger dividends down the road.

A Democratic Flub

Our country's sluggish pace at the turn of the 21st century could not be wholly blamed on George W. Bush. In the 1990s, Bill Clinton and Al Gore had a chance to be generational leaders, and for a time, the prospects were promising.

Early in his second term, President Clinton warned us about global warming: "We see the train coming, but most Americans in their day-to-day lives can't hear the whistle blowing...."

Unfortunately, when it came to climate change, Clinton tended to retreat at the first sign of significant political opposition.

Inhibited by his fealty to Clinton and his aspiration to be the next president, Al Gore made only symbolic forays into environmental activism during his tenure as second-in-command. He was not the same person who wrote the fiery, best-selling environmental tome, *Earth in the Balance*. Gore's muted behavior as vice president raises a fundamental question. Is our political system—built on compromise—compatible with making hard choices on serious environmental problems when there is little time or margin for error? Are we capable of being proactive when the full magnitude of the threat is not obvious and a reactive response would be too late? Or are our leaders always doomed to be so subservient to immediate gratification that only a catastrophe can jolt them into action? Rep. John Dingell, D-Mich., chairman of the House Energy and Commerce Committee, had a cynical take on those questions. In mid-2007, he exuded confidence that his colleagues wouldn't have the courage to stick their necks out by supporting a new tax aimed at curbing global warming.[5] An unwavering defender of the American auto industry, located in his district, Dingell introduced a bill authorizing a carbon tax opposed by his corporate constituents. His strategy was to call the bluff of House Speaker Nancy Pelosi and other lawmakers seeking aggressive legislation to reduce the energy use and air pollution associated with the burning of fossil fuels (and in Dingell's view, to possibly put a crimp in the profits of his automobile magnate friends).

Dingell knew there was little risk that his scheme to kill the idea would go awry. And sure enough, his fellow legislators, at least then, lacked the moral backbone to impose a new tax, no matter how environmentally beneficial such action would have been to society. A Congressional debate on how a new carbon tax would make a major dent in greenhouse gas emissions never occurred. There was no public discussion about how the levy could be structured to provide a rebate system to offset the hardships low-income earners would otherwise incur—and how the levy could be introduced in graduated fashion to ease the public's fiscal burden. A further egregious sin of omission was committed by ignoring Sweden's successful implementation of a carbon tax since 1991. That tax had reduced the country's greenhouse gas emissions by nine percent between 1991 and 2008, even as the Swedish economy grew by 48 percent. Finland also had success with such an impost, and like Sweden, returned the revenues to taxpayers in the form of a rebate. So much for a pollution abatement tax sounding the death knell for economic growth.

Manhattan Don Quixote

Courageous politicians who have pushed a broad swathe of daring, groundbreaking environmental reforms have been few and far between. Early in the 21st century, one of the most notable examples was New York City Mayor Michael R. Bloomberg. He proposed a bold blueprint to make the "Big Apple" the "first environmentally sustainable metropolis."[6] What made his dramatic and instantly controversial plan for the city so impressive was that he outlined specific, attainable steps to achieve his goals by the year 2030. One might argue that it did not take much political courage for Bloomberg to unveil a bold blueprint, since his enormous personal fortune insulated him from ruin if his ambitious plan wound up aborting his political career. Yet for most people of prominence, loss of reputation is something for which great wealth cannot compensate. Bloomberg ran a substantial risk of repudiation, yet he pressed forward undeterred, even after the New York State Legislature promptly jettisoned the most revolutionary of his 127 different proposals: a traffic "congestion-pricing scheme" in which an $8-a-day charge would be levied on vehicles driven into downtown Manhattan during the week. Already a mainstay in London, the arrangement would have saved energy, decreased pollution, and reduced the horrendous congestion that often brings Manhattan traffic to a standstill. Unfortunately, the legislature killed the proposal on the trumped-up excuse that the measure discriminated against low-income motorists when in reality they, like most sensible New Yorkers, used public transit when traveling throughout Manhattan.

Other visionary Bloomberg reforms that were still on the drawing boards included a plan to ensure that every city resident lived no further than a ten-minute walk from a park. Bloomberg hoped to accomplish that arrangement by converting some schoolyards and reclaiming for parkland every other bit of open space in the city's five boroughs. He also proposed to eliminate city sales taxes on hybrid vehicles, use mussels to suck pollution out of municipal waterways, plant a million trees, and provide tax incentives for making roofs "green." Nor was Bloomberg finished. Less than 18 months before his term's official expiration, he commissioned a study to determine how windmills, solar panels, and tidal turbines could be installed in and around the city. His farsighted vision: electricity generation in New York would stem primarily from clean, renewable energy.[7]

Was Bloomberg a man ahead of his time? Most environmentalists would say that his master plan was an embodiment of contemporary pragmatism. He should at least be lauded for seeking to achieve his goals through a framework compatible with the natural environment and the concerns of future generations. And if the city ever adopted all his ambitious proposals, historians surely would canonize him at some later date.

Alarmed at the growing body of evidence pointing to environmental deterioration from global warming, a number of officials in other cities, various states, and even corporations have begun to challenge the status quo. Consequently, some of these individuals initiated progressive greenhouse gas emission-reduction programs long shunned by the Bush administration. By the fall of 2009, one thousand mayors representing 85 million Americans had signed a U.S. Conference of Mayor's Climate Protection Agreement first introduced in February of 2005.

So the good news is that localized efforts have materialized, fragmented though they might be. The bad news is that valuable time has been wasted in the absence of a centralized approach to accelerate the remedial process and provide the necessary national cohesion. It remains to be seen how much of a penalty the nation will pay for that delay in confronting climate change.

Mayor Bloomberg—Urban visionary

Administrative Spinelessness

The U.S. Environmental Protection Agency's record has sometimes not been much better than those of uncaring individual politicians. The EPA is statutorily charged with being an independent decision-making body serving the American people. Shortly after EPA was established in 1970, its first administrator, William D. Ruckelshaus, declared that the agency was starting out "with no obligation to promote commerce or agriculture." Yet all too often, the EPA ended up deferring to politically influential corporate entities opposed to more stringent environmental regulations because of increased compliance costs. This was especially true under the Reagan and George W. Bush administrations, although the Democrats were not immune.

There is no better illustration of this shameful capitulation than EPA Administrator Stephen Johnson's March 2008 decision to ignore his scientific advisory board and issue a less stringent ground-level ozone standard than the board recommended.

The Clean Air Act (CAA) requires that the economic cost not be taken into account in setting the standards, only in complying with them. Health and public safety constitute the sole criteria for formulating anti-air-pollution standards. Johnson insisted he had abided by the law. But his dismissal of the tougher anti-smog recommendation of his scientific team in the wake of industry protests suggested otherwise. Indeed, in announcing the new ozone regulation, Johnson brazenly made a pitch for incorporating economic as well as health considerations into the drafting of antipollution standards, thereby advocating a flagrant violation of existing law.

Let's not lay the perversion of the EPA's mission in this instance totally on Johnson, however. It was subsequently disclosed that President Bush and Vice President Dick Cheney, ever solicitous of their corporate cronies' concerns, personally intervened. They ordered the pliant EPA administrator to select the weaker standard for smog, despite the respiratory health threat it would pose to hundreds of thousands of Americans.[8]

Bush's misguided priorities were exposed by the EPA scientists' own research. They calculated that the less stringent ozone standard the president demanded would prevent 1,300 to 3,500 premature deaths annually, while the standard they recommended would avert an estimated 3,000 to 9,200 fatalities, albeit with somewhat higher compliance costs, softened by a gradual phase-in of requirements.

It should be noted that as an alternative to mollifying industry by diluting a proposed regulation, the EPA on occasion has simply not enforced the rules on the books.

Whistle While You Work

The EPA's periodic coziness with the industries it regulates has occasionally led the agency to punish whistleblowers within its ranks. Some EPA staffers who disclosed improprieties in agency operations received demotions designed to drive them out of government. Such retaliation violated the spirit, if not the letter, of the federal law designed to protect them, and was usually successfully contested in court. Occasionally, the staffers who exposed irregularities chose to resign in protest rather than battle from within to retain their jobs. One of the first instances of this occurred more than 30 years ago when three highly respected attorneys quit the EPA's General Counsel Office because the agency dragged its feet in regulating pesticides.[9]

Although the law to protect a federal employee who discloses misconduct has been on the books for decades, a whistleblower can still incur risk by informing on colleagues' wrongdoing. Retribution for bringing to light any internal malfeasance can be subtle and hard for an informant to prove.

We thus owe a debt to the informers, who put conscience ahead of career advancement when encountering skullduggery within their ranks. One such hero was Joe Mehrkens, a U.S. Forest Service (USFS) employee who gave up job security and pension benefits accrued during 17 years of government service and took a pay cut to join an environmental organization critical of his agency. The year was 1987, at the tail end of the "Reagan Revolution." Mehrkens, the USFS regional economist in Alaska, could no longer stomach the agency's disregard of its conservation responsibilities. Under the pro-industry Reagan regime, the USFS was ignoring its statutory obligation to manage 191 million acres of national forest in a manner that balanced wilderness conservation with commercial recreation and timber harvesting. The 39-year-old Mehrkens watched in dismay as the agency pandered to politically influential lumber companies by allowing them to treat a significant portion of the national forests in Alaska as a glorified tree farm. Trying to push reform from within, he ran up against a bureaucratic stone wall. His defection didn't change things overnight, but it did draw attention to USFS practices that have moderated modestly over the years under pressure from newfound public scrutiny.

In 1995, Brian Holtzclaw was delegated by the Environmental Protection Agency to conduct a survey of the industrial pollution and health problems in the northeast corner of Kentucky. Lo and behold, Holtzclaw discovered that there were significant pollution problems, including ones in which low-income and minority residents bore the brunt of the exposures, with their health suffering accordingly.

Not surprisingly, Holtzclaw's assessment did not sit well with the Ashland Oil Company and other politically influential local industrial interests. They wanted to build two chemical plants in the region, where serious pollution already existed. Under pressure from Ashland, the EPA agreed to suppress Holtzclaw's report and transfer him back to regional headquarters in Atlanta to assume relatively mundane duties. Outraged, Holtzclaw sued the EPA for wrongful termination. The lawsuit was eventually settled for a modest $20,000, with the agency denying any wrongdoing. But Holtzclaw had made his point, and a decade later he became an EPA project director who actually won an "environmental justice" award for his work.

Other Personal Acts of Courage

Those who have challenged environmental abuse have often risked not just their position, reputation, and financial condition but even their personal safety. A number of U.S. Forest Service employees who upheld the law and dutifully limited commercial activity on public lands in the Rocky Mountain West received death threats and had their cars torched and home windows shattered. Citizen activists have been subjected to bombings, arson, and assault in retaliation for efforts to stymie commercial interests engaged in environmentally degrading activities.[10]

Political Firebrands

As has been duly noted, rare is the politician who is willing to take an unpopular environmental stance that he or she believes is in the people's best long-term interests. One such extraordinary person was Rep. Butler Derrick, D-S.C. Back in the 1970s, in an action uncommon to this day, he condemned in his own district, the long-accepted Congressional practice of funding "pork barrel" projects to win the support of influential special interests. Derrick committed the heresy of opposing construction of a local dam after concluding that the structure would do more harm than good. He took the position that the proposed $326 million project would generate expensive electric power that wasn't needed, eliminate more jobs than it created, and destroy valuable timber and wildlife resources.

The representative's principled stand challenged the unwritten code of reciprocity between incumbent congressmen showering goodies on their respective districts and voters showing their gratitude at the ballot box. His negative action might have initially outraged his constituents, but after hearing his reasons, they were supportive, suggesting that voters' approval of new development in their own backyard is not a given.

Former Rep. Pete McCloskey, R-Calif, was a more recent profile in environmental courage. At the age of 78, the decorated ex-Marine chose to come out of retirement, leave his small California ranch, and use his own modest savings to mount a 2006 primary challenge against a powerful incumbent in his own party. The reason to make this sacrifice and take on a seemingly hopeless task in a neighboring district: the incumbent, Rep. Richard Pombo, chairman of the House Natural Resources Committee, was in the hip pocket of developers, and bent on weakening the Endangered Species Act that McCloskey had helped usher through Congress 30 years earlier. Although McCloskey did not win the GOP primary, his bold, principled effort drew public attention to Pombo's anti-environmental record and sleazy cronyism, thereby contributing significantly to the Democrat opponent's victory in the general election.

Sen. Mark Hatfield, R-Oregon was not afraid to speak his mind, even if it clashed with his party's official line. During the 1970s, this iconoclastic senator defied conventional wisdom with his early opposition to the Vietnam War. In the environmental field, he was ostracized by many fellow Republicans for daring to warn of the dangers of over-consumption and the need to live in harmony with the natural world.

Hatfield dismissed President Nixon's blind reliance on finite fossil fuels as unrealistic, not to mention environmentally hazardous. Instead, he promoted the concept of "net energy." A former political science professor, Hatfield told his Senate colleagues that "the true value of energy to society is not the gross amount that exists in the world. It is net energy—the amount remaining after one subtracts the energy costs of extracting and concentrating that energy."

Hatfield went on to say that "at some point soon, man must shift from rapid growth... to a steady-state economy. Just as all other living things must reach an equilibrium point in balance with other living things and be governed by the constraints of the natural world, so must man." Clearly, renewable energy sources were in Hatfield's sights as an alternative to fossil fuel.

When Hatfield took this tack, many of his fellow Republicans looked upon him as though he was an alien from outer space, but the Oregonian lawmaker was a true visionary. We would have been spared a lot of grief at the start of the 21st century if our policymakers had adopted the philosophy he advocated instead of belittling him as an eccentric.

Russell W. Peterson also had a keen eye for the future, as well as a penchant for putting common sense ahead of dollars and cents. The former Delaware Republican governor was chairman of President Gerald Ford's Council on Environmental Quality (CEQ) when he articulated his "revolutionary" views about human beings placing themselves in jeopardy through their neglectful relationship with the environment. That occurred in 1975, when in official (and not-so-official) circles, Peterson's assertions were greeted at best with bemused disdain, and at worst as demented rambling. He avoided dismissal because President Ford's focus was elsewhere. Regrettably, the general public was also oblivious.

What exactly was Peterson saying that was so radical it could have cost him his job if anybody had been paying attention?

"Traditional economics underestimates the value or 'cost' of natural resources," the CEQ chairman declared, "and in some instances, it does not represent the values at all."

Peterson had the gall (and good conscience) in the midst of our prosperity to warn we were on an environmentally unsustainable track. Natural resources were being consumed at a faster rate than they could be regenerated. Left unchecked, such a deficit would lead to material shortages and higher prices. If complacency still reigned and consumption rates were not scaled back, he warned, conditions would further worsen, and society in all likelihood would experience major destabilization. Quite a mouthful for a Republican, even a moderate one.

Peterson lamented: "Why does man, alone of all the creatures, seem to believe that there is no natural check on his activities, that he is free to convert natural resources to his own use without limit? Why is it so difficult for us to realize how quickly short- term complacency and business-as-usual thinking can bring us to disaster?"

His words were not what anybody wanted to hear, but as the global environmental scenario has unfolded, it is clear that everybody should have been paying close attention.

CHAPTER ELEVEN

—

MORE UPSTARTS

Foreign Bravura

EXAMPLES OF THAT UNIQUE POLITICIAN who exhibits moral fortitude in defense of environmental protection are not limited to the United States. In the 1980s, Mexico was fortunate enough to have Manuel Camacho Solis as Minister of Urban Development. Holder of a master's degree from Princeton, Camacho tackled the seemingly insoluble pollution problems of smog-besieged Mexico City with gusto. He shut down factories, including several owned by the government, because they were violating antipollution standards. He also forced a chemical plant to relocate from Mexico City as penalty for failing to cut back production that discharged excess toxic emissions into the fetid atmosphere. Previously, as mayor of Mexico City, Camacho instituted a mandatory automobile-inspection program that for years had been operated on a voluntary basis.

Outside of Mexico City, he established a 40,000-acre ecological reserve to protect the wintering grounds of the ecologically stressed monarch butterfly, and created a number of nature preserves to assure the survival of the country's remaining tropical forests and nesting sea turtles.

These actions did not endear Camacho to many in Mexico's moneyed class, and even among those at the bottom of the economic ladder, there was some discontent about removing land from commercial exploitation. But Camacho was focused on the larger picture and remained resolute. Unfortunately, not all of his successors matched his commitment and intensity, and Mexico has had its share of setbacks. Among them is Mexico City's air quality, which remains hazardous to health on numerous days of the year. Antipollution measures have not been able to keep pace with population growth in the Mexican capital, whose air mass is trapped in a valley surrounded by high mountains.

The short life span of many of Camacho's accomplishments in Mexico City illustrates well the reality that there is never a guarantee that victory will be permanent in environmental controversies. To maintain the advantage requires eternal vigilance and the willingness to intervene at the first signs of recidivism

Then there were the European visionaries in the persons of two prominent elder statesmen. In the 1970s, Dutchman Sicco Mansholt and

Mexico City: There's something (bad) in the air

Italian Aurelio Peccei foresaw the environmental challenges of the 21st century, yet they were truly voices in the proverbial wilderness. European leaders many years their junior were so preoccupied with post-World War Two economic recovery that they frequently seemed unaware of current, much less future, environmental concerns.

Not so Mansholt, who headed the fledgling European Common Market, nor Peccei, who founded the world-renowned environmental think tank known as the Club of Rome. Despite their prominence, the aging statesmen found that their prophetic words of wisdom were ignored by all save a few young backbenchers in the fledgling European Parliament, which wielded little power at the time. The typical European bureaucrat regarded the two elders as eccentric mavericks. You thus had a topsy-turvy situation in which daring new ideas were being articulated by senior citizens while the younger generation was fixated on an outdated status quo.[1]

What were the views that these two distinguished men in the autumn of their lives chose to express at the risk of ridicule? Mansholt pulled no punches. "Europe's present leaders have shut their eyes to the reality of waning resources in order to promote an economic growth which cannot be sustained."

His solution consisted of five basic strategies: centralized planning and decentralized production; reduced consumption by rich countries and a redistribution of some wealth to poor countries; elimination of planned obsolescence; tax incentives to encourage smaller families; and an international body that would settle environmental disputes between nations. Does any of this sound familiar? If it doesn't, it will in the not too distant future.

Peccei preached the importance of attaining an economic equilibrium. "Zero growth is politically impossible," he declared, "but exponential growth is physically impossible. We must grow only within an ecological framework so that every increase is matched by a decrease somewhere else."

This prescient prescription is still widely scorned, despite the power of its logic and the fact that the 21st century is in the process of proving it on the mark.

At the grassroots level overseas, there have been numerous individuals who have defied convention at some personal risk or sacrifice in order to combat environmental degradation. Most of those singled out in this book made their mark prior to the turn of the 21st century, when citizen environmental activism was not as prevalent as it is today.

Let's start with Frenchman Brice LaLonde, whose environmental claim to fame did not stem from being a first cousin of Sen. John Kerry of Massachusetts. LaLonde gained international recognition by being plucked from the minority Green Party to run (unsuccessfully) for

President of France in 1986 and two years later to serve as France's Environmental Minister. But it was as a citizen activist that he first earned his environmental spurs. LaLonde was president of the French Chapter of Friends of the Earth in the mid 1970s, when his country not only lacked environmental consciousness but also often viewed environmental concerns as inimical to economic growth. That parochial official posture did not deter him from bold action. LaLonde challenged France's unquestioning decision to rely primarily on nuclear power for its energy source. He had copies made of U.S. Congressional hearings on the radiation dangers of nuclear power and distributed the materials to every member of the French National Assembly. Although that didn't sway France from its original energy strategy, it did help to instill greater public awareness of the country's environmental vulnerabilities. LaLonde could be proud of that achievement in later years when he led a more sedate life as mayor of the village of Saint-Briac-sur-Mer, that is until he was appointed France's chief climate change negotiator by President Nicolas Sarkozy in 2008.

On rare occasions, an environmental activist has paid for his cutting-edge advocacy with his life. Chico Mendes won worldwide acclaim for his efforts to organize his fellow Brazilian rubber-tappers and persuade them to harvest their crops from the Amazonian jungle in an environmentally sustainable way. But his brave efforts to save the vegetation antagonized loggers and livestock operators eager to raze the forest (with the exposed land eventually becoming desert under the searing heat of the equatorial sun). Mendes's international renown from exploiting the Amazon without destroying it ultimately failed to shield him from his enemies. A wealthy cattle rancher had Mendes assassinated, and the assassin was brought to justice two years later.

At least in theory, Mendes's activism was in line with his national government's policies (even if that didn't spare him from local vengeance). No such luck for Marina Rikhvanova. Her national government in Moscow was inimical to her cause. Nevertheless, as co-director of the citizen Siberian conservation group, Baikal Environment Wave, Ms. Rikhvanova successfully faced down the government of Vladimir Putin, no mean feat for a Russian citizen. In 2006, she was able to organize widespread support both within and outside of Russia to reroute the government-sponsored Siberia-Pacific gas pipeline away from Lake Baikal, a world heritage site, which is the planet's oldest and deepest body of water of its kind.

This was an environmental coup, but the 47-year-old Rikhvanova paid a price for defying the all-powerful Putin on behalf of the lake's thousands of unique animal and plant species (not to mention human neighbors). She and her followers were constantly harassed, and her son was arrested without any formal charge and sent to prison where he

Lake Baikal—Russia's great lake

languished for nearly a year before being released.

The only reason Rikhvanova was able to outmaneuver Putin and not end up in a gulag herself can be traced to that old adage, "there's safety in numbers."[2]

In 1982, African leaders, with few exceptions, considered environmental protection a luxury that only wealthy industrial nations could afford, and in some extreme cases deemed it a plot to keep them in perpetual economic servitude. Considering the autocratic rule that dominated the continent, it took a courageous individual to challenge the widespread institutional suspicion and often outright hostility towards environmental activism.

Simon Muchiru was just such a man. Serving as assistant national organizer for the 50,000-member strong Wildlife Clubs of Kenya, the 28-year-old Muchiru promoted an agenda aimed at saving African wildlife jeopardized by encroaching development. Halting erosion, deforestation, and runaway population growth was also his concern. He traveled around Kenya, and elsewhere in Africa, delivering his provocative messages regarding those widely unrecognized threats to all too many uninformed students right up through the university level. He was one of the few people to publicize the African conservation ethic in its embryonic stage, often under the indifferent—if not disapproving—eyes of government officials. To this day, Africa doesn't have enough "Muchirus," and has suffered accordingly.

Pioneer Science: Homegrown Courage

In the United States, Herman Daly boldly challenged conventional thinking. While an economics professor at Louisiana State University in the 1970s, Daly was a major force in formulating the theory of a "steady-state economy" along the lines of Peccei's zero-growth formulation. We would have to establish such an economy, Daly explained, to maintain continuing prosperity in a world under increasing ecological stress.

A steady-state economy is essentially one in symmetry with nature. The number of people and supply of goods remain fairly constant, though within those limits, the composition is always changing. Workings of the market remain dynamic. Economic growth is constant, but it is more qualitative than quantitative. Renewable resources are used at a rate no faster than they can regenerate. There is an equilibrium between births and deaths. Behind it all is the belief that unchecked quantitative growth on a finite planet is a prescription for disaster.

Daly derived much of his inspiration for his "steady-state" formulation from reading Rachel Carlson's *Silent Spring* and taking a teaching assignment in northeastern Brazil, where he witnessed first-hand the adverse environmental ramifications of explosive population growth.

"Steady-state" received only a modest welcome from an America enamored with a "more the merrier, bigger is better" lifestyle. But despite the snickers, Daly (who later became an economics professor at the University of Maryland) has persisted over the years. The limitations that nature imposes on humanity have begun to dawn on us, witness the gradual integration of recycling into our culture. A lot more people now take "steady-state" seriously, even if the majority of Americans are not yet ready to abandon their addiction to conspicuous consumption.

Dr. James Hansen, head of New York city-based Goddard Institute for Space Studies, an offshoot of the National Aeronautics and Space Administration, was one of the earliest scientists to sound the alarm about global warming. What set him apart was his well-publicized testimony during the 1980s before droves of skeptics in Congress, and the indifference, if not outright antagonism with which his employer, the federal executive branch, responded to his admonitions. Even 20-odd years later, with the preponderance of the scientific community behind Hansen, his repeated warnings that time was running out were spurned by the George W. Bush administration.

Challenging the Corporate World–Alpha Female

Shareholders' challenges of corporations' environmental policies are not uncommon today. But they were back in 1973, when Alpha Smaby, a spunky, 63-year-old former Minnesota state legislator, sought to win a seat on Northern State Power Company's board of directors. A coalition of environmental and consumer groups recruited Smaby to run for the board as a representative of the general public, with the aim of leading the protest against the company's plan to build a nuclear power plant on the banks of the Mississippi River. The late Ms. Smaby was clearly an ideal choice for contesting—on behalf of "small" shareholders—the wisdom of locating a nuclear facility on an environmentally sensitive site, as well as for questioning the safety of the energy source itself. She had been Sen. Eugene McCarthy's choice for a running mate in one of his unsuccessful tries for the Democratic presidential nomination, and she was actually the first elected official to come out publicly against the Vietnam War, so you get an idea of her populist feistiness.

Smaby did not win a seat on the board of directors, but her well-publicized campaign helped set the stage for the modern-day gadflies adept at using annual shareholders meetings to pressure management to clean up its act.

Palmiter's Way

You would think that George P. Palmiter, an outdoorsman skilled at getting the most out of nature, would have had his offer of free help

accepted by the federal Soil Conservation Service (SCS) to further its
mission of reducing the widespread erosion and flooding along rivers in
western Ohio.

It was the late 1970s, and the SCS opted to resolve matters by
tampering, rather than working with, nature as Palmiter envisioned through
manual removal of debris that was clogging up waterways. The agency's
solution was to use energy intensive machinery to transform meandering
streams into straight, artificial channels so as to speed the rate of flow
and eliminate the buildup of rising flood waters. By wiping out adjacent
wetlands and their absorptive capacity in the process, the SCS succeeded in
merely shifting the flooding problem further downstream at an exorbitant
cost to taxpayers.

Palmiter's alternative—which the SCS initially snubbed—presented
quite a contrast. The 50-year-old railroad brakeman proposed to organize
citizen volunteers to clear by hand the debris that had caused rivers to
back up and spill over their banks during heavy downpours. Palmiter had
already demonstrated elsewhere in the state that by preserving waterways'
natural twists and turns and establishing vegetated buffer zones, he could
often achieve far better results than the SCS, and at a fraction of the cost.
At the time, neither Palmiter nor the SCS were aware of another valuable
benefit derived from retention of a stream's natural curvature. Michigan
State University researchers recently discovered that the sinuous routes
function in a manner that filters out pollutants that create oxygen-deficient
"dead zones." By contrast, when human intervention straightens out
streams, they become little more than glorified drainage ditches that act as
conduits for pollutants.

Since federal agencies were not particularly receptive to non-
structural solutions in the 1970s, implementation often rested with private
citizens like Palmiter, who helped modify officials' outdated policies by
means of a volunteer approach in harmony with nature.

The Unholy Grail

The Vatican has tested many Catholics' faith with a rigid behavioral
code for human sexuality. It is a code that if followed to the letter would
increase the risk of harm to reproductive health and environmental quality.
The church deems condom use sacrilegious, even for a person whose spouse
has AIDS. Family planning to avert unintended pregnancies (and stabilize
population) is only sanctioned if it involves using the natural, "rhythm"
method. Given the power of the sex drive to override any preordained
period of abstinence, it is a wildly unrealistic papal decree. The Church
wants abortion prohibited, even when the life of the mother is at stake. Nor
does the Vatican's opposition soften when the fetus is the product of incest
or rape.

The response of the majority of American Catholics to this doctrinaire thinking has been to consider it both their right and responsibility to follow their conscience, even if it conflicts with Vatican teachings. Yet rebellion takes courage. Catholic laymen who publicly disavow Rome's formal edicts on abortion and contraception and openly urge their fellow parishioners (as well as the general populace) to follow suit risk excommunication from the Church and possibly even alienation from relatives and friends.

The prospect of retribution has not deterred the Catholics for a Free Choice (CFFC). Established in 1973, this private, non-profit organization has openly challenged the Vatican's dogmatic opposition to artificial contraception and legalized abortion. It promotes the view that it is consistent with Catholic belief for women to follow their conscience in matters of sexuality and reproductive health. At least in this country, the CFFC has derived satisfaction (and confidence) from the fact that a large percentage of Catholics see things its way. Surveys have long confirmed that American Catholic women utilize artificial contraception and abortion at approximately the same rate as the general population.[3]

Still, it took backbone for CFFC president Frances Kissling in the mid 1990s to proclaim that "misogyny is alive and well at the Vatican; women's lives still rank at the bottom when it comes to respect, much less value."

As was mentioned earlier in this book, marginalizing women is—among other things—bad news for environmental protection. Women's natural inclination to nurture the environment, perhaps stemming from their maternal instinct, tends to be squelched when they are relegated to a subservient role in society. In such cases, the fairer sex needs help, not an implacable orthodox paternalism from the Catholic Church.

"No-Win" Proposition

There is no greater manmade threat to the environment and human survivability than thermonuclear war. The consequences of even a limited exchange would be catastrophic. In addition to the incineration of those close to the blast, the lethal effects of radiation poisoning would likely spread thousands of miles from the explosion and make life a living hell for survivors of the conflagration in the days, weeks, and years to follow. If the Earth's protective stratospheric ozone shield were damaged by the detonation, crops laid bare to the unfiltered ultraviolet rays of the sun would wither, and mass starvation would follow. Even if the ozone shield remained intact, a much higher incidence of cancer and birth defects would likely occur because of people's exposure to the long-lived radioactive elements infiltrating the soil, food, and water.

According to a recent computerized study by a team of researchers at the University of Colorado, even a small-scale, regional nuclear conflict could alter the global climate for at least a decade, causing severe agricultural losses and as many fatal casualties as in World War Two.[4]

These nightmarish projections demonstrate why political leaders around the world must articulate loud and clear that there can be no "winners" in a nuclear war, even with a preemptive first strike. In this pronouncement, there is no implicit acquiescence to unilateral disarmament, just an underlying sanity and conveyance of a strong sense of responsibility for the fate of the human race.

Nevertheless, to harp on the prospective advent of Doomsday is a difficult exercise for any politician. Elected officials know full well that acquiring a "grim reaper" reputation is not the optimal way to win friends and influence voters. Officials therefore rarely refer to nuclear warfare as "unthinkable," fearing that such terminology would be construed as a sign of weakness. Thus, it is hard to find any politician astute (or brave) enough to openly and repeatedly declare that attaching legitimacy to the insanity of waging nuclear war even in the most limited of ways is an insane act in itself.

World leaders must have the courage to overcome this barrier and depict the horrors of nuclear war with brutal frankness. The verbal imagery alone would provide a powerful incentive for halting proliferation and scaling back arsenals.

SECTION FIVE

—

HONESTY

CHAPTER TWELVE

—

BRAINWASHING

The Ad Game

INDIVIDUALS WHO DISTORT information to downplay credible environmental threats (usually to further personal agendas) are neck deep in morally indefensible behavior. Given the well-publicized gravity of most of these threats, any claims of ignorance by the purveyors of deceit should carry no water.

That brings us to advertising that twists environmental truth to minimize industrial pollution. Free speech and oodles of money can combine to concoct a toxic brew that possesses the potential to impede societal progress if taken seriously. The only antidote is acquisition of enough basic knowledge to recognize—and repudiate—such insidious propaganda.

Hence, when an ad paints a misleading rosy environmental picture regarding a controversy in which the future quality of life, if not survivability, is clearly stake, the print or electronic media receiving compensation for carrying the message have a moral obligation to provide full disclosure. Otherwise, the uninformed could be lulled into complacency that could delay urgently needed reform.

That was why further clarification was required of ex-oil man H. Leighton Steward's seductive ad in the October 5, 2009 edition of the *Washington Post* (as well as on a number of TV stations) claiming that the human-generated rapid rise in atmospheric CO_2 was not a concern but a blessing because of the resulting accelerated plant growth. Not much was actually needed to discredit the Steward ad's implicit defense of industrial polluting emissions, given the refutation by the overwhelming weight of scientific evidence. Carbon dioxide does nourish plants, but in excess, it is too much of a good thing. A thorough review of the science in 2009 by the executive branch's U.S. Global Change Research Program confirmed the inescapable conclusion that the increase in human-generated carbon dioxide—mainly from industrial sources—was not a verdant boon to Mother Earth. Excess CO_2 is an incontrovertible global warming catalyst that dilutes the nutritional content of crops and forage for livestock, favors weeds, including a particular penchant for poison ivy, and increases production of allergy-inducing pollen. Steward's ad—distributed by his organization euphemistically labeled "CO2 is Green"—also conveniently omitted any mention of skyrocketing atmospheric carbon dioxide precipitating expansion of drought, rising sea levels, and dangerous heat waves that would dramatically diminish our quality of life.

When an ad attempts to downplay legitimate threats to mankind's very survival, why knowingly give it any exposure in the first place? One answer is that there are those who place ad revenue ahead of civic integrity and social conscience, and the First Amendment allows them to exercise their prerogative. Yet media responsible for displaying such a potentially disruptive message can recapture some integrity by inserting at the bottom of the ad a can't-be-missed codicil, putting the misleading claims in their proper perspective.

In the case of Steward, a former vice chairman of Burlington Resources, the postscript to his ad should have revealed the exact origin (and self-serving bias) of his pro-fossil fuel "CO2 is Green" organization as well as the fundamental scientific flaws in his beatific depiction of escalating carbon dioxide concentrations.

Explanatory caveats to dangerously misleading ads will at the very least raise a red flag for unsuspecting members of the general public and provide an incentive to become more knowledgeable about the vital issues at hand.

It might not have been as all-encompassing as climate change, but another brazen example of environmental falsification was a coal industry ad boasting of successful mine reclamation through depiction of a former site transformed into an idyllic pastoral pond. Adjacent slag heaps were excised from the photograph.

Then there was the oil industry's attempt to quell public fears of despoliation of the marine environment from offshore drilling. Its ad featured a photograph of a school of fish swarming around a deep-sea rig's pilings, suggesting that far from polluting ocean waters, the structure was serving as an artificial reef. What the ad omitted was that the fish congregating around the rig lacked the biodiversity of species normally frequenting natural coral reefs. (Only species less sensitive to turbidity in the water were present.)

The myth that oil rigs are a bonanza for marine life continues to be perpetuated not only by energy barons but also by politicians either in bed with the industry or convinced that offshore drilling will further their career ambitions. A notable example of the latter case involved Arizona Republican Senator John McCain, who during his 2008 presidential campaign announced his support for offshore drilling that he originally opposed. He justified his reversal on the basis that drilling would increase oil production that would help lower soaring gasoline prices, and expressed assurances that such activity could be done in an environmentally benign manner. He was wrong on both counts, but then, anything to get elected. Any oil from offshore rigs would need a ten-year lead-time and be a blip in the nation's long-term energy picture. And as sturdy as the rigs are purported to be, there is a record of major hurricanes damaging them and causing widespread pollution of surrounding waters.

Even McCain's victorious opponent, President Barack Obama, was not immune to bending to political pressure. During his presidential campaign, Obama insisted that the output from offshore oil drilling was not worth the environmental risk or costly technological effort. Yet only a year after taking office, he reneged on his campaign message and proposed selective limited new offshore drilling. His rationale: offshore drilling was not a panacea but was one short term element in easing the transition from a society dependent on imported oil to one reliant on clean, renewable, home-based non-fossil fuel energy.

Only time will tell whether he shall be forgiven for backtracking on his campaign disavowal of offshore drilling as a viable national energy policy alternative.

The effectiveness of industry ad campaigns can be extraordinary. Detroit's success with its promotion of gas-guzzling SUVs was a case in point. Accused of flooding the marketplace with these oversized vehicles when it was in the national interest to improve fuel economy and reduce dependency on foreign oil, American auto executives claimed they were just responding to customer tastes. To characterize themselves as the passive party in this relationship was laughable. Much of the consumer demand for their gas-inefficient, rollover-prone monstrosities was generated by paid advertising's clever psychological manipulation. The vehicles were usually pictured in a bucolic setting to reinforce an "outdoorsy," sporty marketing image. Their safety due to size was overstated, and their roomy interiors were glorified until even those with no need for that much space suddenly viewed the vehicle as a necessity. It took the price of gasoline soaring to $4 a gallon in the summer of 2008 to puncture Madison Avenue's illusion. The public was jolted back to reality regarding the finiteness of oil supplies and the virtues of energy efficiency. At that point, SUV sales plummeted.

To make matters worse, one American auto manufacturer played down the existence of a relatively environmentally friendly product it preferred not to have on the domestic market. In the 1970s, the Ford Motor Company told members of Congress it did not possess the technology to reduce polluting engine emissions in commercial vehicles, even as it was producing energy efficient jeeps overseas for the military with that technology—and no one in authority called Ford on it.[1] The added expense of retooling its domestic assembly lines, and the possibility of the public being diverted from buying gas-guzzlers possessing the highest profit margins, took precedence over any moral obligation by Ford to offer an environmentally superior product. It was a typical auto industry decision springing from a lack of imagination and a surfeit of greed. Decades later, those attitudes came back to haunt Ford and its American competitors when the price of gasoline abruptly skyrocketed. They suddenly found that they were outflanked by far more clairvoyant, conservation-oriented Japanese carmakers.[2]

America's once–mighty "Big Three" automakers discovered that in effectively lobbying to block a legislative mandate for greater fuel efficiency, they had undercut their own future. Late in 2008, Chrysler and General Motors stood on the brink of bankruptcy, and in 2009 received a multibillion-dollar bailout from Congress, with no guarantee that even that subsidy would rescue them from ultimate collapse or ever be repaid. Ironically, it was Ford that in the wake of this disaster was the first of the "Big Three" to make a radical break with the past and belatedly commence retooling its assembly lines for the 21st century.[3] It alone avoided bankruptcy and a federal bailout.

It's Not All in a Name

Corporate polluters have a habit of choosing environmentally friendly titles for their professional associations and programs to obscure any negativity of their handiwork. The technique is known as "green washing," and it embodies both motive and deed that are short on ethics. A typical example is the National Wetlands Coalition. Sounds like an organization dedicated to preserving the nation's original wetlands not yet overrun by development, doesn't it? Don't let the cadence fool you. Actually, the Coalition is a front for corporations and developers seeking to weaken laws that are impediments to projects which would destroy remaining wetlands, as well as wipe out endangered species.

Green washing occurs in the public sector too. The Bush administration labeled its air-pollution cleanup program "Clear Skies," although the initiative required less industry compliance than the regulations it would replace. Similarly, Bush's "Healthy Forests" proposal gave lumber companies carte blanche to harvest old growth timber stands on public lands that had been off limits to commercial activity because of their rich biodiversity and substantial carbon dioxide sequestering capacity. Only the companies found this arrangement "healthy."

That these green washers felt compelled to resort to euphemisms showed a lack of confidence in the merits of their programs. If their cause could not be sold by an honest exposition of the facts, it should not have been sold at all. "Green washing" is a reminder to pay more attention to what officials and merchants do than what they say.

Timber cutting—Timberrrr

Of Mice and Men

One of industry's most reprehensible tactics has been its attempts to discredit the science that raises questions about the safety of various products. A prime target has been laboratory experimentation with mice and rats that has served as a basic tool of researchers in evaluating the toxicity of chemical compounds scheduled for release into the marketplace.

Results of these experiments have sometimes thrown a wrench into industry's marketing plans, prompting a number of companies to question the validity of the methodology. Bristling at even the hint that something is amiss with their products, the corporate chieftains in question have asserted that rodents "are not little people." Any health problems that their brands produce in test animals were thus irrelevant. Yet surely, their own scientists must have told them that rodents have enough genetic similarities to human beings to make laboratory tests meaningful. It is hard to believe, but rats and mice contain millions of mammalian cells similar to our own and subject to the same biological processes.

Animal testing may actually underestimate human risk, since laboratory rodents are subjected to high doses of suspected toxic chemical compounds for only part of their lives. By contrast, human beings' exposure to such chemicals in commonly used products tends to be a chronic, cumulative experience that can result in unhealthy concentrations accumulating over many years.

Defamation as a Weapon

Character assassination is an ugly exercise, and it takes on added malevolence when used to demean not only the credibility and character of environmental activists but also the important reforms they are promoting. Critics of the environmental movement frequently try to tag their opponents with the "extremist" label. So-called green radicals are pilloried for being against economic growth, the use of fossil fuels that runs our cars and keep us warm, and drilling for oil under any circumstances. Were these pernicious false charges to stick, they would be capable of impeding the societal unity necessary for us to meet global, national and individual environmental challenges.

Fortunately, this defamation receives short shrift from the majority of the public at home and abroad; after all, common sense dictates that mainstream environmentalists value their basic creature comforts as much as anyone else. Moreover, environmentalists gain credibility from the fact that they, unlike their polluting adversaries, rarely stand to reap large financial rewards from the ax they grind. Finally, when it comes down to it, just about all of us believe we are "environmentalists."

Undaunted, the most implacable of the environmental movement's political and corporate adversaries incessantly malign it as a thinly veiled socialist crusade that would phase out private enterprise. Again, nothing could be further from the truth. Mainstream environmental activists view the dynamic, entrepreneurial creativity of capitalism as civilization's best hope. The difference is that their version of capitalism includes appropriate regulatory restraints to curb any excesses in the market's highly focused dash for short-term profits.

Environmentalists favor strong economic growth, but here is the ethical distinction between them and the champions of pure laissez-faire economics: the growth must be environmentally sustainable; that is, sufficient natural wealth and a high quality of life must be preserved for future generations. To achieve such goals, fossil fuels must be gradually replaced by renewable energy sources such as wind, solar, biomass, hydropower, and nuclear fusion, assuming fusion can ever be perfected. Qualitative values have to eventually take precedence over quantitative ones. Conservation must temper consumption. Recycling and reuse need to displace planned obsolescence, and would provide the added dividend of a reduction in greenhouse gas pollutants. That's because an enormous amount (44 percent in 2009) of American emissions have stemmed from the manufacturing and one-time use of materials employed in consumer products and their packaging.[4] The throwaway society is one of which Americans are becoming increasingly leery as the cost of energy and goods steadily escalates and the public appeals for environmental sensitivity grow ever louder.

Still, the allegation that environmentalists seek to turn back the clock to the Stone Age has sometimes gained traction among our most gullible citizens, especially when they have been seduced by the argument that antipollution regulation produces those rising prices at the pumps as well as unemployment.

In actuality, environmentalists recognize that fossil fuels—significant pollution impacts notwithstanding—for the moment constitute a mainstay of our energy supply. They simply point to the inevitability that these carbon-based fuels will become a dwindling part of the energy mix as their supply diminishes, pressures mount for pollution reduction, and the use of renewable sources becomes more practical and expands.

Along these same lines, environmentalists are criticized for opposing domestic oil drilling when that drilling would allegedly decrease our reliance on imports from unstable sovereign states. Again, this is a spurious allegation. The vast majority of public lands in the United States remain open to oil and gas development, and environmentalists have raised no objection to exploiting those resources as a holding action while renewables gain momentum. Environmentalists do resist proposed energy exploration in lands designated off limits because of their extraordinary wilderness values. Their position could hardly be classified as extreme, considering acreage of that sort equals less than 10 percent of the public lands open for leasing.

Sieg Heil

What is really scurrilous is when radical critics of the environmental movement assert that it is an offshoot of Adolf Hitler's Third Reich. This is a malicious attempt not just to minimize environmentalists but to criminalize them.

Originally, the portrayal of the "greens" as ideological heirs to Hitler and his Nazi followers was limited to occasional rants by rabid right-wing fringe groups with no real audience outside their own tiny constituency. But then this grotesque mythology began to be publicly promoted by some supposedly responsible mainstream academicians. Two libertarian college professors wrote a 1993 tome in which they asserted that ecological concern was a major element of the Third Reich, making it "the first government to be dominated by radical environmentalists."[5] To further expand on their guilt by association thesis, the professors cited the Nazi SS's choice of "an oak leaf as its symbol, its motto of 'blood and soil,' its mantra of the possible need to sacrifice mankind to nature, and a fixation with tree planting."

Another academic, Anna Bramwell, went into more detail and provided further convoluted "evidence" for the smear merchants to use against the environmental movement. Bramwell, a British historian, made a big deal out of the fact that prominent Nazis Rudolph Hess and Heinrich Himmler were keen on organic farming.[6] What that had to do with the modern environmental movement eludes me, unless she was suggesting there was something inherently subversive about growing organic produce.

Another nugget offered by Bramwell was that "SS training included a respect for animal life near Buddhist proportions." Too bad it didn't extend to human beings classified as Jews, gypsies, and other non-Aryans. Was she implying that animal rights activism was a philosophical Petri dish for Nazi brutality?

Bramwell recounted how some members of Hitler's entourage convinced him not to drain German wetlands. Does that make today's wetland preservationists ideological progeny of the Führer?

The author eventually revealed the ideological stimulus behind her tortured analogies. "Like ecologists today," she wrote, "the Nazis opposed capitalism and the consumer-oriented market mechanism." Hello, what kind of historian is Bramwell? Didn't Hitler court and eventually win the support of German (and some American) industrialists in constructing his regime's massive war machine and death camps? Didn't the pre-war, private industrial activity nurtured by the German despot lift his nation out of a depression, temporarily create jobs, put more money in people's pockets for consumer goods, and contribute to a rise in the Nazi Party's popularity? And what of Bramwell's gross misrepresentation of the modern environmental movement, which is counting on dynamic, though well-regulated capitalism to lead civilization into an era of ecologically sustainable development?

There is nothing wrong with disagreeing over the issues, but to use scurrilous allegations to denigrate an opponent is morally reprehensible. To the extent that this defamation gains even a little traction, it could become a thorn in the side of environmental progress, which is one of many reasons why such slander should be promptly repudiated as vicious invective with no legitimate place in literature or anywhere else.

CHAPTER THIRTEEN

—

TOOLS OF THE TRADE

Code Words

W E NEED NOT LINGER OVER a person who knowingly lies and is the only one victimized by the falsehood. Justice has been served, and let's leave it at that. The same cannot be said for a person who deliberately engages in an immoral act that harms innocent people. Every effort should be made to assure that such a perpetrator is the recipient of highly visible public retribution to discourage, if not prevent, repeat performances.

Reference has previously been made to the administration of President George W. Bush and its semantic sleights of hand aimed at diverting attention from defaults on promises to protect the environment. A favorite technique of Bush (also used by previous presidents, though not nearly to the same degree) was to invoke code words that sounded reassuring but were vague and open-ended. When action was called for, Bush and company could interpret the words any way they wanted without danger of explicit contradiction. Bush's Interior Secretary, Gale Norton, was unusually adept at this sort of chicanery. When asked by preservation-minded senators whether she favored widespread drilling on previously pristine public lands, Norton would reply cryptically that "it is important to have a balance [between environmental protection and economic development]."

Given the Bush administration's track record, "balance" became a classic euphemism for giving industry virtually carte blanche. The senators knew it and Norton knew it, but unfortunately there was no chance to pin her down until the giveaway was formally set in motion, at which point it was extremely difficult to reverse.

Bush himself was a master of gaining tacit acceptance of ostensibly insipid caveats that gave him leeway to breach statutory and other environmental commitments. The president often touted energy conservation as an important part of the effort to wean us away from dependency on oil imports. Yet in the very next sentence, he proceeded to downplay its significance by emphasizing that conservation was no panacea. This gave us insight into his true intentions, since no one disputed conservation's limitations. He was building a case for drilling for domestic oil on a massive scale in wilderness areas previously designated off limits.

Another favorite ploy of Bush was to exploit (and sometimes create on his own) a phony crisis that advanced his interests. He did just that when first taking office and having to confront an energy crunch manipulated by corporations in California. Bush seized the opportunity to push his ideological agenda: the state's energy shortage, he declared, resulted from too few power plants and too many regulations. He urged that strict environmental safeguards be relaxed so that power companies— such as corrupt, later-to-be-defunct Enron—could operate with virtually no constraints.

Bush was in thick with the chief executives of those companies, including the soon-to-be-disgraced Enron chairman, Ken Lay. That friendship evidently allayed any misgivings Bush might have had about playing along with industry's creation of an artificial California energy crisis through price manipulation. The president's philosophical opposition to a regulatory solution (i.e. California's request for federal imposition of price controls) reinforced his determination to use the trumped-up crisis to advance deregulation. A genuine crisis—Wall Street's and the banking system's meltdown—largely due to a lack of federal regulation under Bush's watch, was still years away.

Bush's move to blame environmental safeguards for the California energy shortfall was a classic exercise in scapegoating, but it was not very convincing. California environmental officials, electric utility regulators, and even the president's own EPA chief, Christine Todd Whitman, all disputed his allegation. Indeed, California's environmental regulations had ample flexibility for dealing with the operation of old power plants and the construction of new ones.[1]

Corporate Chicanery

As for the scions of industry, they have hardly been getting shortchanged in the marketplace, though you would never know it from the rhetoric of many in their crowd. A favorite ploy has been to complain to the federal bureaucracy about an "imbalance" between economic growth and environmental protection. I don't have to tell you how the businessmen have defined the imbalance. Nor, I suspect, would you keel over in shock when informed that credible evidence to back up their one-sided version was hard to come by. Indeed, throughout much of our history, conditions have pointed to an imbalance that favors commerce at the expense of environmental protection. Don't shed tears for a corporate America that has experienced years of record profits. Despite the presence of supposedly oppressive environmental regulations, our gross domestic product, which was estimated at $13.8 trillion in 2007, was increasing at a steady rate until the major recession late in 2008, on the eve of Bush's departure from office. Much of official Washington and its corporate clientele chose to ignore that approximately 95 percent of the lands in the Rocky Mountain's mineral-rich belt that industry contended government kept off limits were anything but. Nor did environmental regulations stifle the chemical industry's output of synthetic, often highly toxic pesticides, although you would never have guessed it from the frequency with which authorities acceded to corporate complaints of excessive regulation.

If American economic interests have been subordinated to environmental ones, as some business executives maintain, how come most of our commercial fisheries have long been in decline, and more than 58,000 acres of precious original wetlands have been lost to development each year? Compromised by corporate campaign contributions and personal ties to industry, many of our officials, especially those serving in recent Republican administrations, have treated as gospel the business community's bogus claims of inequitable treatment.

Glaring Omissions

It's equally reprehensible for those in the public eye to promote a particular ideological viewpoint without taking into account the public health risks involved. You would think that the late White House Press Secretary, Tony Snow, would have known better. But then again, he was not battling cancer in 1995 as he was in 2008 when in a tragic twist of fate the disease ultimately took his life. It was in 1995 that he staked out a morally irresponsible position in regard to radioactive pollution in American homes. Then a newspaper columnist, Snow dismissed the carcinogenic threat of radon radiation as a "huge, costly government-bred hoax." His perfunctory rejection of potential danger juxtaposed nicely with his ideologically driven zeal for deregulation and a reduced federal government presence.

Snow's editorial stance relied on a scientific study that could not definitively link radon exposure to lung cancer. While such uncertainty was enough for him and like-minded ideologues to make light of the threat, he neglected to mention that the study's researchers had warned that "a clear picture of the level of risk associated with lifetime low-level exposure to radon is not known."[2]

If ever there were a case for "being better safe than sorry," that was it. And guess what: Snow forgot to tell us that the authors of the study included the caution that incompleteness of data on the radon exposure of the subjects they monitored should not deter erring on the side of caution. In fact, the study actually did detect a correlation between home radon exposure and the incidence of a potent cancer other than malignant lung tumors—another detail that eluded Snow.

Cancer Cover-up

Unfortunately, the cancer threat has been disingenuously

downplayed on even a broader scale. Some representatives of industries emitting carcinogenic pollutants have assured us that we need not fear their companies' operations, and as proof, they have cited the declining mortality rate from malignant tumors. What they didn't say was that the incidence of many types of cancers—including leukemia, non-Hodgkin's lymphoma, pancreatic, thyroid, kidney, and liver—has been spiraling upward. Fewer people have been dying from some of these diseases, but more have been getting sick, and manmade causal factors are prime suspects. It should also be noted that childhood cancer increased 10 percent between 1999 and 2005, a statistic that strongly contradicts what industrial emitters of carcinogenic pollutants would have us believe—namely that the disease is totally age-related.[3]

George W. Bush was a frequent practitioner of Machiavellian omission as well. For example, the president claimed credit for a net gain in the nation's wetlands after years of loss. But to justify the assertion, he had to count artificially constructed decorative ponds that bore scant resemblance to biologically prolific natural wetlands. Meanwhile, under Bush's watch, an estimated 130,000 acres of irreplaceable original wetlands were being lost annually to developers.

The president also boasted of an increase in our nation's forest cover in recent years. What he did not mention was that this expansion was comprised mostly of scrub and brush, which had overrun abandoned farmland. Commercial interests were extracting the most ecologically valuable timber—old-growth forests—at an alarming rate.

It is blatantly dishonest to use the absence of absolute proof (that is most likely unattainable) as an excuse to throw caution to the winds and jeopardize public health for monetary gain. Yet as we have seen, that excuse is frequently employed by unscrupulous politicians and businessmen to minimize the incriminating evidence associated with such threats as global warming and tobacco use.

The Old Under-funding Gambit

Budgetary sleight of hand has been used by all presidents to advance their policies, but few, if any, have applied the technique in the systemic way that Ronald Reagan, and to an even greater extent, George W. Bush did. President Bush knew that the conservative doctrine of government being part of the problem rather than the solution was not a widely popular notion, as well he should. Hadn't the voters elected him to make the Washington bureaucracy work? Hence, he used budgetary smoke and mirrors to conceal attempts to reduce the domestic (but not the military) responsibilities of the government he headed. A favorite technique was to follow Reagan's example and delegate federal responsibility to state officials, local authorities, or private interests who were known to lack the monetary resources or political inclination to fill Washington's shoes. Another favorite Bush ploy was to ask Congress for an outlandishly large appropriation, knowing his request would be denied. Then, he could privately celebrate while publicly shedding crocodile tears and blaming Congress for obstructing progress.

Still another gambit was to gradually starve a federal program by spending money previously appropriated, but not request any significant new funds. An illusion of fiscal responsibility was created. That it was no more than an illusion quickly became apparent when the program began to falter. Bush used this technique to distract from his broken pledge to provide sufficient dollars to reduce the National Park Service's maintenance backlog. His much-advertised humanitarian program to combat the AIDS epidemic in Africa also relied on manipulating funds already appropriated, with little new money being allocated for a battle that had no end in sight. A variation of this tactic was to take a previous year's appropriation that had remained stagnant or been reduced and propose an increase that still left the program well short of a truly viable funding level. The Bush administration did that a few years back when the president asked for an increase of a hundred enforcement positions in the EPA to show how tough he was on corporate polluters. The trouble was that even if Congress had granted his request, the agency would still have had a hundred fewer enforcement officers than in the previous year.

Bush was not about to opt for strictly enforced environmental regulation when he could hang a peg on voluntary corporate compliance. He just wanted to muddy the waters, knowing that his true position would alienate many Americans. Empirical studies have shown it would be naïve to expect the average corporate executive to voluntarily adhere to more rigorous governmental cleanup goals that would encroach on profits.[4] Environmental conscientiousness is not always innate.

Sometimes, to escape the blare of publicity, officials make a subtle adjustment to scale back a program that is popular but they view as too expensive. How else to explain the Bush White House taking unobtrusive steps to tighten the eligibility standards for veterans receiving health benefits? Bush proposed at one point to double veterans' co-payments for prescription drugs and health care,[5] and to cut the Veterans Administration budget by three percent in 2008.[6] Here were occasions where he was not waving the flag!

Calculated neglect has been another subversive budgetary tool utilized by the executive branch. Funds that Congress authorized are simply not spent. President Richard Nixon frequently utilized this technique, impounding millions of dollars for water projects he opposed.

Neither is Congress above such budget skullduggery. If it doesn't approve of actions its predecessors took but senses a lack of public support for revoking those provisions, it can amend them by substituting toothless penalties or moving to deny adequate resources for enforcement, tactics resorted to countless times.

Reinventing Reality

The modern national environmental movement in effect was launched on April 22, 1970—the first Earth Day. Since then, many in the corporate world, together with their allies in federal, state, and local government have striven to create a rift between green activists and a triumvirate of organized labor, minorities, and the working poor.

The business community took its cue from the old adage "United we stand, divided we fall." As has already been referenced, part of its propaganda pitch was to stereotype environmentalists as individuals who cared more about natural outdoor settings than people, an argument that lost steam in the 1980s when the targeted audience wised up. Nevertheless, demographic pockets continued to be swayed by this coldly calculated casuistry. Among the most visible holdouts was the aforementioned National Conference of Black Mayors. These African-American officials were under so much pressure from the high unemployment rates in their communities that they were quick to seize on anyone who could serve as a scapegoat.

Then there was the "Alliance to Stop the War on the Poor." This misguided coalition of black civil rights and religious leaders maintained that the efforts to curb global warming would reduce employment and increase the cost of energy for low-income citizens. Reacting to high gasoline prices, the Alliance bought the right-wing argument that environmental protection and conservation were at odds with a robust economy and should take a back seat to massive new oil drilling. The organization's leaders forgot that if our addiction to oil were not brought under control, future generations in low-income communities would suffer the most from the effects of global warming.[7] And the Alliance allowed emotion to overwhelm reason by embracing the false claim that expanded drilling would bring immediate relief to its constituents when in reality, any fiscal payoff was years away.

The specter of higher energy costs is an industry red herring designed to stir up low-income group's opposition to more stringent pollution regulation. In fact, stiffer regulation's fiscal impact would be modest for all income brackets, thanks to more efficient energy use and amortizing additional costs across the entire breadth of society.

Perhaps most important to remember, environmental protection and a sustainable robust economy are two sides of the same coin. A society mired in a severely degraded environment will inevitably see its economy erode. Cleaning up pollution may cause some temporary job displacement, but retraining programs can compensate for the disruption, and over time, the economy should vigorously rebound in its streamlined reincarnation revolving around "green jobs."

Conversely, a nation in desperate economic straits is a poor bet to exercise judicious environmental stewardship. In that circumstance, immediate gratification is likely to be all consuming at the expense of long-term environmental consequences.

During his presidency, George H.W. Bush repeatedly proclaimed that a robust environment and strong economy were compatible (as have all presidents and politicians in recent memory, even if they were only paying lip service.) But under pressure in his reelection campaign and, needing more support from a regulation-averse corporate constituency, the elder Bush bowed to his advisors' counsel. He began pitting a clean environment against economic prosperity—creating conflict where there was confluence. The public didn't buy it, and his philosophical flip-flop was instrumental in his defeat in the 1992 general election.

Crisis Management

Few tactics are more morally despicable than exploiting a crisis in order to advance an agenda that circumvents environmental laws. Unfortunately, President George W. Bush specialized in just such orchestrated exaggeration to intimidate opponents on a broad spectrum of issues. And he didn't wait long to put his methodology into play vis-à-vis environmental concerns.

The *piece de résistance* was the 9-11 terrorist attack on Manhattan's Twin Towers. Bush tried to use that horrific event to convince Americans that failure to extract oil from the Arctic National Wildlife Refuge's pristine coastal plain would put us at the mercy of Islamic extremists. Although that pitch didn't resonate with the public, failure did not deter Bush from resorting to fear mongering to get his way on other matters. Invoking the threat of terrorism and the need to buttress national security continued to be his chief instruments of persuasion. Indeed, as the nation's commander-in-chief, he repeatedly invoked security concerns to justify actions that on their own would never have seen the light of day, either because of longstanding public opposition or contravention of existing law. Those who dared question his wisdom had their patriotism impugned, implicitly by Bush and explicitly by some of his more outspoken subordinates. He cited national security as reason not just to cover the ANWR with oil rigs and suspend pollution curbs on petroleum refinery activity, but also to exempt the military from the Endangered Species Act and other environmental laws.

With the help of the courts and sympathetic members of Congress, a determined green community was able to thwart most of Bush's attempts

Appalachian mountaintop mining

to parlay the terrorist threat into a mechanism for rolling back regulations. Moreover, legislation was introduced in Congress to formally bar military waivers of environmental laws, and no doubt will one day win approval, as it most assuredly should.

Slippery Science

It is bad enough to deceive the public by deliberately suppressing scientific research. But when authorities employ this duplicity to further a policy detrimental to the environment and/or public health, the behavior takes on an added nefarious dimension.

The distortion of AIDS science might not ultimately have as broad an impact as manipulating data to discredit the global warming threat, but it is bad enough. Harvard School of Public health researchers calculated that former South African president Thabo Mbeki's refusal to recognize HIV as the cause of AIDS and therefore block distribution of antiretroviral drugs in his country resulted in 365,000 premature deaths.[8]

Mbeki contended that no proof existed that AIDS was transmitted by sexual activity and at one point recommended ingestion of lemon juice, beetroot, and garlic as a cure. He challenged prevailing science by asserting the disease was a fiction that industrial Western nations had concocted to make money off the sale of unnecessary medicines. At one point, he even suggested that AIDS was introduced to Africa by the Western World in order to thin out the native black population.

What could be more unconscionable than to promote phony racist jingoism to consolidate political power at the cost of hundreds of thousands lives?

Former Interior Secretary Gale Norton was a frequent manipulator of science in order to promote President George W. Bush's agenda. Yet as shrewd an operator as she was, she occasionally outsmarted herself. For example, Norton was caught red-handed bypassing a government study that contradicted her assertion that Alaskan caribou would not be adversely impacted by the proposed ANWR oil drilling. When some angry senators confronted her about her flagrant omission, Norton went on the defensive, smiling sheepishly, shrugging her shoulders, and professing it was simply an honest oversight. The performance spared her from well-deserved censure, but thankfully was not nimble enough to open the door to commercial activity in the ANWR.

On another occasion, Norton failed to release a critical U.S. Forest Service evaluation of a Bush administration proposal to relax wetland protections that were blocking projects dear to some of the president's friends. Her excuse: oops, the evaluation had not been typed up before the deadline passed for eliciting public comments on the Bush plan. What a shame!

The Bush administration's muzzling of the science incriminating global warming was well documented. Facts were withheld, cherry-picked, or just plain falsified to buttress the president's skeptical attitude towards the climate change threat. To further defend their skeptical stance, the Bush people often cited a devastated economy as a likely consequence of any attempts to slow global temperature rise, and to the uninformed, the bogus argument carried weight.

The Bush administration compounded its sins when it sought to suppress evidence implicating secondhand cigarette smoke, also known as environmental tobacco smoke (ETS), as a health hazard to more than 126 million non-smoking Americans. White House officials denied they were attempting to conceal the danger of the fumes. After all, they were self-proclaimed guardians of the nation's moral values. But then again, they were not under oath to tell the truth, and their accuser, Dr. Richard H. Carmona, was. At one time President Bush's own U.S. Surgeon General, Carmona testified before a congressional committee in July 2007 that the president's minions intervened to delay the release of his report on ETS. Carmona's report contained documentation that routine exposure to secondhand smoke increased non-smokers' risk of heart disease by 25 to 30 percent and lung cancer by 20 to 30 percent.[9]

The Bush crowd was evidently more concerned about the profits of the tobacco industry and smoke-filled bars and restaurants than the respiratory health of those 126 million plus Americans involuntarily exposed to the toxic fumes. Tobacco proponents were especially hostile to Carmona's recommendation that mandatory smoke-free zones be established in all public places (happily, a proposal well on its way to being implemented). There was grumbling about infringement on people's freedom to engage in smoking whenever and wherever they chose. It was "do or die" for laissez-faire, hardly a lofty expression of moral values!

Fortunately, suppression of science was a technique that usually did not fly in a court of law. A majority of judges—even conservative ones—turned out to be unsympathetic to Bush's political sleight of hand in defense of corporate "freedom." Between 2004 and 2008, his administration lost ten lawsuits on air pollution issues alone in the District of Columbia Circuit Court. Jurists of all political stripes reacted negatively to the Bush White House quashing research that contravened its business-friendly agenda.

That the president felt compelled to resort to subterfuge suggested he lacked confidence either in the merits of his case, his powers of persuasion, or both. Either way, concealing the scientific facts from the public made a sham out of his professed transparency and morphed into an assault on democracy.

Hypocrisy Supreme – States' Rights Flip-Flop

Many conservatives rail against "Big Brother" in the form of the federal government imposing a "one-size-fits-all" regulatory regime on the individual states. That should not be surprising, given that a preference for states' rights (as opposed to central government dominance) is a core precept of modern conservative ideology. Conservatives label as "socialism" an allegedly heavy-handed central bureaucracy setting mandatory, minimum antipollution standards that curb the autonomy of states to tailor regulations to fit their individual needs.

When the federal minimum standard is more stringent than state regulations, business-oriented, free-market conservative politicians will dutifully emit cries of outrage. Commercial interests detest the idea of the feds ordering states with less rigorous (and hence less costly) environmental protection laws than Washington to tighten regulations. But guess what? When a progressive state such as California wants to exert some independence and enact stricter environmental regulations than the national minimum standards, industry cries foul. In the blink of an eye, conservative politicians and their corporate constituencies shift gears and become centrists, contending that a weaker federal standard should preempt states' rules (to bring about consistency). When California enacted pesticide-emission regulations more stringent than the federal version, states' righters reversed field overnight and called for the rules to be annulled.

In another instance, the Bush administration secretly lobbied Congress and a number of governors to block the waiver that California and 11 other states were seeking for implementation of auto antipollution rules more rigorous than the federal version.[10] Then, not so secretly, the administration on its own denied the waiver, leaving its doctrinaire fidelity to states' rights in shambles. Such a reversal was blatant hypocrisy as well as a cold-blooded dismissal of public health concerns in order to placate corporate campaign contributors.

Finally, when environmental problems transcend jurisdictional borders and require an aggressive coordinated response, common sense, not to mention a moral imperative, dictates that only a central authority should oversee the task.

Tools of the Trade

Let us review some of the principle tactics unscrupulous officials use to camouflage their sellout of environmental protection:

The shell game—Divert attention from unpopular negative acts with positive gestures dwarfed by the harm they are meant to obscure. President George W. Bush was a master of this black art. For example, he attempted to pass himself off as an environmentalist by pledging to restore rundown national park facilities. Not only did he fail to keep his much-bandied-about promise, he simultaneously sought in unpublicized fashion to place a two-year moratorium on government purchases of additional parkland. Had Bush prevailed, the federal government would have missed numerous one-time opportunities to acquire choice parcels desperately needed to meet the recreational requirements of a burgeoning American population.

Vowing disingenuously to wean the nation off its addiction to oil, Bush proposed a research program to develop a hydrogen-powered vehicle, a goal clearly years down the road. At the same time, he was proceeding in a low-key manner to cut funding for conservation programs and development of solar, two alternative energy strategies that could make a difference now. Despite Bush's brave-sounding rhetoric supporting the substitution of renewable, non-polluting energy for oil and natural gas as quickly as possible, his policy tilted heavily toward prolonging his fossil fuel industry buddies' privileged market position as long as possible. Their enormous federal subsidies remained sacrosanct, while renewable energy entrepreneurs received either token contributions or lip service.

Shell games to further personal agendas have by no means been the exclusive province of unprincipled government officials. The Philip Morris Tobacco Company made its money by peddling a product detrimental to people's health, yet orchestrated an ad campaign to discourage youngsters from taking up smoking. Incredible, you say, for Philip Morris to crusade against its own merchandise. Hold on, there was a "method in its madness." The company could behave in an ostensibly high-minded manner knowing full well that tobacco's potent addictive power guaranteed such appeals for abstinence would fall on many deaf ears.

Of even more significance was the industry's ace in the hole—the international marketplace, which was their major source of revenue. Requirements abroad to divulge the dangers of smoking to consumers tended to be much more lax, if present at all. Not surprisingly, then, Philip Morris and other American multinational tobacco companies concentrated their primary marketing campaign on overseas locations—and the merchandising strategy paid off handsomely. More than 80 percent of the Earth's citizenry who smoked made their homes in the developing world, victims of a largely unchecked, life-shortening caveat emptor!

There were indications, however, that those days were numbered for the tobacco industry. In late November of 2008, 160 nations, many from the Third World, convened in Durban, South Africa to evaluate the effect of the international anti-tobacco treaty they had ratified. At the meeting's conclusion, the countries agreed to take a firmer stance against tobacco companies' insidious marketing strategy in order to combat the escalating health costs resulting from widespread cigarette use.[11]

Hail to the private sector—When President Bush was somehow exposed for using an empty gesture to blur the funding cuts in a popular federal program he did not like, his fallback position was often to assure the American people that the private sector would pick up the slack. But the private sector is profit-oriented, whereas serving the public interest can involve activities that are not moneymakers yet are essential to society's well-being. Without an opportunity to realize a decent return on investment, private entities have little incentive to perform at an optimum level. Anyone with elemental observational skills recognizes that, so it was no surprise that Bush's assurances were not especially persuasive.

Delay and lowest common denominator—Going through the motions of complying with a law, while discontinuing its funding, application, or enforcement, works more often than it should. The misconduct either slips past the media or benefits from public gullibility and indifference. The Endangered Species Act (ESA) was an anathema to Bush administration officials, who believed it to be an assault on private property rights. Consequently, the president dragged the government's feet in listing species that deserved protection. Bush's average annual species listing was eight compared with President Clinton's 65 and even the elder Bush's 58. By neglecting designations, George W. Bush spared landowners the legal obligation to preserve endangered species for all mankind—and no one really called him on it until he was about to leave office.

Sabotage—When a president considers a government agency an unnecessary appendage of the federal bureaucracy but hasn't the authority (or nation's support) to dismantle it, he can still sabotage its mission. What better way than to appoint as the agency's head an individual who has had a lengthy confrontational history with it while serving in the private sector? Such an individual will have acquired the knowledge to scale back the agency's mission in subtle, technical ways difficult to discern, much less reverse. That subversive hiring tactic was a favorite strategy of both Presidents Reagan and George W. Bush, who harbored ideologically motivated distrust of the federal government's regulatory scope, especially in matters involving the environment.

Another deceptive technique that anti-regulatory politicians have employed is to make no distinctions between environmental regulations that American people overwhelmingly support and bureaucratic red tape that almost everybody detests. If the public falls for the chicanery and fails to differentiate between the two, the resulting confusion can lead to throwing out the baby with the bath water.

CHAPTER FOURTEEN

—

DEFENDING THE INDEFENSIBLE

Reagan's Follies

IN PRO-INDUSTRY RADIO COMMENTARY during his pre-White House days, Ronald Reagan smugly proclaimed that some doctors thought the nitrogen oxide pollutants in the haze enshrouding North Carolina's Great Smoky Mountains benefited tubercular patients' respiratory health. You have to wonder about those doctors and where they earned their medical degrees. One thing is for sure: there has been no great push to construct sanitariums on the ridges of the Great Smokies or any other site where smog is pervasive.

Nor did sickly individuals flock in droves to the California coastal city of Santa Barbara, despite Reagan's contention that the community's air quality possessed extraordinary curative powers. According to Ron, inhaling winds that blew across natural oil seepage in adjacent ocean waters prevented infectious diseases. As the wind wafted over the oil slick and into Santa Barbara, it picked up traces of chemical pollutants that Reagan asserted had germ-killing properties.

Those were the lengths to which Reagan went to minimize the need for industry to be regulated by the very government he would one day head. His bizarre assertions over the airwaves were spurred not just by his ideological aversion to federal regulation but also by his belief that the marketplace (and his corporate cronies) could best deal with pollution problems on their own. Reagan might not have been the brightest orb in the political universe, but surely he realized he was advocating a highly controversial point of view. Alas, any indecision he might have harbored was quickly dashed by doctrinaire fidelity to his own version of conservative ideological correctness. Being a true believer enabled him to promote with conviction the most farfetched or grossly flawed environmental policies.

When a political leader allows ideological zealotry to prevail over reason and result in the spread of falsehoods potentially harmful to the general public, neither his unwavering loyalty to a cause nor perverse stupidity can serve as vindication.

Despite their ludicrous content, some of Reagan's radio-broadcast assertions are repeated to this day by those sharing his ideological bent. For example, Reagan attempted to justify commercial harvesting of biologically invaluable, old-growth timber on public lands by declaring that when those trees died, they became "pure waste and harmful to the forest." It is highly irresponsible to mislead the public regarding the role of dead trees in our ecosystem, yet we still occasionally encounter people promoting the harebrained allegation that dead wood is pure detritus. Fortunately, such mercenary-inspired propaganda won't win many converts if our educational system does even a passing job. Any basic high-school biology text will tell you that dead trees constitute a vital component of the forest's regenerative cycle. As the trees decay, they return essential nutrients to the depleted soil. The dead trees also provide irreplaceable habitat and forage for species that roam the forest floor and help maintain the woodland ecosystem. Forest fires stemming from natural causes periodically thin out the dead foliage that has not yet decomposed and would otherwise become thick enough to choke off living vegetation.

When woodlands adjacent to communities must be periodically trimmed to reduce fire hazards, human intervention is called for. But that important exception was not enough to satisfy Reagan, who was focused on the harvesting of prized timber deep in the forest.

Reagan's contention that trees are more to blame than human beings for air pollution has been recycled throughout the years by those seeking to stave off tighter regulation. Thankfully, this arboreal indictment has generally been greeted with disbelief, if not disdain. Disingenuous attempts to make nature a scapegoat for human-generated pollution can only gain credibility when the public is unaware of some fundamental principles.

While it is true enough that carbon-dioxide-absorbing trees emit certain pollutants, they do so gradually, and the discharges are widely dispersed. Furthermore, that incremental pollution has been a fact of life for eons, giving all species (including us) plenty of time to acclimate to the exposure. By contrast, toxic industrial emissions are relatively new and often enter the environment in relatively dense concentrations, with the potential to break down the immune systems of human beings and other living organisms.

The ANWR Fable

Deliberate distortion does not stop at the forest's edge. The oil industry had long sought permission to drill in the Arctic National Wildlife Refuge, our nation's last wholly intact pristine wilderness ecosystem that supports a wide range of animal and plant species. With the complicity of sympathetic government officials, primarily members of the Republican Party, the energy executives tried every tactic imaginable to demean ANWR's unique attributes. Photographs were displayed of the snow-

ANWR—The last frontier

covered region in the height of winter and wildlife hibernation to illustrate the area was a lifeless wasteland. No headway was made, thanks to firm rebuttals of this misleading picture, and to the reverence for that region's spectacular wilderness held by an overwhelming majority of Americans. It made no difference that they were unlikely ever to experience its grandeur first-hand.

When attempts to denigrate ANWR failed, the advocates of development dredged up the argument that oil and gas drilling would impact only 2,000 of the refuge's 1.5-million-acre coastal plain. They insisted that their activity would leave virtually all of the area's unparalleled wilderness and bountiful wildlife undisturbed. What they didn't say was that a network entailing more than 280 miles of roads, hundreds of miles of pipelines, 11 production facilities, and two ports would be needed to service the drill sites.

That omission indicated a willingness to place avarice ahead of principle, desecrating the wilderness's eternal values for a quantity of oil estimated to equal what Americans use in a 90-day period. Moreover, it would take some ten years to extract the petroleum from the ground and transport it to the marketplace, with some indications that the destination would be the Japanese—not the American—market! If not Japan, how about Norway? In a Gulf of Mexico offshore-lease sale held in August 2008, the highest bidder was a Houston-based subsidiary of the Norwegian company Statoil Hydro. So much for concern over our own nation's energy independence and national security!

As the 2008 national elections drew near, the Republicans were apoplectic about their low standing in the polls. Out of desperation, the entire party, from Presidential Nominee John McCain on down, rallied behind a demand for a massive increase in drilling on public lands as a way of countering soaring gasoline prices. It was a cynical attempt to embarrass the Democrats by pandering to public emotions at the expense of future national interests. More responsible voices responded that extensive drilling could not—in either the short or long term—deliver appreciable relief at the pump. Furthermore, opening up previously off-limits territories to drilling would inject significant environmental negatives into the picture, mostly in the form of additional pollution that would exacerbate global warming and lower the quality of offshore waters.

Irrepressible Blowhard

A notorious defender of the environmentally indefensible was conservative radio talk show host Rush Limbaugh. One can only hope that few of his millions of listeners, even his regulars, took his assertions at face value. From his honorary seat on the corporate bandwagon, Limbaugh lambasted any regulation that would restrict the business community from polluting, or doing just about anything else.

To that end, he ridiculed the suggestion that secondhand cigarette smoke (ETS) could harm non-smokers. In fact, he even had the temerity to maintain that cigarette smoke might have a protective effect against lung cancer. To support his ludicrous assertion, Limbaugh misquoted a United Nations World Health Organization scientific study and touted a four-year-old Forbes magazine article which made the preposterous claim that cigarette smoking was beneficial to human health.[1]

Contrary to Limbaugh's assertions, the UN study did find a statistical connection between ETS exposure and lung cancer. As for the magazine article, its conclusion was drawn from a few studies that recorded a lower incidence of several major diseases in smokers than in non-smokers. To anyone with a modicum of common sense, these studies had a glaring fatal flaw: the diseases identified in the article—Alzheimer's, Parkinson's, colon cancer, and osteoarthritis—are generally illnesses associated with ripe old age, a period of life that relatively few smokers ever reach.

Limbaugh narrowed his perspective through ideologically crafted intellectual blinders. Maybe he had to do that in order to block any remorse at coaxing others to engage in self-destructive behavior for the benefit of corporate America's balance sheets—and his own.

Specious Climate Talk

Sugarcoating the health effects of ETS is bad enough, but the diehard skeptics who choose to play Russian roulette with the Earth's climate would place the human race in even greater peril.

When the evidence of global warming's existence and human beings' contribution to it are too persuasive for even professional skeptics to deny, the naysayers still find no cause for alarm. Their fallback position is to treat global warming as a boon because of moderation of frigid climates and extension of the growing season in many parts of the world. But the environmental benefits of climate change are extremely speculative, whereas the environmental costs are not. Most scientists believe that, if left unchecked, global warming will cause prolonged droughts, fast-rising sea levels, more intense storms, and the extinction of numerous species unable to adjust to relatively abrupt climate change. What of edible plants that need cold weather to germinate? Suppose the increased carbon dioxide concentrations accompanying global warming cause crops to sprout so rapidly that they outgrow their nutrient supply in the soil, making them far less beneficial for human consumption?[2]

False Analogies

Those who ridicule the idea that overpopulation threatens humanity offer the following anodyne: why worry that there will be too many people for the planet to support when you can fit the world's entire population into the state of Texas? What's more, each individual would have over 1,000 square feet of space!

One would be hard pressed to encounter a more specious analogy. It has as much relevance as the observation that the universe is large enough to provide a galaxy for every person on Earth. True, our world doesn't seem crowded when you take into account all the vacant land, but much of it consists of desert, mountains, ice fields, and other inhospitable terrain. By contrast, the much smaller share of the Earth's landmass suitable for sustainable human habitation has been filling up rapidly. In some regions, unrestrained population growth has already resulted in the number of people exceeding the carrying capacity of the natural-resource base.

The finite nature of our planet alone makes it morally irresponsible to promote the demographic notion of the more, the merrier. But those who do so rationalize that human ingenuity can transcend any limits imposed by natural resources, including the challenge of feeding an exponentially increasing number of mouths. The more people there are, they maintain, the more minds are available to solve the problems afflicting the human race. Lower birth rates could quite conceivably deprive civilization of future Einsteins, Beethovens, and the like, or so the thinking goes.

The delusional disconnection here is failure to recognize the link between human development and the condition of the surrounding environment. A prospective Einstein born in an overcrowded, disease-ridden slum is unlikely to ever reach maturity and is almost certain to be far too preoccupied with daily survival to exploit, much less be fully cognizant of, his or her extraordinary talents.

A Phony Conflict

Industry leaders balking at the expense of proposed antipollution regulations have often sought to gain support by alleging that environmental protection will cost jobs and force closure or relocation of manufacturing facilities. It is a ploy that is, among other things, designed to discourage environmentalists, minority groups, and organized labor from forming alliances to lobby against the business community's interests.

In most cases, the coalitions targeted by corporate propaganda for fragmentation have become too sophisticated for their collaboration to be unraveled by such balderdash. Typical was a national survey of African-Americans which found that more than half considered climate change a serious problem and were willing to pay higher electricity bills and drive less in a concerted effort to combat air pollution and global warming.[1]

But there have been a few groups that have continued to be swayed by the bluff and bluster. One such organization has been the National Conference of Black Mayors, representing more than 600 African-American city officials. The NCBM is understandably preoccupied with widespread unemployment among minorities. That predicament has made the organization receptive to industry's disingenuous admonitions, even though low-income neighborhoods tend to experience the most toxic pollution because of logistic discrimination.

Consequently, you had Vanessa Williams, executive director of the NCBM, at a September 2007 EPA hearing, urging Washington not to strengthen air-pollution regulations. Her rationale? New stringent clean air standards would discourage the arrival of industry and/or its continued presence in minority communities. "Clean air is important," she declared, "but so is economic development."

She and her organization failed to grasp that the relationship between the environment and the economy was not a zero sum game. A society plagued by serious pollution not only wouldn't prosper but would face eventual economic collapse. Also overlooked was that all the well-paying jobs in the world were not worth spit if one were too sick to show up for work. Instead of knuckling under to industry fabrications, which had not swayed the majority of Americans, the NCBM should have focused on the need to aid the 60 percent of African-American children who lived in areas where ozone pollution exceeded existing federal standards.[2]

Although forcing industrial polluters to shell out more money to clean up their act could result in some layoffs, the loss could be largely offset by government-subsidized retraining programs and unemployment benefits. "Dirty" facilities confronted with an imminent shut down would be forced by cleanup mandates to make the necessary upgrades to keep operating. If they chose to flee to a more permissive overseas location rather than comply with stringent domestic pollution abatement requirements, good riddance. It wouldn't be long before they would wear out their welcome on those temporarily more lenient foreign shores, and then most likely be left with the choice of either returning home to play by the rules or face going out of business.

For those who argue that the higher remediation costs will make our industry non-competitive, be reminded that a healthier environment reduces absenteeism due to illness and the enormous expense it imposes on society. Moreover, the demand for pollution-abatement equipment and advanced cleanup technologies invariably generates far more jobs than the closure of outdated facilities would eliminate.

Indeed, as far back as 2004, researchers at the University of California's Berkley campus found that renewable energy (a.k.a. solar, wind, etc.) produced more jobs per average megawatt of power installed and per unit of energy produced than the fossil-fuel-based energy sector. According to the Berkley study, investment in new renewable energy sources would result in roughly ten times more jobs than a comparable investment in the fossil-fuel industry.

In light of that data, there was no credible explanation for the Bush administration shortchanging renewable energy other than fossil-fuel favoritism. It was that sort of myopic pro-industry bias that caused our nation to fall behind—at least temporarily—in transitioning to the 21st century. And it was that kind of data that helped prod our nation to make up for time lost during the Bush era.

Pollution a la Natural

Some commercial polluters maintain that their toxic discharges are a necessary byproduct of industrial progress. Should their argument be rejected as a self-serving attempt to minimize pollution control science and escape liability, the malfeasants go one step further. They assert that pollution is a natural component of the environment, so not to worry about a few more particles in the air!

Nature does emit pollutants, but they are a far cry from the ones discharged by industrial activity. As was mentioned earlier in this book, nature's pollutants tend to be widely disbursed, so that any toxicity is extremely diluted, and the exposed flora and fauna have had eons to build up immunity. Furthermore, some natural pollutants have an important positive role in sustaining the web of life. For example, ash ejected in volcanic eruptions is a rich source of soil renewal after it settles, cools down, and decomposes over time.

By contrast, manmade pollutants (especially from manufacturing facilities) have not been around long enough for biota (including Homo sapiens) to become acclimated. Many of these chemical brews have lengthy shelf lives and possess carcinogenic properties that create risks even in small doses.

Dubious Tradeoffs

If the claim that industrial pollution is harmless or at worst a necessary tradeoff fails to convince, the mythmakers occasionally embrace the old adage that the best defense is a good offense. They have not been above advancing the nonsensical idea that industry contamination is a boon to mankind. Reference has already been made to President Reagan boasting that air pollution cured respiratory ailments, and to representatives of the tobacco industry asserting that cigarettes have a salutary effect on human health.

Just as absurd have been the attempts of some industry types to portray heavily polluted, ozone-laden smog as beneficial because it blocks certain solar ultraviolet (UV) rays that can lead to skin cancer. Again, this strategy is nothing more than an effort to legitimize air pollution in order to avoid extra cleanup costs. Persuading people that they must choose between lung cancer (from smog exposure) and skin cancer is unconscionable. Chemically laced smog can be curbed to make the air cleaner without increasing our exposure to potentially lethal UV rays. Haven't the devotees of smog ever heard of staying out of the midday sun and wearing a hat, sunglasses, long-sleeved shirt, and suntan lotion?

Highway High Jinks

In our society, the more-the-merrier philosophy has not been confined to family size and heirlooms. It has also been very much in evidence in the construction of highways. The supposed raison d'etre for new roads is the alleviation of congestion. Yet they only produce a temporary solution, a vacuum that is quickly filled and ultimately makes matters worse than they were before. Traffic jams end up bigger, air pollution is worse, gasoline consumption rises, and more of the landscape is marred. Are we the victims of unintended consequences, or should transportation planners know better? My guess is that those with a strong vested interest in new highway construction have more than an inkling of what lies ahead but are too monetarily compromised to worry about long-term consequences.

It doesn't have to be this way. There are environmentally friendly solutions for easing traffic congestion and its attendant evils. Relief is at the ready by way of mass transit, telecommuting, staggered work hours, and toll roads. Perhaps most important over the long haul, the nation will benefit from better land use planning in the form of clustered, relatively high density development that de-emphasizes automobile use. That reverse-sprawl trend started as a trickle in the 1980s and has gained momentum in tandem with escalating gasoline prices. Suburbia is beginning to transform itself into self-contained communities rather than remain distant appendages of some municipal core.[3]

For more than half a century, the powerful highway construction and automobile lobbies encountered little resistance as they exploited

Traffic Planning Default

their formidable ace in the hole—Americans' long-time love affair with motor vehicles. It helped that the lobbyists had accomplices in the federal government more concerned with their personal futures than those of the general public. Even politicians not seduced by lobbyists' money weren't eager to tamper with an entrenched automobile-oriented culture and to take the lead in engineering a shift in transportation strategy.

Only the sudden jump in the price of gasoline in the late spring of 2008 showed signs of altering Americans' driving habits and creating a more environmentally favorable national transportation mix. Economics came out of the blue to lead the way where no political leader had dared tread.

Sham Volunteerism

President Bush concocted a fairy tale to spare his corporate constituency the obligation of meeting rigorous antipollution standards. The fiction Bush (and Reagan before him) foisted on the nation—to the detriment of the general public's health—was that corporations' voluntary compliance with pollution reduction goals produced better results than the force of law. All that stemmed from Bush's deep-rooted, ideologically motivated belief that big government was more of an impediment than a facilitator and was highly inefficient when compared to the pressures applied by market forces. Bush and his band of subordinates liked to insinuate that an extensive governmental regulatory approach was nothing but an insidious attempt to sow the seeds of socialism.

It is ridiculous to suggest that as a group, corporations, which measure success in dollars, would voluntarily subordinate their financial welfare to the nation's environmental concerns. And the inanity of this "honor system" theory has been borne out by the evidence. Among the most recent statistics are those contained in a report by our own Government Accounting Office. It found that of the 74 companies evaluated, only 38 agreed to voluntarily set—much less meet—a pollution emission-reduction goal.

In 2007, professors at the University of Michigan's Ross School of Business found that industry's voluntary reporting of greenhouse gas emission reductions failed to achieve its desired effect. In fact, greenhouse gas emissions increased in 323 of the 550 utilities that reported their output to the government and were covered in the study. Without strict enforcement of emission-reduction goals, it was clear that cleanup objectives would not be met.

If Bush were not truly aware that it was in keeping with human nature for corporate volunteerism to tempt entrepreneurs to go astray, then he was unbelievably naïve. More likely, avarice and ideology triumphed over common sense and conscience.

Spare the Children

It is criminal to downplay the extreme vulnerability of young children to environmental health hazards. Nonetheless, influential conservative interests in both the political and business worlds complained that kids were being "used" as propaganda tools to ensure enactment of unnecessarily stringent and expensive antipollution rules.

Once again, right-wing radio talk show host Rush Limbaugh took the lead as a shill for these hardhearted conservative malcontents and their hefty bank accounts. When President Clinton cited youngsters' health as a major reason for approving tougher clean-air standards back in 1997, Limbaugh labeled the rationale "a cheap, lame attempt to tug at our heartstrings." The radio windbag went on to say that "kids are healthier the day they are born than you are if you are 30 or 40. Kids' immune system can ward off far more than the elderly can when you talk about air pollution and other such things. I tell you, kids are the epitome of health. This notion that our children are vulnerable little waifs… is absolute bunk. We were created to live within the systems that exist on this planet. Children are not threatened."

Unfortunately—and unconscionably—this drivel has often been reflected in our policy. Instead of making allowance for children's greater vulnerability, regulators have frequently set antipollution standards consistent with the capacity of vigorous young adults to tolerate a degree of toxic exposures.

A healthy baby is undoubtedly more resistant and resilient to infections than a sickly 80-year-old, and some immunity to disease is transferred from mothers to their newborn for the first three to six months of the infant's life. But young children in general are far more susceptible than adults to a vast array of bacterial and viral diseases and toxic environmental pollutants. How could it be otherwise, given the approximately eight years it takes for a kid's immune system to fully evolve? Lacking mature organs, infants cannot metabolize many kinds of medicines. In fact, there are medications that cure adults but can kill babies.

A national medical conference on the health impacts of air pollution concluded the following: "children are more vulnerable to airborne pollution because their airways are narrower than those of adults. Thus, irritation caused by air pollution that would produce only a slight response in an adult can result in potentially significant obstruction in a young child's airways. Children also have markedly increased needs for oxygen relative to their size. They breathe more rapidly and inhale more pollutants per pound of body weight than adults do."

If ever there were an apologist for polluters, Limbaugh fit the bill. He and those for whom he spoke chose to engage in a callous demagogic exercise that sacrificed child safety for balance sheet embellishment.

SECTION SIX
—
HUMILITY

CHAPTER SIXTEEN

—

RAMPANT HUBRIS

If an individual's hubris brings about his or her downfall, it can be tragic or deserving depending upon the circumstances. If the individual's hubris causes the ruination of others who are innocent parties, there is no personal redemption for the perpetrator.

What Would Jesus Do?

IN THE SERMON ON THE MOUNT, Jesus Christ preached: "In everything, do to others what you would have them do to you, for this is the law of the Prophets."

The United States has fancied itself a standard bearer of Judeo-Christian values, yet its diplomatic stance during the first eight years of the 21st century often ran counter to Jesus' teaching. We stood virtually alone in refusing to sign a spate of international treaties, a number of which pertained to environmental protection. That left us conspicuously isolated in a world where with each passing day, interdependence between nations became more essential to everyone's survival. Under the Bush regime, the beam from our "shining city on the hill" failed to filter down to those below. We lost a great deal of America's luster by defaulting on our moral obligation to shoulder our fair share of the environmental and humanitarian burdens imposed on the global community. Something tells me that Jesus would not have approved of our government's dismissive attitude towards mutual trust and equitable reciprocity in the international arena.

Chances are that Jesus would also have been critical of the Bush administration's core values. Christ warned to "be on your guard against all kinds of greed, for one's life does not consist in the abundance of possessions."[1] But His admonition did not register with the president when Bush called on Americans to engage in shopping binges as an act of defiance against the 9-11 terrorist attack. Nor did Jesus appear to be on Bush's mind during his administration's frequent opposition to strengthening sorely needed environmental regulatory protections. For an avowed devout Christian, Bush was awfully rusty on biblical directives. "O Lord, our Sovereign, how majestic is your name in all the Earth."[2]

It seems obvious that Jesus would have admonished us for

expecting other nations to respect our concerns while we thumbed our nose at theirs. He would have had little empathy for Bush's self-righteous version of "American Exceptionalism," which cast us as the world's moral icon as well as its sole superpower. In reality, Bush's "exceptionalism" was little more than a presumptuous claim of self-serving preeminence, bound to alienate friend and foe alike.

Empty Entreaties

Hence, we had Bush debasing our international image with his egocentric vision. Under his aegis, the United States was a law unto itself, steadfastly refusing to sign off on a global warming pact, the Law of the Sea Treaty, and a biodiversity agreement ratified by the overwhelming majority of the international community. We were one of only two countries that failed to ratify the Rights of the Child Treaty (lawless Somalia was the other holdout) and were virtually alone in our refusal to sign treaties banning discrimination against women and establishing an international criminal court. We were also a solitary dissenter to a pact halting the manufacture of antipersonnel mines, and dragged our feet in implementing military arms-reduction treaties we had already ratified. For Bush, the mere idea of accommodating to interests other than our own was an affront to his notion of American supremacy. It stoked his paranoid fear of loss of national sovereignty rather than presented an opportunity for the international cooperation essential for any advancement towards world peace and stability.

Was that why we were one of the few countries that failed to sign off on a treaty to discourage the sale and use of tobacco products throughout the world? This 2005 agreement contained such "threats" to our sovereignty as provisions for more conspicuous labeling, smoking bans in public places, stronger programs to kick the destructive habit, higher user taxes, and limitations on advertising. The Bush administration twiddled its thumbs while some 5.4 million poor souls around the world were dying prematurely each year from addiction to the poisonous weed.[3]

Yes, we eventually ratified the treaty, but not before insisting on the inclusion of language that in effect exempted any nation from compliance if they so chose. Does anyone think Jesus would have been so solicitous of the tobacco industry's fiscal fortunes when the health of millions of people was at stake?

Our obsessive accumulation of armaments when we already possessed enough weaponry to decimate any adversary many times over didn't make sense in a number of ways. It fanned insecurity throughout many corners of the world, with people worried that such a military buildup reflected more than just a defensive posture. American militarization set a bad example for other countries, some of which tried to emulate us as best they could by allocating disproportionate sums for weaponry at the expense of domestic needs. Excessive funding of the armed forces shortchanged public health, education, housing, and environmental protection, especially in developing countries with far less fiscal margin for error than in the more industrialized states.

A Superiority Complex

A less imperious definition of American exceptionalism than Bush's would be something like the following: our country and others vary in political behavior and public opinion. Furthermore, cultural differences lead to divergent, sometimes clashing, views about morality. We should respect these differences (provided they are not used to foster genocide or export conflict), as well as candidly acknowledge our own imperfections and the limitations they impose on our sphere of influence. Otherwise, we risk establishing ourselves as a pariah throughout the community of nations, an unenviable position when international cooperation is crucial for surmounting the challenges of the 21st century. Of course, we need not be ashamed to acknowledge that our vibrant democracy and national wealth make us a world leader—provided we keep our leadership and power in proper perspective, a strategy much better understood (and implemented) by Bush's successor, Barack Obama.

The risk of alienating other nations was not taken into consideration when Bush's Washington moved to impose American mores on Third World countries with different behavioral norms. Promiscuity and marital infidelity were tolerated publicly in these countries in contravention to the established societal climate in the United States. As was noted previously, the Bush administration's moral indignation at such "aberrant" behavior led to constraints being placed on financial assistance to vital family planning and AIDS-prevention programs in Africa, causing much unnecessary suffering as a consequence.

American hypocrisy acquired an added dimension when we penalized others for behavior legitimate in our own country. Withholding American fiscal aid for foreign family planning programs to protest the would-be recipient country's acceptance of legalized abortion had the opposite of its intended effect. The ensuing reduction in family planning services on foreign shores was repeatedly shown to lead to abortions that could have been averted. Not only that, these abortions often took place under medically unsupervised, unsanitary conditions, increasing the likelihood of fatal outcomes for the patients. Hopefully, President Obama's reversal of this misguided Bush policy is destined to be a permanent one. Another shameful American government decision under the Bush aegis was to deny desperately needed financial assistance to Brazilian peasants because of legalized prostitution in their country. Our moral outrage rang hollow since in our very own state of Nevada, courtesans are permitted to legally ply their trade.

We condemned China for its one-child policy and Nepal for encouraging voluntary sterilization. What gall to chastise these countries when population growth was overwhelming their natural-resource base and a reduced birth rate was crucial to self-sufficiency, if not survival!

An episode during the Reagan administration demonstrated the potential mayhem our arrogant parochialism could unleash. A Chinese couple who wanted to have more than one child sought political asylum in the United States. Under Chinese law, the couple could have had another baby, but they would have faced stiff economic penalties. In the context of Chinese law, they were not being singled out for persecution, only persuasion. So if they had been given asylum, as some Reaganites wished to do, we would have been opening the floodgates. If one Chinese couple who wanted to have more than one child were entitled to political sanctuary, why not other Chinese with the same intentions?

Pride Goeth Before Iraq

President Bush's unswerving belief in America's infallibility was graphically on display in Iraq. The wisdom of his military intervention will not be the focus here. Let's just say that he unilaterally started a war of "liberation" without fully taking into account the consequences to his own nation as well as to Iraq. There was little long-range planning devoted to the toll that might be paid in American lives and treasure. Nor did Bush appear to make provision for dealing with the effects of war on the health and environment of the Iraqis.

Iraqis suffered grievously due to his messianic arrogance, which was built on the shaky premise that Americans could democratize the Middle Eastern nation and in the process do no wrong. His ideologically rooted tunnel vision prevented him from anticipating that the Iraqis might soon perceive us as occupiers rather than benefactors. He and his advisors did not seriously contemplate the extent of our responsibilities for repairing the damage in a post-war Iraq. It did not seem to dawn on them that, as wealthy as we were, we might not have sufficient assets to both rehabilitate the country and battle insurgent rebels without severely undercutting our global military capabilities, other foreign policy initiatives, and our own domestic programs and economic vitality.

Certainly, our intelligence agencies were cognizant of potential post-Saddam Hussein pitfalls. From an environmental perspective, they warned that two of war-torn Iraq's major rivers would have to be cleaned up if political stability were to be restored. Intelligence analysts also pointed out that providing adequate drinking water supplies and electricity to a battle-weary populace would pose a major challenge, especially while seeking to maintain security in an unstable post-Saddam Hussein environment.

Sure enough, the analysts' worst fears were realized. In the invasion's aftermath, chemicals and untreated sewage poured into the Euphrates and Tigris Rivers in ever-increasing volumes, intensifying health hazards.[4] Thousands of abandoned contaminated industrial and military sites left over from the fighting polluted the land and water. The rehabilitation of sanitation and other public health facilities lagged far behind schedule, and in some instances was nonexistent because of militants' harassment. Diversion of U.S. personnel and funding from reconstruction to security also contributed to further deterioration of the war-torn nation's public facilities.

Even without security concerns, the Bush administration would have fallen far short of its moral obligation to help rehabilitate the country our forces invaded. The White House has allocated $2.4 billion since 2003 for Iraq's perilously rundown water and sanitation facilities, whereas the World Bank calculated it would take at least $14 billion to rehabilitate them.[5] These were numbers the Bush people didn't want to hear, having run up a gargantuan national budgetary debt that they effectively downplayed by keeping the total Iraq war-related sum off the books.

Needless to say, the Iraqis suffered mightily: more than one million lost their lives in the course of the war,[6] and their death toll mounted as we gradually withdrew our forces from the country. An on-site survey by a UN-sponsored, Norwegian think tank found that in Southwestern Iraq, malnutrition and disease among children aged six months to five years had actually risen after our invasion.[7] And this was in a country where before the war, the mortality rate of Iraqi children under five years was 16 times higher than that of comparable American children.

President Bush shrugged off Iraq's casualties and the destruction of property; taking solace in the belief that he was doing God's will by "liberating" the Middle Eastern nation from tyranny. Meanwhile, more than two million Iraqis had fled their homeland in the wake of Americans' act of "mercy."

Inflated Stature

History is full of humans' presumptuous efforts to remake nature more to their liking.

A classic illustration: the U.S. Army Corps of Engineers' straightening out meandering rivers with riprap to make them more "agreeable" destroys adjacent wetlands and their absorptive capacity. It also accelerates the flow of the current that then produces flooding downstream as well as erosion along the banks in a series of disastrous unintended consequences.

Our efforts to restore wetlands to their original biodiversity, after we have drained them, fall pitifully short. Their complexity is generally beyond our capacity to duplicate. Clearcutting old-growth indigenous forests, replacing them with monolithic tree plantations, and then boasting that deforestation has been avoided is the height of hubris and a disservice to society. Lacking diversity, these homogenous tree plantations are highly susceptible to blight, and their uniform character eliminates the habitats of species that occupied the original forest.

Back in the 19th century, large predators in most parts of the country were considered threats to domestic animals, unacceptable competition for hunters, and just plain pests. Efforts were made to exterminate them, and that shortsighted goal came close to fruition in the lower 48 states, unleashing a series of negative consequences. Deer and their hoofed relatives, the favorite prey of large predators, proliferated and overran a number of habitats. With their ravenous appetites, the ungulates denuded a substantial amount of the foliage and ravaged crops in numerous parts of the country. In the Eastern United States, the combination of deer's high density and tendency to carry infection-laden ticks resulted in human outbreaks of a formerly rare, serious ailment that doctors eventually named Lyme disease.

Humanity has long been aware of the risks inherent in upsetting the balance of nature. Yet a mix of hubris, greed, and denial has all too often prevailed over good judgment. The arrogance persists that we can routinely compel nature to do our bidding when total control of natural forces is beyond even our considerable cognitive skills.

A byproduct of this hapless overconfidence has been the conviction that technology will allow us to do what we please to Mother Earth without fear of retribution. It is a conviction that is nothing more than a dressed up rationalization to justify plunder. What does it take to recognize that the natural world is not subject to our every whim?

Property Rights

"To thine own self be true," opined William Shakespeare, and excellent advice it is. But every person also has a responsibility to society. Individual and collective rights must be weighed to achieve a moral balance; and if that requires a touch of humility, so be it. To treat private property rights as absolute is an unwarranted extension of individual rights and potentially a wrongful act against future generations.

To claim, as some private landowners do, that they should be compensated for not violating the Endangered Species Act is the epitome of audacity. That having been said, the law provides plenty of leeway for working out a non-monetary arrangement to minimize the intrusiveness of endangered species on one's property. But for some politicians, it's not enough. They still want to pay landowners for being law-abiding citizens.

Again, what a perversion of justice, an invitation to anarchy, and a budget buster of an idea!

Abuse of Nature

Plants are often viewed as expendable, lifeless objects. People who harbor that perception think nothing of bulldozing a tree that lies in their path and doesn't suit their fancy. They seem unaware that plants are living organisms providing the shade which is nature's air conditioner, absorbing greenhouse gas pollutants, supplying us with food,[8] and last but not least, producing the oxygen on which all life depends. When failing to recognize that lower life forms—be they animal or plant—have a purposeful niche in the Earth's complex biosphere, humanity is setting itself up for some nasty consequences.

This interconnectedness of species has inspired formation of a school of jurisprudence that argues that nature should have legal rights. Advocates of this proposition maintain that a guardian should be appointed to seek restitution on nature's behalf when she has been wronged by human activity. As it now stands, the law considers rivers and plants to be objects, not subjects, leaving them open to a wide range of exploitation with no protection against human excesses. Meanwhile, corporations and ships are frequently treated as persons by the law.

In a 1972 case, Supreme Court Justice William O. Douglas wrote a dissenting opinion in which he declared that "protecting nature's ecological equilibrium should lead to the conferral of standing upon environmental objects to sue for their own preservation."

Unfortunately, Douglas's views have not made much headway, with courts as a rule still refusing to recognize that nature has directly enforceable rights or that anyone demanding damages on her behalf should have standing to sue. Lower life forms and the basic components of nature (air, water, and soil) are still regarded for the most part as commodities to be bought or sold at will, a condition that makes the job of protecting and preserving the biosphere infinitely more difficult (and that includes the task of combating global warming).

South African environmental attorney Cormac Cullinan was on target when he wrote: "The day will come when the failure of our laws to recognize the right of a river to flow, to prohibit acts that destabilize Earth's climate, or to impose a duty to respect the intrinsic value and right to exist of all life will be as reprehensible as allowing people to be bought and sold into slavery."[9]

(Ecuador became the first country to award nature legal rights that could be enforced in a court of law when in September of 2008, two thirds of its citizenry approved a new constitution to that effect.)

Arboreal Personalities

Scientific evidence indicates that trees can communicate with each other. No, they can't argue about politics. But experiments suggest that in times of stress, they release chemical compounds and/or electrical impulses that seem to act both as pest repellents and/or electrical impulses and warning signals to their neighbors, which immediately begin manufacturing chemical-defense mechanisms of their own.[10]

All of this reminds us that, despite our cognitive superiority over other organisms, there is no merit to the brash notion that nothing on Earth has intrinsic value or an existence of its own other than what we arbitrarily assign to it. To embrace that self-centered point of view is to legitimize people running roughshod over nature. An example of this obtuse posture was the Bush administration's opposition to a proposed rule protecting the North Atlantic right whale, one of the most endangered species left on Earth. The White House objection, overruling the government's own scientists, supported the shipping industry, which protested that it would lose money if required to slow its vessels in waters through which the whales were migrating. Authorities were more concerned with saving some corporate campaign contributors a few dollars than preserving an irreplaceable component of our lonely little planet's precious gene pool. Once again, people in positions of power were demonstrating they knew the cost of everything and the value of nothing.[11] Thankfully, a federal court ruled against the administration, which then begrudgingly extended protection to the whale, although with a troubling caveat that the regulation must be reevaluated in five years.

The Fixers

Our technological prowess frequently imbues us with a false sense of invincibility in manipulating the environment. We convince ourselves that our ingenuity will allow us to do pretty much as we please. At first blush, our technology may indeed seem so potent that it need not be bound by nature's parameters. After all, many of our technological initiatives seem to be designed not only to protect us from being penalized for any environmentally stressful activity but also to allow us to continue engaging in it.

The problem is that the best all those ecologically undisciplined technological advances can do is shift or postpone disruption of natural systems, a Faustian bargain bound to weigh heavily on future generations. For example, synthetic, highly toxic pesticides are no substitute for environmentally sound agricultural practices such as no till farming, crop rotation, and the use of biological pest controls. If there is over-reliance on synthetic pesticides to provide a "quick fix," their use will backfire. Target pests will build up immunity, "good" insects and other non-target species will suffer losses, and toxicity will seep into plants and soil. Petroleum, which is a base for the bug sprays, will be diverted from the manufacture of gasoline, medicines, and other important products.

Nuclear power as a solution to our energy woes remains economically daunting because of the immense construction, maintenance, and decommissioning costs associated with new plants. Safe disposal of the radioactive waste has yet to be achieved. But that has not stopped some in positions of authority from pushing for construction of new nuclear power plants, despite no such facilities having been built here in over 30 years due to the aforementioned obstacles.

Although dams and levees may offer some relief from nature's more intense climatic outbursts, they cannot provide reliable, long-term protection of development located in low-lying flood plains. Left in their original state, those areas serve as natural sponges that soak up significant overflow from torrential rainfall. Such lands are not meant to be covered with houses, and where they have been, the structures face an uncertain future.

Even if "miracle" drugs developed in our laboratories have minimal or no detectable side effects, the medicines cannot match the effectiveness of preventing disease in the first place by reducing exposure to manmade toxic chemicals in the environment.

We are fooling ourselves when we think we can thumb our noses at nature ad infinitum by virtue of our technological prowess, and any political leader who knowingly allows us to behave in this fashion is likely to be judged harshly by future historians. Enduring progress cannot be achieved without the recognition that technology will ultimately be counterproductive unless compatible with the ebb and flow of Earth's natural life-support systems.

Waste Not, Want Not

It is shameful to treat wasteful behavior as a privilege of affluence. Yet consciously or subconsciously, Americans have allowed this attitude to permeate their daily lives. Even among those of us who are barely making ends meet, one-time use is more prevalent than recycling. Where did that leave the United States? As the world's leading wastrel and a primary catalyst of the global economy's meltdown in the autumn of 2008!

In many nations, electric lighting is timed to shut off automatically when not in use. Such arrangements remain few and far between in our country, where most people would consider attempts to install "motion lighting" a brazen intrusion on personal freedom.

Where else could you find global warming skeptics proclaiming a "Carbon Belch" day in which they urged fellow Americans to waste fuel for one hour in a symbolic protest against a policy of stepped-up conservation? The originator of this brilliant idea was a conservative grassroots organization, Grassfire.org, that spread its asinine message over the Internet. As you might expect, there were few takers, especially at a time of volatile gasoline prices.[12]

Our profligate behavior becomes even more unconscionable when subjected to statistical comparisons with other nations. We generate almost twice as much municipal waste per capita as Japan and Belgium. Americans have been using twice as much water and energy per capita as their European counterparts, who still manage to enjoy roughly the same standard of living, with life expectancies equal or superior to ours.[13]

Our country has been a comparative laggard in moving forward with recycling, farmland preservation, and waste treatment plants. According to the latest data, the percentage of paper and cardboard that we recycle has been roughly 50 percent, in contrast to Germany (73 percent), Belgium (60 percent), and England (56 percent). The difference in the percentage of glass we recycle is even more glaring. Our grand total amounted to approximately 28 percent, whereas Belgium recorded a stunning 92 percent, Germany 86 percent, and France and Italy 62 percent.[14]

America's indulgent lifestyle has strained not only our own natural resources but also those of other nations, many of which export their riches to us despite their economically disadvantaged populations and shrinking raw material base. We have been shirking our responsibility to set an example for the rest of the world by failing to show greater restraint. Our inability to lead could have catastrophic consequences considering that the resources of three Earths would be needed for everyone on the planet to engage in a consumptive lifestyle at our level. (The World Overpopulation Awareness organization disagrees. It calculates that five Earths would be required to support the U.S. rate of consumption.)[15]

Both present and future generations suffer grievously when wasteful behavior is elevated to a status symbol, which is what happened with an explosion of unprecedented American prosperity at the end of World War Two. A hyper-consumption-oriented value system took hold and gathered momentum. A one-use, throwaway mentality and planned obsolescence of material goods became trademarks of our culture, with scant attention paid to conservation and the damage inflicted on the environment. Only in the last decade, with oil supply's volatility and widespread global poverty capturing more headlines, have systemic wasteful habits come under intense public scrutiny. As a result, recycling and reuse of material goods have finally gained some traction on our shores. That's all to the good, but full integration of these elemental processes across American society has a long way to go, especially in the face of a still well-entrenched obsession with conspicuous consumption and stubborn adherence to planned obsolescence.

Humbled by Nature

Exposure to pristine wilderness tends to put life in proper perspective by reminding us of how puny we are alongside the unshackled forces of nature. This surge of humility often results in greater empathy towards other human beings, and in many instances to lower life forms as well.

Wilderness can also inspire us by conveying a sense of order in a world that sometimes seems torn asunder by chaos. If one is patient and pays attention, it becomes clear that nature is ultimately geared to perpetuating life in an exquisitely balanced structure that arguably refutes the idea we inhabit a random universe. Although we frequently confront the inexplicable in our lifetimes, it is comforting to realize that whatever force is behind the system in which we reside is a force that wants us collectively to "belong." It is a realization that can be uplifting to the disillusioned and dispossessed, and it has given rise to a new field of study dubbed "eco psychology" that focuses on the therapeutic benefits of nature.

In the meantime, wilderness, together with the regenerative evidence it parades before our eyes, can provide a spiritual connection to the miracle of creation. That may explain why pristine settings frequently have a calming effect, and why so many of us feel an intense desire to preserve them for posterity. No wonder the public has soundly repudiated hyper-aggressive entrepreneurs when these businessmen have floated the idea of locating plush hotels and other swanky recreational facilities in such pastoral houses of worship as the Grand Canyon and Yellowstone National Parks.

SECTION SEVEN

—

LOYALTY AND BETRAYAL

CHAPTER SEVENTEEN

—

AFFIRMATION—AND BREACH—OF TRUST

Violation of Trust

WHAT ARE WE TO THINK when a person who has held a position of public trust tells us that noxious, lung-choking smog, technically referred to as ground-level ozone pollution, is beneficial to our health? That question arose when former Office of Management and Budget Administrator Wendy Gramm contended that the health benefits of pollution-laden smog far eclipsed any advantages derived from cleaning the air.[1] Gramm's convoluted rationalization was derived from a study conducted by economists, not medical researchers. The economists concluded that the smog's dilution of the sun's ultraviolet rays associated with skin cancer outweighed any relief that the lessening of smog would bring to "temporary" respiratory distress.

First of all, the premise that lung damage from repeated exposure to ozone-permeated smog is short lived is very much in dispute. In fact, there is a growing body of evidence that frequent exposure to high ozone levels can lead to serious health problems, including lung cancer and heart attacks.[2] Even assuming smog can provide some protection against ultraviolet rays, must we accept an increased risk of lung cancer or heart disease as the price for alleviating the threat of skin malignancies? Don't tell me that a grim Hobson's choice is the best that our trusted public servants can offer! The truth is that ground-level ozone pollution varies widely, and in most places is not sufficiently concentrated to provide meaningful protection from the sun (although it can sear our lungs). But even if smog-free air allowed more unfiltered solar rays to reach the Earth's surface, the skin-cancer threat would be manageable. Repeating an earlier point, whatever happened to the simple strategies of wearing a hat and long-sleeved shirt, using sun block, and staying out of the midday sun?

Moreover, if we are worried about ultraviolet rays, wouldn't the more prudent course be to focus on preservation of the stratosphere's "good" ozone, which filters out the lethal solar radiation so damaging to our skin? An excellent start has been made in that regard through a treaty (the 1987 Montreal Protocol) to halt the high altitude ozone layer's deterioration from manmade chemicals.

Using the threat of skin cancer as justification for not cleaning up smog is a scam created to ease the pressure for tougher regulatory restraints on polluting industries. It is as simple as that.

Gramm, the wife of former U.S. Sen. Phil Gramm, R-Texas, was out of the government at the time and lacked official authority to promote her no-win tradeoff when it made the headlines. But don't rest easy. Chances are there will always be somebody in the federal bureaucracy willing to curry the favor of industrial polluters at the expense of the general public.

Defender of the People

The Environmental Protection Agency was established to protect the public against pollution and other forms of ecological degradation, just as the Department of Agriculture was formed to champion farmers' concerns and the Commerce Department to promote the business world's interests. If you have any doubts, review the EPA primer's own definition of the agency's mission. Published in 1970, when the agency was established by President Richard Nixon, the primer contained the following: "EPA is an independent regulatory agency that has no obligation to promote agriculture, commerce, or industry. It has only one mission—to protect and enhance the environment."

Unfortunately, that has not always been the way the agency has operated during its brief history. As was previously pointed out, the stance taken by President George W. Bush's first appointee to head the EPA, former New Jersey Governor Christine Todd Whitman, was all too commonplace. On the eve of assuming her post, Whitman pledged to employ a "balanced approach" in resolving conflicts between corporate polluters and the general public. It appeared lost on her that the EPA administrator was supposed to be the people's advocate for stronger environmental protection, not a mediator who granted concessions before negotiations had even begun. Although the president appoints the EPA administrator, the latter's primary obligation, at least in theory, is to protect the environmental health of the American public, not follow a president's pro business, partisan dictates.

Setting the Stage

President Ronald Reagan was elected to head a government he believed should be largely dismantled aside from military and police functions. He quickly set out to implement that ideologically inspired conviction and, in doing so, created a blueprint for George W. Bush's assault on environmental protection more than a decade later.

Reagan certainly opened himself to the accusation that he acted unethically in accepting the support of voters who expected him to deliver—not curtail—the government's full range of services. But by putting Reagan into office, the public also had to share the blame for

Reagan—Environmental miscommunicator

the deterioration of the federal bureaucracy under the former California governor's presidency. Remember, Reagan made no secret of the inherent contradiction in his candidacy. Many a time, he declared that the federal government was part of the problem rather than the solution.

How did he get away with it? Reagan's "feel good," campaign theme, which pandered to people's self-indulgence, diverted the electorate's attention from his dismissive attitude towards a wide-ranging role for government. From an environmental perspective, Americans paid dearly for their early inattentiveness. They soon witnessed the abdication of their nation's environmental leadership abroad and acceleration of environmental degradation at home.

One of Reagan's most insidious acts (carried out with even greater verve by George W. Bush) was to fill environmental posts with individuals who in private life had made a career of trying to weaken the very departments they were chosen to head.

Reagan's first EPA administrator was the late Anne Gorsuch, an ultra-conservative ideologue who dutifully answered the president's call to arms by launching a rollback of many of the regulations her agency was supposed to implement. She sought acceleration of regulatory exemptions for manufacturers who had been prime targets of statutory restraints, did her utmost to slow the agency's rule-making process, and reveled in slashing the EPA'S budget. Typical of her *modus operandi* was the regulation of formaldehyde, a gas used as a disinfectant and preservative but found to cause cancer in laboratory animals. Not willing to "inconvenience" formaldehyde manufacturers, Gorsuch ruled out regulatory restrictions until and unless the chemical was proven incontrovertibly hazardous to human beings. She did not consider it particularly significant that lab rats consistently exposed to low amounts of formaldehyde developed cancer. In fact, her assistant administrator for pesticides, John Tod Hunter, declared that formaldehyde should not even be regulated because "it did not cause significant risk of serious or widespread harm of cancer." (Think how those victims who were stricken against the odds felt about their government, which was supposedly charged with minimizing health risks to all Americans.) Hunter went on to say that the EPA's preliminary decision in 1980 to regulate formaldehyde was "incomplete and flawed."[3]

Fortunately, the agency eventually acknowledged its responsibility, revised its evaluation of formaldehyde's potency, and declared the chemical a "probable human carcinogen."[4] So did the U.S. Department of Health and Human Services and the International Agency for Research on Cancer. Both concluded that formaldehyde "can reasonably be anticipated to be a human carcinogen." Lab rats were, in the final analysis, a legitimate red flag. A National Cancer Institute study found a significant link between formaldehyde exposure and cancers of the blood and lymphatic system.[5]

While formaldehyde today is subject to at least some regulation, government stonewalling against restrictions on other toxic substances has continued. Is this the best that American people can expect? More often than not extending the benefit of the doubt to the potential polluter rather than the prospective victim? Elevating corporate profits ahead of public health? Placing the burden of proof on the party at risk to show there is a reasonable cause for concern rather than on industry to demonstrate a product is reasonably safe? If the former, corrective action may be too late since it is essentially predicated on responding to harm rather than preventing it.

Gorsuch's blatant pro-industry bias caused highly qualified, difficult-to-replace, mid-level career EPA personnel to resign in droves. They recognized what she was up to and would have none of it. Yet despite Gorsuch coming under increasing criticism across the nation for shortchanging environmental protection, Reagan steadfastly defended her actions. To put it charitably, his doctrinaire loyalty remained blind to the very end. Even when pressure from an outraged public eventually forced her ouster, Reagan accepted her resignation with regret.

Just as invidious was Reagan's appointment of James Watt to be Interior Secretary. A zealous evangelical Christian, Watt quickly gained national notoriety for his dismissive attitude towards conservation. We have noted that he subscribed to a biblical interpretation of the Second Coming, in which all Earth's resources are deemed ripe for exploitation by human beings. Watt therefore leased or sold off prized undeveloped public lands to private commercial interests at bargain-basement prices. Until stopped by the courts, he awarded management responsibilities over federally owned rangeland to ranchers whose livestock had often been overgrazing the terrain in question. Nor did Watt's religious fervor produce any benefits for Native Americans, who were angered when the Interior Secretary issued leases to strip-mine their sacred burial grounds and archaeological sites located on public land.

Watt never seemed overly concerned whether the facts justified his decisions. More important in his eyes was whether his decisions conformed to his religious principles. It was in effect an end-justifies-the-means formula ironically made famous by the communist thinker Karl Marx, whom Watt so despised; and its application resulted in some radical decision making that alienated most of the nation.

Watt's blatant disregard for conservation of natural resources soon made him the most unpopular figure in the Reagan administration (which took some doing). Eventually, his critics found cause for dismissal that even Reagan could not ignore: an offensive, offhand remark by Watt that one of his departmental advisory boards was comprised of "a black, a woman, two Jews, and a cripple." The great Christian unmasked! Although Reagan felt compelled to ask for Watt's resignation, he characterized the Interior Secretary as a victim of a witch-hunt. If Watt were a victim, how should we have classified the American people, who were forced to watch the Interior Secretary go about shredding their wilderness heritage?

Gorsuch and Watt were "faithfully executing" the will of Reagan, not the laws of the land (unless the two by chance happened to coincide). The "Gipper's" jovial demeanor may have spared him direct public censure, but it could not obscure the environmental damage inflicted by his subordinates. Although the prime responsibility for Reagan's appointees' actions lay at his doorstep, they took the brunt of the blame and even diverted public attention from the president's atrocious foreign environmental policy. It was a policy in which Reagan spurned a number of international environmental treaties, including a pact that required warning labels on all toxic substances.

At home, Reagan procrastinated in combating acid rain. He tried to turn the law upside down by making economics rather than environmental protection the primary consideration in setting health standards and endangered-species listings. He chose to ignore the legal dictate that fiscal concerns could only be factored into the application of environmental rules, not their formation. He insisted that strengthening protection against pollution had to be justified by incontrovertible proof when that was virtually an impossible standard to meet. His corporate allies were delighted with his prescription for easing their liability. Moreover, the president allowed companies to police themselves for environmental violations, an open invitation for unscrupulous executives to cut costs by cutting corners. In short, Reagan paved the way for George W. Bush, who proceeded to carry his predecessor's destabilizing, conservative environmental agenda to an even greater extreme.

Bush's Betrayal

Illustrative of President George W. Bush's betrayal of the public trust was the difference in the way he dealt with environmental concerns inside and outside the confines of his Crawford, Texas ranch. That he could be so dedicated to the conservation ethic on his own property while displaying little or no commitment to preservation on undeveloped public lands reeked of hypocrisy. It was clear where his loyalties lay, and they were not with the "great unwashed masses."

Within the borders of his 1,583-acre ranch, Bush was the epitome of environmental correctness. His Crawford home fully utilized passive solar energy and featured geothermal heat pumps that circulated water to warm or cool the house, depending upon the season. He waxed lyrical about the large trees, endangered species, variety of birds, and unpolluted streams on his property.

This was the same guy who had sought to increase timber harvesting in previously protected wilderness reserves on public land and had extended legal protection to far fewer endangered species than did preceding presidents, even as scores of animals and plants were going extinct. He opted for renewable energy at Crawford, yet his budgets repeatedly shortchanged federal funding of solar energy research and development for the nation.

Bush may have been intensely protective of the pristine waterways on his ranch. But he fought relentlessly to remove barriers for developers seeking to pave over off-limits wetlands and forest habitats. His administration sanctioned the proposed dumping of mining wastes into unpolluted Appalachian mountain streams, a move tantamount to permanent ecological desecration. The practice was vigorously challenged in the courts as well as in the scientific community where a 2009 peer-reviewed study definitively found mountaintop mining to be an unmitigated environmental disaster. Authors of the study recommended that absent some miraculous new remediation technique, the mining should be banned for the sake of the people, freshwater streams, and wildlife in the project's path.[6] The Crawford ranch was indeed a shrine to the double standard.[7]

As was previously mentioned, the U.S. Constitution requires the president to "faithfully execute" the laws of the land. But faithfully execute was frequently absent from Bush's lexicon in his handling of environmental regulation. That was especially true if you interpreted the phrase to mean "keeping faith" with the electorate. For example, his proposal to reform the Clean Air Act would have allowed more lethal industrial-mercury contaminants to be released, and lengthened the time before the owners of a polluting power plant would be required to take remedial action. Even worse, Bush tried to remove the "hazardous" label from mercury. Had he succeeded, the danger quotient would have escalated for children and the chronically ill, both of whom are particularly vulnerable to the trace elements of this toxic chemical present in many products.

Sometimes, Bush and his subordinates chose to circumvent existing law altogether. The president was particularly fond of invoking "national security" to exempt the military from a slew of environmental laws, especially the Endangered Species Act. He resorted to the national security refrain in granting a waiver that allowed the Navy to ignore regulations protecting marine mammals from harmful sonar-signal exposure off the Southern California coast. A federal district court judge took exception to those strong-arm tactics and ordered the regulation to stand, noting that the Navy had plenty of opportunity to practice sonar detection of submarines without disrupting whales and other marine mammals.[8]

Unfortunately, the story did not have a happy ending. On appeal, the U.S. Supreme Court's five-member conservative majority, which tended to be extraordinarily deferential to presidential power, reversed the district court's decision. For these justices, the higher authority lived in the White House, not the heavens.

Bush's Secretary for Homeland Security, Michael Chertoff, carried out one of the most flagrant circumventions of existing law. With a swipe of his pen, he released his department from any requirement to comply with 19 environmental statutes while constructing a 470-mile-long anti-immigration fence along the United States-Mexican border. Concerns over clean air, clean water, and safe drinking water were scuttled, despite the fence's location in an area of southeastern Arizona inhabited by more than 200,000 people. That whole episode prompted Karen Wayland, legislative director of the environmental activist organization Natural Resources Defense Council, to remark that "it's frightening that one man, not elected by anyone, could take 40 years of laws that keep America safe from toxic pollution and throw them out the window."[8] Although national security is obviously a legitimate concern, it does not justify a peremptory invalidation of the laws and freedoms of the land.

When Bush chose "No Child Left Behind" as the catchy slogan for his education policy, the symbolism did not apply to children's health. In a startling lapse of conscience as well as execution of official duties, he sought to terminate federal oversight of the screening of low-income youngsters for lead poisoning. Consider that more than 300,000 kids aged one to five had already been identified with blood-lead concentrations above safe levels. Keep in mind that some 24 million housing units in our nation had dangerous lead levels (mostly from dust and peeling paint). More than four million of those homes—located primarily in low-income neighborhoods—were occupied by one or more young children. Finally, take note that minorities were especially at risk, with an estimated 3 percent of black children under age six afflicted with elevated blood levels compared to 1.3 percent of their white counterparts.[9]

Confronted with these statistics, even a frequently compliant Congress could not go along with the president and rejected his cold-blooded decision to dispense with the screening oversight program.
The elderly fared no better under the Bush regime. Some in industry argued that it was not cost effective to strengthen pollution-abatement rules to give extra protection to the elderly, especially those in frail condition. Clearly, these were business interests looking for a way to keep a lid on compliance costs. They wouldn't say so explicitly, but what they were really suggesting was that it was foolish to spend extra money on people who didn't have that long to live. The administration actually embraced this de facto euthanasia and only recanted in the wake of politically embarrassing publicity and resistance in Congress.

That, however, represented a rare retreat from Bush's deregulatory proclivity. For the most part, his administration dutifully stuck to a heavily weighted, pro-business script. For example, the EPA sought to relax the proposed rule to curb polluting emissions from industrial laundries— another perplexing maneuver for an agency responsible for environmental protection. Motivation in that instance became clearer when one learned that a major supporter of the president owned a leading company in the industrial laundry field.

But nothing was more galling than the Bush EPA's rejection of its own scientists' recommendation for strengthening the ozone (toxic smog) standard and instead submitting a weaker version that would appease industry but cost lives. (The EPA even dismissed any link between smog exposure and respiratory disease until a report by the National Academy of Sciences forced the agency into a retraction.)[10]

There is a long tradition of newly elected presidents seeking to alleviate post-campaign rancor by pledging that they will be the president of all Americans, regardless of political persuasion. George W. Bush publicly expressed that sentiment on numerous occasions. Unfortunately, his policies in the environmental sector and elsewhere made him a president of many Americans in name only.

Putting America First

Presidential contenders also often assure voters that they will foster national unity by "putting America first." That was GOP presidential nominee John McCain's campaign rallying cry in the fall of 2008, and a hollow pledge it was. McCain was willing to place his country in long-term jeopardy for the possibility of short-term political gain by naming as his running mate an individual who had very few, if any, qualifications to be vice president, let alone president. If McCain really had Americans' interests at heart, would he have chosen a person who refused to acknowledge the definitive cause of global warming, the most profound societal challenge of our time? Since McCain himself appeared to recognize the enormity of the global warming threat and humanity's culpability in exacerbating it, how in good conscience could he name someone with diametrically opposed views to be just a heartbeat away from the presidency?

McCain's choice, Alaska Governor Sarah Palin, may have fulfilled his objective of energizing the hard-core conservative GOP base, but she rejected the scientific consensus that global warming was in large part due to human activity and instead viewed accelerated temperature rise as most likely a natural phenomenon. According to that line of thinking, we could do little more than attempt to adapt to warmer temperatures— perhaps a necessary interim measure but ultimately temporary relief when mankind desperately needed a cure. Moreover, it was a cure that could only come through mitigation of industrial and other manmade pollutants that scientists had identified as the primary force behind rising global temperatures.

Palin's skepticism reinforced the argument that it made no sense to impose major regulatory restraints on the energy industry's polluting ways, and dovetailed nicely with her pro-business bias. Unfortunately, her stance would almost certainly have spelled disaster for the United States if it had ever become national policy; so it was unconscionable for the 72-year-old McCain, a four-time cancer survivor with an uncertain health prognosis, to gamble with the American people's future. McCain's vice-presidential choice left him with an image that didn't add up to "putting American first," and not surprisingly in the White House contest, he came in "second."

Democratic Inclusion

It is only fair to note that the environment did not escape unscathed during President Clinton's years in office. Only in the final days of his tenure did "Johnny Come Lately" Clinton muster the courage to cease buckling at the first sign of significant political opposition and to sign off on bold initiatives to control pollution and preserve wilderness.

Perhaps most disappointing was the relative passivity of Vice President Al Gore, who had made environmental protection his signature issue from the start of his political career. Gore had generated lofty expectations with his rousing call for ecological activism in his best-selling tome Earth in the Balance. Yet as second-in-command, he consistently deferred to a president with a relatively undistinguished environmental record. Those disappointed in Gore's vice-presidential performance anticipated that at least when he ran for president, he would champion the progressive ideas he so often soft-pedaled while serving as veep.

But to the chagrin of the faithful, once Gore took to the presidential campaign trail, he accepted his advisors' flawed recommendations to rein in his environmental advocacy. They warned him that it might alienate more voters than it would attract, given people's instinctive distrust of being led into uncharted waters.

Gore's pullback was arguably a factor in his razor-thin election loss to George W. Bush. Many disenchanted environmentalists deserted him for third-party candidate Ralph Nader, and they were not insignificant in number, especially in the pivotal swing state of Florida.

Although Gore's advisors did him no favors, they required a willing accomplice, and when the vice president most needed to heed his own counsel, he failed to do so. Gore the author was a very different breed from Gore the presidential candidate. In his best seller, he warned against the "subtle and pervasive temptation of leaders in a democracy… to attain and hold on to power, even when doing so means avoiding hard choices and ignoring the truth." Such introspection rarely went beyond the printed page

Sarah Palin—Shoot first and ask questions later

Al Gore—Global warming guru

while he was vice president or campaigning for the presidency.

What "revolutionary" ideas did Gore's campaign brain trust fear would offend voters? Earth in the Balance provided these samples: our technological revolution had its limits, so we could not destroy nature with impunity; material consumption was undermining our spiritual values as well as the environment, and our political, business and intellectual leaders had done little to discourage this indulgent lifestyle; the mining of fossil fuels was being conducted in an environmentally unsustainable manner; the strict fuel-economy standards the Clinton administration failed to get through Congress should be enacted; and environmentally destructive subsidies to industry should be discontinued.

The ex-vice president should have publicly promoted those concepts during the campaign. His reluctance to do so suggested more concern about career advancement than principle. Gore clearly lacked confidence that voters would acknowledge the wisdom of his cause.

On returning to private life, Gore did make some amends for his muted environmental persona during the White House and presidential-campaign years. He finally spoke out forcefully and at great lengths about climate change, and his crusade (with the help of his Academy Award film documentary) won him a Nobel Peace Prize. But at that point, his sense of urgency lacked the authority to promote change other than through propaganda. Powerful though media messages might be, it was in the White House where he would have had the authority to institute some immediate mandated reforms that would have set an example for the rest of the world. As a private citizen, he had to rely solely on his rhetorical powers of persuasion to convince heads of state to be more activist. Actually, where Gore experienced his most tangible success was at the grassroots level. It was there that he was able to effectively mobilize people to exert pressure on world leaders to address climate change.

CHAPTER EIGHTEEN

—

IDEOLOGY, DEVALUED INTENTIONS, AND GOOD DEEDS

Blind Loyalty

LOYALTY IS USUALLY an admirable trait, but exercised blindly, it can ultimately be self-defeating. In Congress, lawmakers who stymie passage of legislation out of knee-jerk partisan fidelity rather than objective evaluation of a proposal's substantive merits are shortchanging their constituents. On numerous occasions and with varying degrees of success, small groups of legislators have sought to bury important environmental legislation by nitpicking it to death for ideological reasons that lacked substance. Let's bring up again one of the most glaring examples: in the 1970s, opponents of government regulation in principle and the Clean Water Act's strong language in particular tried to torpedo the entire bill by singling out a provision requiring a zero discharge of pollutants. Such a goal was impossible, they maintained, and any corporation attempting to comply would go bankrupt.

This transparent ploy won few converts. The legislative language accompanying the bill made clear that zero discharge was an aspirational goal rather than a mandatory target (although there are rare circumstances in which the source of pollution can be completely eliminated and zero emissions achieved). The higher the bar is set, the better people perform. Here was an occasion in which dissenting politicians chose to make the perfect the enemy of the good because they considered the "good" too much of a restriction on industrial activity. Driven by partisan politics, naysayers sought to deep-six the legislation on phony, semantic grounds. It was a morally unconscionable and thankfully unsuccessful strategy that would have posed a threat to public health.

A more recent example of vindictive partisanship was Republican politicians' behavior towards President Obama in the immediate aftermath of the thrashing their party took in the 2008 election. It appeared that GOP lawmakers cared more about making Obama look bad than the nation look good. In blatant dereliction of their official oath to serve the public, these politicians focused on doggedly obfuscating, or opposing outright, the president's initiatives, regardless of their merits. No serious efforts to find common ground were forthcoming. It was simply a raw attempt to regain political power, the nation be damned.

Yet even if a cause is noble, loyalty to it can be counterproductive if so rigid as to exclude compromise when such an outcome may be all that's achievable. Obstinacy is no virtue when it is more pigheaded than courageous. A case in point was the political gyrations of Rep. Ken Hechler (D-W. Va.) in the mid 1970s. Hechler led the congressional crusade for a ban on strip-mining, an environmentally damaging practice that was ravaging his district. He even gained 110 co-sponsors for his bill, a modified version of which was ultimately passed.

Nevertheless, when President Ford vetoed the bill, Hechler voted to uphold Ford's decision, which was sustained by a mere three votes in the House of Representatives! Why would he vote against the very legislation that had been his personal crusade? Because in his view, the modified bill contained too many loopholes. For him, doing nothing was better than accepting the lowest common denominator. He especially objected to enforcement being left to the individual states. But demanding an unachievable, all-or-nothing resolution when people desperately needed at least a foot in the door was a selfish ego trip, not a display of admirable resolve.

Fatal Trafficking Jam

The Catholic Church is not alone in imposing its own orthodoxy on sexual behavior. A conservative-dominated Congress passed the Trafficking Victims Protection Reauthorization Act in 2003. While the law had the commendable objective of cracking down on the abominable practice of selling young girls into sexual slavery, right-wing legislators inserted a provision denying artificial contraception assistance to any foreign government, group, or organization that sanctioned legalized prostitution. Conveniently omitted was any reference to our own Nye County, Nevada, where so-called "houses of ill repute" were not only legal but a bulwark of the local economy. It should also be noted that prostitution carried out in private by consenting adults is lawful and government-regulated in most countries around the world. Given that backdrop, citing the 2003 statute to withhold $48 million in contraception assistance to impoverished areas of Brazil because authorities there would not criminalize long-standing legalized prostitution was the height of parochial-driven hypocrisy—and insensibility.

Fiduciary Limitations

During the mid-1990s, Sen. Christopher Bond (R-Mo.), chaired an appropriations subcommittee and sought to economize by reducing the EPA's enforcement budget by more than 22 percent. How could he justify such a cut, considering that the EPA's broad regulatory responsibilities were perennially under-funded? Bond's answer: eliminate "low-priority actions when there is the least risk to human health and the environment."

It was all well and good for Sen. Bond to talk detachedly about "low priorities" from his rarified niche on Capitol Hill. You won't find much pollution (other than verbal) in Congressional corridors. But what constitutes "low-priority" is in the eyes of the beholder. Those in the general public victimized by human-induced environmental hazards—however remote—would hardly consider their plight deserving of such a paltry classification. There is no good reason why those people should be sacrificed in a society where a moral imperative, at least in theory, elevates health above profit and where enough resources exist to provide the maximum possible protection to every segment of the populace.

Because most exposures to health hazards from industrial pollution are involuntary, and therefore beyond the capacity of any individual to curb single-handedly, primary responsibility for prevention rests with the government. It alone has the sophisticated monitoring systems and full range of police powers to rein in the broad array of toxic industrial emissions.

Note, however, that the government's moral obligation to protect the public against environmental and public health threats has limits. When human exposure to external risk is largely voluntary and can be avoided, or at least dramatically minimized if the individual so chooses, the government's fiduciary responsibility to provide protection is much more modest. Even though driving, cigarette smoking, alcoholism, and poor nutritional choices claim many more lives than toxic pollutants, democracy draws a line against government intrusion into voluntary high-risk behavior. In those situations, the authorities' role is limited to notifying the public of the magnitude of personal risk involved and how to reduce the dangers through acts of good judgment.

Of course, when individuals' voluntary risky behavior also jeopardizes the health and/or safety of others, government regulators should intervene. That is why an alcoholic who drinks himself silly in the privacy of his home is doing nothing illegal, whereas if he ventures onto the highway and drives erratically, he is ripe for prosecution. It is why as long as cigarettes are legal and people choose to smoke themselves into an iron lung in seclusion, all authorities are morally obligated to do is warn of the nasty medical consequences of such action. When the fumes impact non-smokers in public places, however, government has to be more proactive. That explains the increase in ordinances banning cigarette use in such locations.[1] Moreover, it is only a matter of time before government regulators inevitably tighten the screws on industry's marketing of addictive toxicity to our youth, starting perhaps with a ban on free handouts to juveniles.

Timely Fidelity

We have seen how environmental concerns can bring out the best, as well as the worst. It can prompt people to make bold conciliatory moves they would otherwise have never contemplated. Another case illustrative of this point is water scarcity in the Middle East. It has the potential to either inflame tensions between ancient enemies and culminate in a military confrontation, or serve as a unifying force for reluctant cooperation born of mutual need for survival. So far, expedience appears to be prevailing over deeply entrenched enmity. Israel and its hostile Arab neighbors have participated in a durable, if uneasy, water-sharing arrangement. In addition, Israel and many of its foes lining the Mediterranean have long cooperated in a program to cope with the marine pollution plaguing that body of water. More recently, Israeli and Palestinian villagers discreetly bypassed the animus between their peoples and collaborated in managing a river system running through their respective territories.

The environment's unifying effects extend beyond the Middle East. While diplomatic relations between the United States and Cuba have been suspended for decades, the two countries have had no difficulty in agreeing on a strategy to combat oil spills in the Caribbean. Even when Great Britain and Argentina were engaged in a military face-off over control of the Falkland Islands in the South Atlantic, they continued to cooperate in a program to protect the Antarctic environment.

Private Foibles

You don't have to be a government bureaucrat to be entrusted with special environmental custodial responsibilities. The American Museum of Natural History is a testament to that. Enter the New York City-based institution's exhibition halls and you will be surrounded by advocacy for conservation woven into most of the displays. This is as it should be. Environmental protection leans heavily on education, and the museum provides an invaluable complement to classroom teaching and field experience.

Yet this same museum in 1979 agreed to sell to a developer a 100–acre, heavily wooded tract in densely populated Huntington, Long Island. A wealthy widow had bequeathed the site with the stated intention that it be used as a nature "field laboratory." The museum justified the sale by citing the need for revenue to fund research. Its director contended that his institution's primary function was to analyze the past, not promote conservation in the present. As has been noted, that philosophy has undergone sorely needed revision. These days, the institution strives to be a contemporary spokesman for sustainability and survival—and not a moment too soon.

Disoriented Captives

Whales and dolphins roam freely over vast expanses of ocean. That being the case, it is criminal to capture these large creatures and confine them to a tiny, artificial lagoon where they are often treated as circus animals. Nonetheless, many aquariums and marine-themed amusement parks do just that to attract audiences.

Although incarceration seems inhumane, what of these institutions' declared intent (and responsibility) to educate the public about threats to wildlife and instill an appreciation that will translate into societal support for conservation?

These institutions can reconcile their fiscal survival and educational goals without depleting the natural environment of wild creatures unsuited for captivity or on the verge of extinction. They can serve as halfway houses for treatment of sick or injured animals, temporarily putting the creatures on display during the convalescence period preceding release into the wild.

Lacking an incapacitated cetacean or injured rare species for exhibit, the institution could use film to convey the essence of the animals while promoting the importance of preserving and/or restoring their native habitat. With the miracle of electronic virtual reality, the audience can often get a better understanding of how the animal functions in its natural habitat than they would by witnessing its cramped movements in captivity. If the captured species has no viable wild habitat left to return to, the zoo or aquarium should establish an in-house breeding program. The idea would be to use captive propagation to save the species from extinction with the hope that the creature could some day be returned to a restored natural habitat. To their credit, some zoos are actually collaborating with foreign countries to preserve or revive the natural habitat of wildlife held in captivity.[2]

Where natural habitats remain intact, some endangered species resettlement efforts have proved successful. The Detroit Zoo was able to raise and ultimately release 40 endangered Wyoming toads back into their natural habitat in 2007. Zoos in Toronto and Calgary increased the numbers of Vancouver Island Marmot (found only on that Canadian island) from 50 to 150 through captive breeding. The San Francisco Zoo was instrumental in removing the American bald eagle from the endangered list by raising and subsequently freeing more than 100 of those birds into the countryside.[3]

Let's assume a species that is abundant in the wild can also reasonably tolerate confinement. The zoo can then make a legitimate case for sacrificing some specimens' freedom through permanent captivity so as to cultivate greater public appreciation of the creature's untamed cousins and support for preservation of their native habitat.

Prisoners of Dogma

Conscientious individuals can end up in an ethical quagmire
when they engage in an all-consuming embrace of ideology in which
unquestioning adherence trumps reason. Such believers can find themselves
working at cross purposes from the intended good deed.

That brings us to the current chief prelate of the Catholic Church,
Pope Benedict XVI, who from the very start of his tenure issued stirring
entreaties on behalf of environmental protection. Unfortunately, he
undercut his sage counsel by advocating policies that, if strictly followed,
would increase the chances of irreparable harm to public health and the
environment. For example, the Vatican, under both Pope Benedict and
his predecessors, has not viewed either explosive growth of the human
population or the subsequent stress on natural resources as problems. In
fact, Pope Benedict dredged up the aforementioned canard that without
runaway population growth, there wouldn't be enough young people to
support their elders and the economy, or provide a sufficient gene pool
to produce a bumper crop of future geniuses.[4] It is a viewpoint that just
happens to be in sync with the Church's desire to expand its flock.

Consistent with his ill-conceived enthusiasm for soaring birth rates,
Pope Benedict failed to acknowledge the well-documented association
between rapid population growth and environmental degradation in
developing countries. Such growth can be curbed by family planning
programs that the Church has disavowed because of Vatican opposition to
artificial contraception.

Sure, the Church has exhibited token support for family planning
in the form of "natural" birth control via the so-called rhythm method,
which relies on abstinence during ovulation. But that method is woefully
ineffective. The sexual drive in people of reproductive age is often too
powerful to be restrained by vows of chastity. In any event, the Vatican's
espousal of the rhythm method has not been motivated by a wish to curb
the birth rate. Why? Because in the Church's eyes, a couple who uses the
technique to remain childless rather than space the births of their kids is
misusing the technique.

Meanwhile, Third World nations with the highest population
growth rates have the lowest per-capita agricultural acreage and least
access to safe drinking-water supplies of any sovereign states on the planet.
Population growth has outpaced food production in many of those nations,
with more than 800 million people chronically malnourished. Per-capita
cropland worldwide decreased by more than half between 1960 and 2008,
and of the remaining acreage, only 16 percent was free of soil degradation.[5]
It should thus come as no surprise that per-capita grain production has
been declining as more than 90 million people are added annually to the

Vatican: When In Rome....

global population.

One of the most disturbing facets of Vatican policy has been its refusal to relent on the contraceptive ban contained in the 1968 papal encyclical, Humana Vitae, even when one member of a married couple is known to have AIDS. The Church's stance towards the nuptial bond in this instance seems to be, "You've made your bed, now die in it."

Seems incomprehensible, doesn't it? Yet what can you expect when you have Pope Benedict declaring that condoms "actually increase the AIDS problem," and that engaging in sex solely within the confines of marriage is the only way to prevent the disease. Yes, fidelity of two healthy parties in a monogamous relationship is effective protection against the AIDS virus. Unfortunately, pre-marital and extra-marital sexual relations are endemic in most societies, and are actually an established part of the culture in most of Africa. It is a state of affairs that reduces the Pope's well-intended but naïve counsel to painful irrelevance and depicts him as tragically divorced from reality. (Contrary to the Church's insistent claims, condoms are highly reliable in preventing transmission of AIDS.)

What is the practical effect of such perverse advice? We have seen the scenario unfold numerous times throughout history. An old man indoctrinates much younger impressionable followers with misguided ideology that is mindlessly adopted and puts the "true believers'" lives at risk. It has produced people like Simba Teresa, a 45-year-old mother in the crowd lining the streets to greet Pope Benedict on his visit to the African nation of Angola. In a continent where AIDS is rampant, Teresa paid tribute to the Pontiff by volunteering that "the only people who use condoms are those with no faith."[6]

While the Church has not done its flock any favors by failing to confront the impacts of unrestrained population growth, an enlightened Catholic rebellion has materialized both within and outside the ranks of the clergy. Many laymen have been far more insightful than their spiritual leaders in evaluating the pros and cons of family size and artificial contraception. Some Catholic priests stationed in destitute backwaters of developing countries have made the connection between overpopulation, poverty, disease, and environmental degradation. In good conscience, they have defied Vatican official policy and distributed condoms to the populace.

Individual Conscience

Individuals must share the custodial responsibility for protecting the nation's natural resources. In theory, at least, each of us has a moral obligation to preserve the environment for future generations. While our personal actions alone might not have much impact, they do in the aggregate, which is why we all should strive to interact with the world around us in a sustainable manner.

What would that entail? The fundamentals of such a lifestyle are conservation, recycling, and reuse, which at present are being integrated into our conspicuous consumption-oriented society at a maddeningly slow pace. Indeed, our country has lagged so far behind so much of the rest of the world in adopting this lifestyle that it is getting harder to ignore the increasing negative publicity about the discrepancy. Signs of national guilt have even begun to emerge with regard to our wasting more natural resources per capita than any other nationality. A recent "green guilt" nationwide survey found 22 percent of Americans bothered by their lack of an environmentally sensitive lifestyle (up 2 percent over the previous year).[7] Unfortunately, such regrets have tended to be expressed through action only when forced by extenuating circumstances (e.g. American motorists flocking to mass transit and smaller, more fuel-efficient cars because of soaring gasoline prices in the spring of 2008).[8]

It is not just the quantity of what we consume, but also the marketplace choices we are making that is putting undue stress on the Earth's natural-resource base. In a 14-country survey conducted by the National Geographic Society and the international polling company GlobeScan, the United States finished dead last regarding the ecological wisdom of its consumption patterns.[9] Americans had on average the largest, most energy-inefficient homes and were the least likely to walk, bike, or use public transportation to reach their destination, opting compulsively for automobile travel. Food consumption patterns weren't any better. Americans trailed other nationalities in cultivating locally grown foods and patronizing their producers (thereby benefiting from the fuel saved), even in season. And they surpassed other countries in diets heavily oriented toward meat at the expense of more nutritious fruits and vegetables. Raising livestock rather than plant food is also more fuel inefficient, and the domestic animals' methane gas emissions rise into the troposphere and exacerbate global warming, in contrast to produce's benign environmental impacts. Furthermore, Americans led the international community in excessive packaging and the purchase of environmentally unfriendly products.[10]

It stands to reason that necessity drives many individuals in developing countries to be more conscientious about controlling personal consumption and eliminating waste. How else to survive in the midst of sub-par living conditions and environmentally degraded surroundings? Yet why have relatively affluent Germany, the UK, Australia, Japan, and Spain scored better than Americans? Post-World War Two frugality and a lesser natural-resource base provide some of the answers. Whatever the reasons, conservation and thrift for the moment are more prevalent in those countries, which consequently have had a less feverish association with conspicuous material consumption.

Our consumptive lifestyle is an anachronism in an ever more crowded world of diminishing resources. We need to recognize the perils of that lifestyle and set an example that convinces other countries—rich and poor—not to be seduced by the promise of our seemingly open-ended wealth. Meaningfully modifying our lifestyle—not just in hard times but as part of our daily routine—would at least give other nations second thoughts about following in our current footsteps and squandering finite natural resources.

Thus looms what may be the most formidable challenge of the 21st century for our incoming leaders and American society as a whole. We must acknowledge that our lifestyle puts at great risk the best interests of future generations, and somehow find a way to alter it accordingly.

The Generosity of Elders

Many senior citizens have an opportunity to preserve the country's natural wealth for future generations. Private interests own nearly half of our remaining 800 million acres of forest, and more than 200 million of those acres are in the hands of seniors. What they do with their property when they retire has increased in importance because developers are frequently chomping at the bit to take title and turn rural land into subdivisions. Moreover, the Bush administration sought with some success to sell off public forest tracts to private commercial entities, mostly in the Western United States. Its motivation was ostensibly to raise money to pay for rural schools, but it really stemmed from the president's ideological conviction that land could be better (and more profitably) managed by private interests than by government bureaucrats. The attempt to deplete the public natural-resource base was significantly thwarted by Congress and environmental activists. Yet who knows what the future will hold if this base is not protected for posterity? And that is where the seniors come in. They can pretty much assure preservation of the woodlands they wish to relinquish if they transfer the property to a member of the family committed to keeping it in its natural state for future generations, sell the tract to a public governing body for use as a park or nature preserve, or grant a conservation easement. In the case of an easement, the original owner remains on the land but transfers management rights in perpetuity to a conservation-oriented government agency, a responsible environmental organization, or a local land trust.

SECTION EIGHT
—
INGENUITY, CONSCIENTIOUS INDUSTRIOUSNESS, AND WILLFUL
NEGLECT

CHAPTER NINETEEN

—

THE GOOD

A Lot Out of a Little

MOUNT TRASHMORE is no majestic, snow-clad peak in the Canadian Rockies. Yet in its own way, it is every bit as much a tribute to nature (courtesy of Homo sapiens' ingenuity) as an awe-inspiring mountain range. Trashmore came into existence in the early 1970s when officials from Virginia Beach, Va. compacted more than 400,000 tons of solid municipal waste, added topsoil, and formed the first landfill park in the world.

It sits on 165 acres and rises more than 60 feet above ground, providing a panoramic view of the surrounding flatlands and the city of Virginia Beach in the distance. Grass covers its slopes, and it is surrounded by recreational facilities that attract more than a million visitors a year.

The transformation of waste into a valuable asset that is environmentally sustainable to boot represents a triumph of human intelligence. Nature's recycling capability was harnessed to assure that the region's landscape would not be marred by scores of open waste dumps and the potential health hazards they would pose. The way the Virginia Beach city fathers chose to keep their jurisdiction from being fouled by litter made them pioneers in challenging America's "one-time-use, throw-away" mentality.

Also in the 1970s, forward-looking entrepreneurs responded to an emerging environmental sensitivity by developing and marketing ecologically friendly technological innovations. These included transformation of waste oil into high-grade lubricating oil without any pollution residue and conversion of municipal garbage into fuel.

Concerns have been raised about the huge swathes of arable land that ethanol and other biofuels would divert from agricultural activity, thereby creating the specter of food shortages. Along came Shell Oil Company to experiment in Hawaii with a system that produced diesel fuel from pond scum. If Shell and other researchers in the field can perfect this procedure, fast-growing algae could be cultivated daily in manmade coastal ponds that would generate 15 times more fuel than equivalent cropland and ease the pressures on agricultural productivity (although not necessarily on greenhouse gas emissions).[1]

Whether these businessmen have any altruistic motivation or are purely profit-driven is irrelevant in the big picture. What is important is that their efforts—if successful—will contribute to a growing national conservation ethic, and regardless of intent, exude an inherent moral ambiance.

That's not to say there haven't been numerous instances when pure idealism rather than profit clearly was the driving force behind efforts to improve the environment. Save Our Streams is a classic example. SOS began life as a citizens group administered by the Isaak Walton League in the "kickoff" environmental decade of the 1970s. Its goal was to relieve rivers and streams of ecological stress. Volunteers removed litter and debris from the waterways and seeded riverbanks with vegetation to halt erosion. The satisfaction of restoring natural processes was their compensation.

More Fruits of Genius

Employing human ingenuity to synchronize the fruits of production with the rhythms of nature has not been limited to conversion of waste products into renewable materials. To their dismay, scientists discovered that the sunscreen used to protect our skin actually bleached and eventually killed coral reefs.[2] Researchers estimate that some 10 percent of the world's reefs are threatened by the 4,000 to 6,000 metric tons of sunscreen that are washed into the ocean annually. A temporary solution is to use sunscreens containing physical filters that reflect ultraviolet radiation. But the permanent answer, as always, requires finding a way to work in concert with nature, and Australian scientists are hot on that trail. Their goal is to develop a sunscreen based on a natural, ultraviolet-ray-blocking compound found in corals.

The use of highly toxic poisons to control predator raids on domestic livestock can have a devastating residual effect on the environment because of the indiscriminate toll on wildlife. Non-target species can suffer even greater mortality than the intended predators, whose viable numbers, by the way, must be maintained to ensure an ecosystem's balance. And there is always the danger of these lethal chemical compounds leaching into the soil and contaminating groundwater tables.

To avoid the slaughter of innocent wildlife and the eradication of an important predator population, scientists have experimented successfully with bait laced with lithium chloride, a chemical agent that causes temporary nausea and vomiting. The technique not only spares the animal but also, in the case of a predator, conditions it in Pavlovian fashion to give domestic prey a wide berth. Nature remains intact, as does our moral obligation to keep it that way.

Individual Heroics

Rarely does an individual have a positive environmental impact on an entire region, but Charlie Munn was creative and dynamic enough to accomplish that feat. A Princeton-educated biologist, he almost single-handedly succeeded in getting more than 15 million acres of tropical wildlife habitat set aside for preservation in Peru, Bolivia, and the Pantanal region of Brazil.

Dr. Munn first visited the area to conduct research on macaws and eventually became one of the world's foremost authorities on those tropical birds. From 1986 to 2000, he served as the senior conservation zoologist for the Wildlife Conservation Society (WCI) in the region. And in that capacity, he operated as a successful one-man lobby for preservation of South American wilderness. Munn's principle strategy for saving the region for posterity was to convince the national governments of the profitability of eco-tourism. This eventually led to his leaving WCI to form his own eco-tourism company serving the area. Munn put his money where his mouth was in a smooth transition that allowed him to retain conservation as his top priority, even as he became a businessman. An increasing number of "Dr. Munn types" are making their presence felt in modern-day society by melding business and conservation into sustainable ventures that are important building blocks for a prosperous future.

Biomimicry

Biomimicry is the paramount means of furthering environmentally sustainable economic progress. The term refers to the technique of duplicating the functions and balanced structure of nature as closely as possible in order to solve human problems. It evolved into an official field of study in 1997, with the publication of American biologist Janine Benyus's book, *Biomimicry: Innovation Inspired by Nature*.[3] Our purest forms can be found in recycling and reuse, the very tools nature employs to regenerate life without creating surplus waste. While Mount Trashmore, addressed a few pages earlier, stands as a monument to biomimicry, less dramatic examples of the practice abound. A case in point: the work of scientists who replicated materials manufactured by mollusks, which produce a clear, virtually indestructible coating. The scientists' synthetic version has been used to fortify windshields and airplane bodies.[4]

The Japanese have excelled in biomimicry. Among their most notable accomplishments: creation of tiny solar batteries patterned after the way leaves turn sunlight into energy; modeling self-cleaning tiles after snail shells; and improving their bullet train's velocity through aerodynamic applications derived from observation of kingfishers' beaks and owls in flight.

Many in industry increasingly seek to turn their manufacturing processes into exercises in biomimicry. Among the growing number of major companies that have successfully simulated natural systems in their operations are AT&T, 3M, DuPont, General Electric, and Royal Dutch Shell.[5] No doubt their degree of success in replicating nature will be instrumental in determining the future prosperity of their respective businesses.

A list of the hundred most successful biomimicry technologies was issued in October 2008 under the auspices of the United Nations Environmental Programme, the International Union for Conservation of Nature, and two private sector groups, the Zero Emissions Research and Initiatives Foundation and the Biomimicry Guild. Selected from a list of 2100 entries, the winners included: vaccines that borrow from Africa's 'Resurrection' plant; antibacterial substances derived from marine algae; and a water harvesting system patterned after the way the Namib Desert Beetle of Namibia extracts moisture from desert fog.[6]

CHAPTER TWENTY

—

THE BAD

Backfire

Y EARS AGO, a group of Stanford University engineering students produced a study indicating that eucalyptus tree plantations could solve our energy problems. The students noted that the trees grew rapidly, adapted to a wide range of climates and soils, and were exceptionally resistant to insect pests. Most importantly, the students said, eucalyptus wood was a renewable resource that could be burned to generate electricity at a cost slightly higher than coal but less than nuclear energy.

Human ingenuity appeared to be working in tandem with nature. But any such collaboration needed to be fully vetted to avoid unintended consequences. If the research had been more comprehensive, the students would have discovered that eucalyptus tree plantations were highly flammable and drained moisture from the soil to an inordinate degree. The trees (which were originally imported from Australia) displaced native plants and eliminated wildlife habitat for many species. Agricultural production would suffer from the profusion of plantations that would have to cover an extensive portion of our arable land to contribute significantly to national energy needs. An idea that had once seemed so promising shriveled on the vine.

The moral of the story is that new technologies can only be successful in the long haul if they fall within the parameters imposed by nature, and therefore must be thoroughly researched in that regard. It is important to remember that even with our extraordinary degree of ingenuity, we have little chance of restoring air, water, or land on a massive scale once they have been severely degraded.

This was graphically illustrated by a mid-1990s experiment with the closed environment facility known as Biosphere Two. Despite the hundreds of millions of dollars spent to build a sealed artificial environment, scientists were unable to create a miniature life-support system that could provide eight people with adequate food, sufficient potable water, and healthy air for a two-year period. Oxygen concentrations declined to levels ordinarily associated with elevations at 17,500 feet, barely enough to keep the occupants of the biosphere functioning. Carbon dioxide levels soared, causing vines within the facility to proliferate at such a rapid rate that they overwhelmed other plants within the capsule, including those on which the crew depended for food. Nitrogen dioxide concentrations in the airtight enclosure rose to levels high enough to damage the human brain.

The rate of extinction in the 3.15 acre Biosphere Two was alarming, with 19 out of 25 vertebrate species failing to survive the artificial environment. All pollinating insects also died out, thereby dooming the majority of edible plants. Doesn't sound like we were ready to set off on a journey to Mars, does it? Indeed, scientists monitoring the project concluded that "no one yet knows how to devise systems that provide humans with the life-supporting services that natural ecosystems furnish for free."

That venture imparted a profound message: we have a special moral obligation to make certain Earth's natural resources remain intact because chances are there are no immediate substitutes waiting in the wings ready to be unleashed by human genius.

The Derelict Government

In the winter of 1985, President Ronald Reagan was reading a Cold War novel about the defection of an officer from the Soviet Nuclear Submarine Corps. To the best of anyone's knowledge, neither Reagan nor anyone on his staff had even glanced at the cover of The State of the World, 1985, which was released during that same period by the widely respected, Washington-based Worldwatch Institute.

If Reagan and company had bothered to skim the pages of the WWI's well-documented work, they could not have remained oblivious to the deteriorating relationship between humanity and the natural systems that sustain life. They also would have been alerted to viable solutions that sadly continue to be frequently neglected to this day. But Reagan was not interested in what Worldwatch researchers and other environmental scientists had to say. Instead, in a myopic display of irresponsible sloth, the president missed out on the crucial connection between environmental degradation and our national security. No recognition was evidenced that deteriorating environmental conditions overseas generated social unrest and civil strife that eventually would produce a negative ripple effect upon our shores. Let's just say we would certainly be in a better place at the start of the 21st century if he hadn't been asleep at the switch.

It should be noted that the White House was not the only branch of government that failed the American people during the Reagan years. In 1986, a Senate hearing explored the adverse effects of human activity on accelerated temperature rise around the globe. The sparsely attended session earned scarcely a mention in the media compared with other Congressional hearings conducted that day. Sen. John Chafee (R-R.I.), chairman of the climate hearing, declared at the end of the session that enough evidence had been produced to identify an environmental problem which, if left unattended, could conceivably result in catastrophe.

"To take no action when options are available is to play planetary Russian roulette," Chafee warned. Inexcusably, his prophetic words of wisdom did not resonate with intellectually lazy—and cowardly—White House officials or fellow members of Congress. Although the calls for action to slow global warming have come more often and with greater intensity in recent years, all too many government officials have continued to respond in tepid fashion, even as time is running out.

Consistent with this apathy towards environmental conditions was the stance taken by George W. Bush's Secretary of State, Condoleezza Rice, on her first official visit to foreign capitals. She sought to firm up international support for the war on terror without making reference to the global threats posed by environmental degradation, especially in developing countries. Rice seemed unmindful of the roles that ecological deterioration played in fomenting the global tensions and strife that threatened the international political order, and by extension, our national security. Dwelling solely on military-oriented geopolitics, she set the tone for her boss's shortsighted limited focus throughout the span of his administration.

We shouldn't be surprised at her dutiful regurgitation of Bush's skewed vision. Rice displayed her own myopic outlook even before entering government. In an article in *Foreign Affairs Journal*,[1] Rice wrote that "National interest is too often replaced by humanitarian interest or the interests of the international community." Instead, she continued, the United States should promote its own interests—democracy and free trade, for example.

Talk about unilateralism! To view "humanitarian interests," either at home or abroad, as contrary to the national interest was seminal isolationism and made a prima facie case for disqualifying Dr. Rice for the post of Secretary of State (or any other federal office for that matter). It exposed a morally deficient posture and the ultimate expression of a dangerously narrow-minded, fortress mentality in an ever more interconnected modern world.

Rice's blinders vis-à-vis the causative factors of civil unrest were emblematic of the Bush administration's ideology and intellectual indolence. As the world's only superpower, we should have been leading the efforts to end the food shortages and reverse the environmental degradation that were contributing mightily to social instability in developing nations. Instead, Secretary Rice jetted around the world calling for more market-based economic growth, naively advancing that as the panacea for turmoil in and between poor countries. Lost on her was the fact that a combination of groundwater depletion, global warming, and rapid population growth was a significant source of international tension. She appeared to view national security solely through an economic and military prism.

Considering that the connection between environmental conditions and national security was no military secret, ideological correctness could not serve as a legitimate excuse for Rice's lapse in judgment. Hopefully, we shall have learned from this sorry chapter in our history and rely on diplomacy rather than partisan posturing.

CHAPTER TWENTY-ONE

—

THE UGLY

The Great Procrastinators

IN THE MID 20TH CENTURY, National Weather Service computer models predicted that if New Orleans were struck by a category five hurricane, most of the city—much of which lies below sea level—would be under water. Fast forward to August 2005, on the eve of massive Hurricane Katrina's direct hit on New Orleans. Woefully little had been done to enable the city and its inhabitants to withstand the destructive force of such a storm. Some work had been completed to fortify the protective levee system, but not nearly enough. Congress, the Louisiana state government, and New Orleans civic leaders had permitted the energy industry to dredge and fill wetlands that would mitigate a fierce storm surge, and little progress had been made in restoring the vanished marshes or expanding evacuation routes. The authorities responsible for addressing New Orleans' vulnerability to the elements had essentially treaded water for decades, and Katrina made the city pay dearly for the neglect.

Unwillingness to rile influential developers and energy industry executives played a role in federal, state, and local officials' feeble preparations for a worst-case scenario. It was a shoddy performance, compounded by the fact that authorities possessed the documentation that justified a highly aggressive strategy, and had at their disposal the means and resources to implement the plan. Specifically, we are talking about: prohibiting the oil industry's destruction of surrounding wetlands; curbing development and encouraging relocation away from especially vulnerable, low-lying urban flood zones in the city, instituting tough building codes; strengthening levees; creating space to store excess water, as the Dutch have done for centuries; and establishing additional evacuation routes. Instead, the officials chose to turn a blind eye to the inevitable, bolstered by the favorable odds that a catastrophic event would not occur on their watch. Out of expedience, tough choices were deliberately left for future generations.

When Hurricanes Katrina (2005) and Gustav (September 2008) battered New Orleans and nearby coastal areas, the chickens came home to roost. The interval between the two storms provided some time for heightened defensive preparation. But it was too little, too late. Three

City Under The Sea

years of intensive remedial activity could not offset the longstanding procrastination and gross neglect. Restoration of degraded wetlands that could serve as a buffer against a hurricane's storm surge had barely gotten underway. Moreover, too much development was allowed to return to flood-prone areas where permanent structures did not belong.

In the case of Gustav, officials knew they could not make up for lost time and ordered a mandatory evacuation of the city. Fortunately, Gustav did not match Katrina's intensity, and even more importantly, swerved west of New Orleans at the last moment, sparing the city the storm's most lethal effects.

How will the city fare when the next giant hurricane appears at its door? One can only hope that New Orleans will have better luck with its officials in the decades to come. For that to occur, those officials will have to heed a 2009 report by the National Academy of Engineering and the National Research Council. Its conclusion: there is no way to protect the most flood-prone areas of below-sea-level New Orleans from a direct hit by a catagory five hurricane. The scientists went on to recommend that any of those vulnerable sites free of permanent structures should be kept that way. Where development existed, either from having survived previous storms or through restoration, the difficult decision had to be made to relocate the buildings to higher ground, regardless of how well entrenched they had been in the neighborhood.

Whistling Past the Gasoline Pump
Throughout the last three decades of the 20th century, scientists produced a spate of studies documenting the need for the United States to reduce its dependency on imported oil, as well as outlining strategies for doing so. They recommended more stringent auto fuel-economy standards as a significant step toward loosening dependence on imported energy. The American automobile industry responded with disingenuous equivocation, and whether out of complicity or gullibility, our politicians went along with Detroit's marketing of shortsighted caveat emptor.

The American manufacturers only stirred when they belatedly recognized they were behind the curve compared to their Japanese competitors. By 2008, when they realized they needed to produce low-gas-mileage, low-emission, durable vehicles en masse to stay in business, the years of tunnel vision left their future very much up in the air, an enormous federal government bailout notwithstanding.

Foot Dragging on Renewables
Giving American automakers a free pass for decades was hardly our elected officials' sole energy-related offense. As was noted, the 1970s saw no shortage of well-documented yet officially ignored analyses of

environmentally friendly energy strategies necessary for our long-term well-being. Many of these strategies were brought before Congress by major environmental organizations, including the Natural Resources Defense Council, Environmental Defense Fund, Friends of the Earth, the Sierra Club, the now-defunct Environmental Policy Center, the National Wildlife Federation, the National Audubon Society, Defenders of Wildlife, the Wilderness Society, the World Wildlife Fund, the Worldwatch Institute, the World Resources Institute, and Greenpeace, to name but a few. Among the leading recommendations were far greater roles for energy conservation, recycling of nonrenewable resources, development and expanded utilization of "clean," renewable energy, and "clustered," high-density land use planning that would minimize disturbance to nature and maximize preservation of open space, especially wilderness and prime agricultural acreage.

According to public opinion polls, Americans reacted favorably to these suggested reforms. More than 90 percent of those queried in the 1980s were receptive to stricter fuel-economy standards for motor vehicles. In 1989, a national poll[1] found a majority of Americans willing, if necessary, to subordinate—at least temporarily—some economic growth to increased environmental protection. More recently, a public opinion survey disclosed that a majority favored development of clean, renewable energy over increased oil drilling—despite the fossil-fuel industry's self-serving warning that renewables were too exotic to be of widespread practical value.[2] Perhaps the majority was influenced by the official disclosure that in 2008, domestic production of renewable energy accounted for more than 10 percent of the total energy in the country, even with lackluster federal support. (By contrast, nuclear energy contributed only 11 percent.)[3] That was not the only favorable trend in 2008. In an examination of global energy markets, researchers found that for the first time, more renewable energy than conventional electric power capacity was added in both the United States and European Union.[4]

Why were our federal officials in absentia when the American people appeared primed to move in a new direction? Much of the answer lies in human nature. Bold vows to take actions that alter fixed habits often amount to little more than talk. Indeed, there are outspoken supporters of change among the general public who openly renege—and then rebel—if pressed too hard. Pragmatic politicians instinctively have recognized this and found the path of least resistance irresistible. Why rock the boat when the water is calm, even if deceptively so? It is a rationalization that heaps shame upon elected officials entrusted with the responsibility of safeguarding society's long as well as short-term interests.

Entering office in 2009, President Barack Obama gave every indication that he would end the inertia and greatly expand the nation's use of renewable energy. He certainly had plenty of potential to tap. Wind-energy resources in 12 Midwestern and Rocky Mountain states alone were estimated to equal approximately 2.5 times the entire electricity production in the nation. Some 45,000 square miles of barren desert in the American Southwest could conceivably accommodate solar panels without encroaching on environmentally sensitive or populated areas, and the structures could provide a third of the country's energy by 2050.[5]

SECTION NINE
—
ARE WE UP TO THE TASK?

CHAPTER TWENTY-TWO

—

FORMULA FOR SUCCESS

NEAR THE END of the first decade of the 21st century, a looming environmental crisis in the form of climate change jarred leaders of numerous countries out of their lethargy of convenience. Yet all too often, the leaders' responses were reactive rather than proactive, resulting in the loss of valuable time in dealing with unsettling changes in the biosphere. Early victims were residents of coastal Arctic Inuit villages that were sinking into melted permafrost and were threatened by rising sea levels. The Alaskan Inuits had no choice but to pull up stakes and relocate inland in response to the warming-induced thaw.

Even if governments had taken the initiative, they were simply not capable of engineering an abrupt halt to the retreat of glaciers as well as a record-breaking temperature rise. Nonetheless, "better late than never" justified beginning the process of stabilizing, if not reversing, the warming trend. Whether the catalyst for reduction of greenhouse gas emissions turned out to be panic or conscience seemed unimportant at the time, considering the consequences of inaction.

Apart from a decrease in industrial pollutants to slow global warming, the most formidable environmental challenge confronting mankind is to engage in the sustainable use of the Earth's finite natural resources. Without these resources, life as we know it ultimately cannot exist. A materialistic American public has to be persuaded that the more-the-merrier mentality must no longer personify the national character. Given our track record, you have to wonder how long it will take before such an appeal resonates when applied to family size or personal consumption habits.

Although many Americans have said in polls and private conversations that they subscribed to such a value shift, the level of their conviction has remained unclear. Talk can easily serve as a cover for deferring reductions in material consumption in a nation notorious for worshipping excess. The sad fact is that many people are more responsive to matters of money than conscience. That is why government regulators will almost certainly be needed to provide some powerful incentives—fiscal and otherwise—that steer us towards modification of freewheeling lifestyles. Any concerns that officials might have about public rejection should be tempered by the thought that though the country's commitment to change may sometimes be wobbly, chances are that the reality of needing to abandon the frequently profligate status quo will eventually set in. The question is whether it will be in time.

Saving the Farm

It should be our collective commitment to prevent the nation's remaining prime agricultural lands from being swallowed by development so that future generations will have the capacity to feed themselves. While some admirable efforts have been made to keep working farms in operation, we have still been losing more than half–a million acres of our most fertile cropland each year.[1] Because developers rarely feel any obligation to preserve the nation's most productive agricultural land, it is imperative that the government keep them at bay.

In some jurisdictions, tax breaks have been offered to farmers as inducements to continue tilling their acreage instead of selling it to a developer. Other locales have used zoning laws to preserve agricultural land, but these ordinances often have loopholes. It's time for new laws that assure the preservation of our national bread basket in perpetuity, with the government assigning and subsidizing management of cropland that an owner is no longer willing to farm. Some might consider such an arrangement an abridgement of private property rights. But when collective survival clashes with individual freedom of choice, the former must take precedence.

Environmental Price Tags

Free enterprise cannot be allowed to run roughshod over the crucial benefits that nature bestows. The only solution is regulation to protect natural resources—and not just fertile farmland—from being diminished by entrepreneurial excesses. An effective strategy for making such restraints politically palatable in a democratic capitalistic system is to demonstrate that their financial benefits surpass any short-term dividends from a *laissez-faire* approach.

As was previously mentioned, the late Eugene Odum, director of the University of Georgia's Institute of Ecology, pioneered the methodology to justify environmental preservation in monetary terms. In the 1970s, he devised a formula for attaching dollars-and-cents values to various natural resources threatened by human activity. His work earned him recognition as the father of "environmental accounting." Others followed, making a powerful case for conservation through a hard-cash vernacular that resonated with a materialistic society. These sorts of calculations strengthened the hand of national environmental organizations in the pioneering 1970s. Armed with extensive documentation, they were able to successfully lobby Congress to pass stringent, landmark antipollution laws and win widespread public support that persists to this day.

Odum calculated an acre of productive marshland to be worth $50,000 a year (in 1978 dollars) by virtue of fishery production, flood protection, and the purification of air, water, and raw sewage. Some 50 countries now use environmental accounting methodology in varying degrees to arrive at the true extent of their national wealth.

In 1997, University of Vermont ecological economics professor Robert Costanza, in a study published in the journal Nature, estimated the Earth's ecosystems to be worth $33 trillion—virtually double the world's gross national product at the time! Costanza's computations served as a basis from which many economists sought in ensuing years to further arrive at the value of wetlands, coral reefs, forests, and other natural resources.[2]

In May 2007, for example, economists commissioned by the New Jersey Department of Environmental Protection assessed the value of the sand dunes on the popular recreational Jersey Shore beaches at $42,000 an acre, based on projected storm protection and coastal stabilization benefits. Eighteen months later, the World Resources Institute released a study appraising the value of coral reefs and mangroves along the coast of Belize at $395 million and $559 million a year, respectively, because of their storm protection, lure as a tourist attraction, and fish-spawning productivity.[3]

Attaching a dollar value to natural resources that provide valuable benefits to society can thwart the incursions of developers, and we should be grateful for such interventions. But environmental accounting is superfluous in locations where the natural resources are so unique, so irreplaceable, that they are priceless, and by extension, untouchable. Unfortunately, the incalculable worth of such hallowed ground has not deterred greedy entrepreneurs from constantly seeking to encroach on the sites. Government vigilance and public condemnation have so far blocked most attempts, some of which have been mounted even in such sacrosanct ecological wonders as the Grand Canyon, the Arctic National Wildlife Refuge, and the Everglades National Park. The last named is the core of the only large, semi-tropical wilderness in the continental United States and a major source of hydration for the southern half of Florida.

Back to the Future

We still have a way to go in establishing a formal government entity that systematically incorporates future environmental risk into the formulation of new legislation. When Al Gore was a young member of Congress, he broached the idea of creating a department for future planning. Not surprisingly, it was greeted with as much enthusiasm as a rogue environmental group received for suggesting that America's Great

Plains be returned to their original wilderness state.

More recently, the official designation of a legal governmental guardian for future generations was proposed by Carolyn Raffensperger, executive director of the Science and Environmental Health Network. She urged that the president appoint an individual to review all regulations for their long-term risks, so as to assure preservation of our common natural heritage. In effect, that proposal would formally integrate the precautionary principle (colloquially termed "better safe than sorry") into governmental decision making, and to that end, Raffensperger suggested that a constitutional amendment might be in order.[4] Considering the magnitude of the challenge ahead, it would come as no great shock if an Office of Long Term Planning became a permanent fixture in the administrations of the post-Bush era. Conservative Republicans, who normally oppose any expansion of the federal bureaucracy, might even recant, swayed by the rationale that "an ounce of prevention is worth a pound of cure."

The New Economy

In an ecologically stressed world, we cannot entrust our future to an economy based primarily on people buying a lot of resource-intensive goods that they really don't need, often can't afford, and—if they reflected at any length—actually don't want. Our country must change the face of commerce by shifting away from reliance on the sale of consumer items built for abbreviated durability and one-time disposal. The U.S. economy must depend more heavily on the marketing of technological innovation. Expansion and maintenance of municipal and transportation infrastructures and alternative energy systems should be major new sources of jobs. Other avenues of employment that should assume a larger role are the agricultural sector and labor-intensive service/entertainment industries, ranging from education and health to arts and recreational pursuits. Our factories should concentrate more on the manufacture, repair, recycling, and reuse of essential products, especially big-ticket items.

As much as possible, all goods should be produced with recycled materials that when exhausted or outmoded could be recycled once again, perhaps for some lesser use. Raw materials utilized in manufacturing should, when feasible, be of the renewable kind, and extracted at a rate that allows adequate time for regeneration.

One way to expedite the transition to sustainability would be to integrate the environmental costs of production (i.e. energy use, pollution impacts, etc.) into the final price of merchandise. The higher price would dampen—perhaps greatly—the impetus for instant gratification and conspicuous consumption.

While monetary disincentives are likely to lead to a decrease in compulsive shopping that squanders resources, such deterrents alone cannot rid our society of its well-entrenched, profligate addiction to materialism. These cash disincentives can lose their clout, at least temporarily, because of a currency devaluation, an artificial supply glut, or some other form of price manipulation. Even more to the point, the acquisitive side of human nature is a product of our innate competitiveness, honed by the driving force for survival that is the essence of evolutionary natural selection and behind virtually all that we do. What's therefore needed is a cultural shift in which achievement is determined more on the basis of personal inner development and intellectual accomplishment than the size of a bank account. Greater value must be attached to the acquisition of knowledge and cultivation of high-quality individual relationships than to ownership of a closet full of designer clothes. The rapid integration of the Internet into virtually every facet of daily life is an ideal catalyst for facilitating this cultural transition. Pervasive computer use invariably has elevated the societal importance of information gathering and retention, with no end in sight.

For an environmentally sustainable value system to gain ascendancy, the notion must be dispelled that moderation is tantamount to penury. Conservation must not be viewed as a dressed-up version of deprivation. Instead, it should be regarded as an affirmation of the truism that less can be more, and recognized as a national status symbol. If you visualize conservation in those terms, what could instill a greater sense of achievement than to obtain more with less?

To reiterate, material acquisition should be de-emphasized by stressing quality over quantity of goods that are purchased. Planned obsolescence should be rendered obsolete. Recycling and reuse should become a way of life rather than a passing fad.

Some exponents have labeled this salutary lifestyle "voluntary simplicity" and have waxed lyrical about its relatively benign impact on the Earth's biosphere. Their words deserve our undivided attention and subsequent activist response, for if some variant of this lifestyle doesn't gather momentum in the first few decades of the 21st century, the future will be bleak.

Urban Morality

Urbanization has the potential to create a more egalitarian, prosperous society. But it also can lead to a more fractious, inequitable one in which wealthy citizens live in tiny, opulent enclaves surrounded by a vast swath of destitute shanty towns. That paradigm is hardly a prescription for long-term political stability. Yet it fits the description of many existing metropolises, especially in the developing world where approximately one billion of the planet's poorest people reside, and where the majority of the human race will live by the end of the century.

Furthermore, cities with dense concentrations of humanity

and enormous demands on natural resources can have a disastrous environmental impact. The extent of the threat becomes clear when one realizes that the 50 percent of mankind currently living in cities produces 80 percent of the greenhouse gases associated with global warming and consumes 75 percent of civilization's available energy supplies.

Whether urbanization ultimately turns out to be a blessing or a curse depends a great deal on how the city of the future evolves. Urbanization generates opportunities for an enhanced quality of life. Bringing people together in close quarters can spur creativity, healthy competition, industriousness, and a communal sense of unity. Social services difficult to deliver in scattered rural areas are usually easier to administer in concentrated population centers. In addition, increased job opportunities and the higher cost of living that are often a product of urban density are conducive to lower birth rates; and these smaller families are an essential demographic first step toward the population stabilization required in a steady-state economy that supports an environmentally sustainable society.

The ideal city of the future will preserve a significant amount of parkland within its borders and be surrounded by ample protected open space in the form of farms and natural forested landscapes. Development will be clustered in a manner that minimizes sprawl and automobile use. An efficient public transit system will serve the community, and there should be a diverse housing mix to accommodate residents of all economic strata. Reliable educational and medical institutions need to be readily accessible to the general population. There must be a decent sewage system and effective recycling of water for drinking and sanitation purposes. Renewable energy will be an important source of electric power.

Early in the 21st century, few cities could boast of even several of these attributes, much less all of them. But if urban centers can manage to implement this full array of amenities, adverse environmental impacts will at worst be negligible.

Some planners envision an additional environmental insurance policy in the form of urban farming. City dwellers would produce a substantial amount of their own food by growing fruits and vegetables on rooftops as well as in greenhouses constructed between translucent glass panes of skyscrapers. Along those lines, Professor Dickson Despommier, a parasitologist at Columbia University, headed a study in which researchers calculated that a 30-story building operated at least partially as a farm could conceivably feed up to 50,000 people through the utilization of hydroponics and aeroponics gardening techniques and renewable energy resources.[5] Cities would be benefiting from year-round, fuel-efficient local agriculture in its most modern utopian manifestation. All that is required is a little imagination and a lot of capital.

Urban farming has already taken root in embryonic form on

rooftops in a number of cities around the world, and the crops have not been limited to fruits and vegetables. Beekeepers have established hives and are producing honey on many of the plant-covered roofs of Paris. Since the sites tend to be pesticide-free, the bee mortality rate has been less than in the countryside, air pollution from heavily congested Parisian vehicular traffic notwithstanding.[6]

A concept labeled "New Urbanism" is fast becoming the ideal matrix for many city planners. It is best described as clusters of relatively high-density development interspersed amid extensive open space and with provision made for preservation of any nearby prime farmland.

New Urbanism certainly has the potential to transform the environmentally unsustainable, car-dependent, sprawling American suburbia of large, detached single-family homes into an anachronism. Indeed, a variation of this transition has already begun in the form of a reverse flight from the outer suburbs to the city center by commuter-weary Americans.[7] During the first decade of the 21st century, downtown residential districts in such major cities as Washington, Chicago, Los Angeles, Atlanta, Philadelphia, Baltimore, Providence, San Francisco, Minneapolis, and Tampa experienced varying degrees of revival, and their property values held up far better than those in outlying areas.

In a 21st century in which energy conservation will be vital to society's ultimate salvation, it makes no sense to have communities without sidewalks and neighborhood commercial centers. Suburbanites need to have their communities reconfigured into self-contained entities to ensure a healthy physical environment and viable economic arrangement for future generations. Aided and abetted by zoning law changes, authorities will have to fill in residential sprawl with stores, schools, medical facilities, modest-sized office buildings, and parks. All facilities will ideally be within walking, biking, or public-transport range of everyone in the community. Automobile use will dramatically lessen, along with accompanying reductions in energy consumption and air pollution. According to estimates by Steve Winkelman, a transportation analyst with the Center for Clean Air Policy, a 60 percent shift of new growth into compact development between 2008 and 2030 would reduce automobile use from 20 to 40 percent. That would remove approximately 85 million metric tons of greenhouse gases from the atmosphere, and drivers would save some $260 billion in fuel costs by the year 2030. (The numbers would be even more dramatic if fossil-fuel-driven vehicles were replaced by electric cars.)

While the concept of clustered development is gathering steam, many interim steps could be taken to enhance life and the quest for sustainability in modern metropolitan areas, especially in industrial nations with the resources to institute those changes. Using the Internet to telecommute eliminates time-wasting, energy-consuming vehicular

travel to work for those still stuck in the distant suburbs and waiting
for fill-in development. It also relieves traffic congestion. Generous tax
breaks could be awarded for installing solar panels, and that initiative has
already been set in motion in many countries, including our own. (At the
time of this writing, our nation's first solar-powered community is on the
drawing board of a Florida developer. A harbinger of things to come?)[8]
Homeowners with large backyards could cultivate crops as at least a partial
alternative to energy inefficient importation of food from distant locations
at home and abroad. Hanging laundry from clotheslines in order to save
energy is making a comeback, with some states already having enacted laws
to block any aesthetic objections to the revival of the practice.[9]

How to further expedite movement in the direction of
sustainability? For one thing, by imposing some version of a graduated tax
on carbon emissions and fossil-fuel use. For another, by granting tax breaks
for recycling, reuse, and, where possible, the promotion of qualitative
values over quantitative ones. In addition, new technologies employing
"clean," labor-intensive renewable energy sources should be integrated
into the operation of electric utilities and transportation, with the goal of
eventually replacing finite, polluting fossil fuels altogether.

While many of these reforms will occur in varying degrees within
the United States in the decades ahead, the same cannot be said with
confidence as far as developing nations are concerned. The best hope for
their metropolitan areas lies in the affluent industrial nations providing
substantial increases in financial and technological assistance. The
immediate objective would be to produce cheap, non-polluting energy,
modernize infrastructure, and create new employment opportunities in the
world's teeming urban slums. This in turn would lead to the major long-
term goal of instilling stability, which as an added bonus would shore up
security for the international community.

Beyond Money

As noted earlier in the book, while monetary disincentives are
crucial, they cannot single-handedly alter a culture wedded to materialistic
indulgence. No matter how things shake out, it is going to be difficult for
policymakers and the general public to abandon the only value system they
have ever really known and substitute one far less self-indulgent.[10]

Conditions have been not been made easier by the presence of a
largely passive mass media. These corporate entities derive their economic
sustenance from revenues generated by advertising that promotes
conspicuous consumption; so an environmentally sustainable lifestyle
works against their financial interest. Nevertheless, at some point, the
American media's full participation will be needed if enduring behavioral
modification and requisite institutional changes are to occur.

Prescription for Morality

The winning formula for morally responsible interaction with the biosphere entails setting priorities that minimize our negative impacts on the environment and, when possible, actually improve the planet's condition. Technologies must be perfected that enable human beings to limit the build-up of greenhouse gases in the atmosphere.

If the protection of public health and the realization of profits come into conflict, the former must take precedence—and remain the top priority. Humanity must adapt to nature. Attempts to interact with the natural world in defiance of its normal flow virtually guarantee disruption and ultimate failure in the form of nasty unintended consequences. Nature's exquisite balance—so integral to the perpetuation of life—is simply too complex for human beings to effectively replicate from scratch except in a rare stroke of dumb luck.

When we place the burden of proof on potential victims to show that a product is hazardous rather than on the potential polluter to demonstrate that it is reasonably safe, the former ends up incurring the greatest risk. They have to be stricken before any form of protection kicks in, and by that time, it may be too late. Since a chemical substance hazardous to human health might be difficult to purge if it is released into the environment, prevention is the superior—and more ethical—course of action. From a pragmatic standpoint, people throughout the ages have acknowledged the superiority of preventive rather than reactive responses to danger, even if they have not always engaged in the former.

Who then adheres to the moral imperative that a chemical be demonstrated to be reasonably safe before being made available to the public? The European Union has done so across the board, regardless of the economic consequences, while we, in deference to the industry's bottom line, have yet to follow suit.[11] Happily, there have been enough rumblings in government to indicate it is only a matter of time before Congress and our federal regulators—despite corporate lobbyists' clout—correct the imbalance that denies adequate protection to American consumers. Health can be protected without stifling entrepreneurial initiative.

Other Components

A responsible political leader should have no qualms about initiating short-term sacrifices that result in substantial long-term benefits for society. All bets are off, of course, if the reward down the road is dwarfed by the immediate hardship. Conversely, short-term benefits that require long-term sacrifice should be opposed unless the former substantially outweigh the latter. Unfortunately, immediate gratification, regardless of the consequences, is a powerful force that politicians find difficult to resist. It thus takes a bold, charismatic leader with extraordinary powers of persuasion to sway the public to voluntarily accept unpopular lifestyle modifications for a distant beneficial payoff.

If we want to be more protective of the planet's biosphere, we should measure a product's worth by the amount of energy used to create it rather than by a price set arbitrarily in dollars and cents. This "new" currency, calibrated in energy units, would internalize the environmental costs of production, better gauge our impact on the Earth, and encourage the transition to a more sustainable pattern of consumption.

When environmental problems transcend sovereign boundaries, they must be addressed by a coordinated international approach rather than in fragmented, unilateral fashion. Otherwise, remedies can easily end up working at cross purposes, with self-interest undermining the common interest.

Because life is complex, it resists cut-and-dried answers. But when every option has been exhausted in a controversy, there is no room for the act of compromise which ordinarily serves as the culmination of our democracy's regular give-and-take. With that in mind, could global warming be fast approaching the point where humanity either assigns emission reduction the highest priority or succumbs to an overheated world? The world's nations first began to seriously wrestle with (if not resolve) this dilemma in a concerted way at the December 2009 Global Warming Summit in Copenhagen, Denmark.

Obvious circumstances exist in which compromise is out of the question from the get-go. Already mentioned is the fate of places like the Grand Canyon. Much of this natural wonder's value stems from its pristine intactness, which makes anything short of total preservation from the start an unpardonable act of desecration.

Any scientific analysis worth its salt tells us that in the long run, sustainable well-being can only be realized when a truly symbiotic relationship exists between the economy and the environment. Corporate polluters who maintain (for their short-term benefit) that environmental degradation is the inevitable price of prosperity are a menace if we take their specious propaganda seriously.

To repeat, responsible management of the environment is grounded in fidelity to the precautionary principle. When threats of serious and irrevocable environmental harm arise, those in charge cannot in good conscience let the absence of conclusive proof delay implementation of preventive cost-effective measures. Should the weight of evidence indicate that a credible threat of severe magnitude is imminent, the best-known defensive steps should be promptly taken, even if their effectiveness—cost or otherwise—has not been incontrovertibly demonstrated. Given the risks, the odds favor a gamble.

A nation that put a man on the moon can surely muster the means and willpower to avoid ecocide. But space travel has so far not intruded on the general public's daily routine and, even more traumatically, on its value system. By contrast, salvaging our planet from terminal environmental degradation will demand a degree of foresight and public discipline that has rarely been evident in the past. It will also require a combination of bold political leadership, aggressive regulation, voluntary population stabilization, grassroots receptivity to change, strong support from the mass media, and groundbreaking technological advances that are labor intensive. (The unemployed are often more inclined to plunder than preserve.)

The role of the mass media is crucial. A recent survey showed that the way in which news organizations present a story has a dramatic influence on public perception. When as often has been the case, news accounts of global warming controversies have placed the tiny group of skeptics on a par with the scientific consensus recognizing the climate threat as real and primarily human-induced, researchers have found the following: faced with an apparent stalemate between conflicting points of view, many in the public chose the path of least resistance—denial. They used the ambiguity to downplay the prospect of any immediate threat—and the need to alter their routine.[12] Providing a balanced news report means conveying both sides of a controversy, not bestowing parity where none exists!

Over the long run, our educational institutions will also have to play a key role in steering our lifestyle in an environmentally sustainable direction. Other than parents, no facet of society has greater access to malleable young minds. Both middle schools and high schools should provide compulsory courses that delineate how a hyper-materialistic lifestyle is a resource-draining anachronism that should be replaced by a culture in which character and intellectual achievement take precedence. Although the integration of environmental studies into the high school and college curriculums is currently voluntary, inclusion has been spreading rapidly throughout much of the nation. Inter-disciplinary academic programs in environmental sustainability are becoming more commonplace in institutions of higher learning. Arizona State University has even established a separate School of Sustainability, featuring a curriculum blending biology and economics.[13]

Arguably the most effective, easily administered mechanism to curb global warming is an outright tax on carbon emissions. Like it or not, a consumer society cannot set the needed behavioral modifications in motion without this disincentive. National leaders can make the levy politically palatable by having its proceeds returned to the public via payroll-tax reductions or an actual rebate. That would mitigate the increased cost the emissions tax would impose on energy use. Indeed, even conservative Republicans, who normally recoil at any mention of a tax increase, have been intrigued by a levy that could accomplish emission reductions without raising the overall tax burden.[14] Moreover, supporters of the proposal talk of attracting further public support by using the much less provocative-sounding term "pollution fee."

The higher cost resulting from a global tax on carbon-based energy would accelerate the nation's and international community's move toward clean, renewable sources such as wind, solar, and biofuels. Progress in stabilization of global warming and enhancement of environmental quality would be realized through a single fiscal maneuver.

Will all of this happen in time? Those in authority must be proactive in anticipation rather than reactive in panic, or there is a risk that the biosphere will deteriorate beyond a point of no return.

CHAPTER TWENTY-THREE

—

FIGHTING THE DOUBTS

Lessons Learned?

IN 2007, CONGRESS HELD DOZENS of hearings on the global warming threat and the viable remedies at our disposal. Turn the clock back to early June 1986, and you would have heard the same testimony delivered to members of Congress at a sparsely attended open hearing. And that 1986 public airing was by no means the first of its kind.

Does our lack of progress over the years mean that we have a tin ear and are congenitally incapable of meeting the all-encompassing challenge of climate change? Are we doomed to falter in establishing a sustainable relationship with planet Earth, even as time is running out on our chances for doing so? Can a materialistic-oriented American society really be persuaded that conservation and non-material gratification—not the more-the-merrier mindset—should form the foundation of its culture?

Throughout history, some pockets of humanity managed to maintain a harmonious relationship with their surrounding environment for a significant period of time. As their populations grew, however, a balance with nature became more elusive. A significant adjustment was required, always a difficult proposition for people acclimated to a familiar daily routine and instinctively resistant to change. Today, there is no unqualified example of a modern society co-existing seamlessly with nature.

The Pressures Mount

A national poll in September 2007 found 84 percent of respondents expressing the belief that the planet was warming, and seven out of ten wanting Washington to assume a larger role in combating that threat. Most of those polled also said they would be willing in principle to alter their lifestyle to reduce carbon emissions and slow the pace of global warming, even if it meant some personal sacrifice.

All well and good, but when faced with the distinct possibility of actually having to carry out their expressed intentions, the respondents displayed a crack in their resolve. Only one American in five supported new taxes on carbon use and one in three an increased levy on gasoline. Again, the results were typical of such polls. When "true believers" were confronted with the actual need to make some specific behavioral modifications for the good of the planet, many tended to backtrack.

Near the end of the 21st century's first decade, 70 percent of the American economy depended on the public's massive consumption of material goods (often on credit), the bulk of which were not recycled or reused. Instead, most of these mountains of "stuff" usually ended up in landfills because of planned obsolescence or consumers' short attention spans.

Unless we change course, this unsustainable drain on our natural resources will narrow our future options to a perilous degree. It has already propelled us towards a fiscal freefall and ecological bankruptcy. That's not all. Our consumptive habits have been driving us into moral bankruptcy as the acquisition of "things" has increasingly overshadowed concern for our fellow human beings, and over the long term, even our own lives.

A 2008 incident that received widespread national publicity vividly exemplified this ethical disintegration. On the hectic post-Thanksgiving shopping day that launched the Christmas season's typical frenzied commercialization, a single-minded mob—in its zeal to snap up early holiday discounts—trampled to death an employee at a Long Island Wal-Mart store, and in the heat of the moment, never looked back.

President Bush's instinctive reaction to the historic 9-11 terrorist attack on the nation was in keeping with this obsessive materialistic bent. He urged Americans to express their defiance by engaging in a massive shopping spree. What did it say about the moral backbone of our society if our principal reply to a catastrophic terrorist strike was to go bargain hunting at the local department store? Whatever happened to closing ranks through material self-sacrifice that would strengthen our military security and diplomatic posture as well as our environmental health?

Despite the actions of countless good Samaritans, environmentally pernicious human behavior persists. Civilization's destruction of natural habitat has continued unabated and doomed some of the most ambitious attempts at resource conservation. Scientists have estimated that a distinct species of plant or animal (primarily insects) is vanishing every 20 minutes, again largely due to habitat loss from encroaching human development.[1] Other than greed and ignorance, a principle factor behind this trend is grinding poverty, which can trigger a desperation that overrides human beings' noblest preservationist instincts. Those unable to achieve a minimal acceptable standard of living have had great difficulty maintaining a sustainable relationship with the surrounding natural environment.

If the basic needs of impoverished people are met, however, they tend to see conservation of natural resources in a much different light. Preservation of resources that provide elemental comforts becomes crucial for them, given their narrow margin of error. Hence, much of the solution lies in eradicating global poverty to the maximum degree possible.

If that challenge cannot be met, the future is grim. For a compelling illustration of what lies ahead if humanity doesn't turn things around, consider the experience of a Harvard researcher in Borneo. In 1997, he was assigned to study the flora and fauna of an ancient swamp in that economically stressed country. The researcher stumbled across an unknown species of tree and took home a branch. When tested by the National Cancer Institute, the tree's sap showed potential for the treatment of AIDS. When he returned to the site a year later, however, all that remained was a stump. In the interim, the area had been stripped clean as a result of avarice-driven indiscriminate logging, and no further specimens of the tree were to be found.[2] Chances for a medical breakthrough had vanished, and who knows how many times this missed opportunity has occurred in the past?

One would like to think we have the moral fiber and foresight to avert ecological calamity. But there is an especially nagging concern about the oft-incremental pace of environmental degradation. Changes can be so subtle that evidence of deterioration may not become obvious until the damage is irrevocable.

That has been a major obstacle for the likes of Al Gore, whose pleas for universal energy conservation and development of alternatives to polluting fossil fuels initially did little to trigger more than a modest response. In reaction to the exhortations of Gore and others, many Americans briefly put on the brakes and experienced that sanctimonious "feel-good" sensation before returning to their old high-volume carbon consumptive ways.

Unfortunately, procrastination is an integral part of human nature. In addition, this trait becomes even more pronounced when individuals are faced with the need to take action outside of their comfort zone. Without prodding (e.g. regulatory mandates) in such cases, most people will invariably put off for today what they can do for tomorrow, oblivious to the reality of time constraints and the possibility that there might be no tomorrow. Global warming often falls squarely into this category. Many Americans take sanctuary in denial because they lack the energy and willpower to confront a cosmic global problem's potential long-range impact while grappling with the immediacy of economic survival. The prospect of having to alter their lifestyle may be daunting. Indeed, they may be too overwhelmed by the enormity of the climate change threat to admit to its existence.

One way to combat this head-in-the-sand mentality is to forego repeated delivery of ominous ecological forecasts that can be rationalized away as too speculative. Instead, communicate with these people in a fiscal language to which they can more easily relate. Make a convincing case that they will experience far more economic hardship if they fail to make short-term sacrifices for long-term gain.

Still, when all is said and done, major environmental disturbances have tended to be far more effective than verbal appeals in influencing human behavior. Among such wakeup calls have been record-breaking droughts and melting glaciers. The collapse of coastal permafrost forced Alaskan villagers to relocate inland in psychologically and financially wrenching moves. Hurricane Katrina was also a marquee occurrence. Even though no one could say for certain that Katrina was attributable to accelerated global temperature rise, many scientists considered the storm's intensity a harbinger of things to come—and that viewpoint produced a lot of lasting impressions among laymen.

Carbon Copies

By requiring a monetary "environmental" investment (such as footing the bill for tree planting) to compensate for pollutants emitted, "carbon offsets" are supposed to lighten our ecological impact on the planet and slow the pace of global warming. Even the United Nations has gotten into the act, however symbolically. In 2007, it used offsets in holding a "carbon neutral" General Assembly debate on global change. The emissions stemming from the debate participants' air travel to the conclave in New York City, as well as from the operations of the UN headquarters itself, were counterbalanced by the international body's investment in a biomass project in Kenya.

Yet reservations persist regarding this ostensibly cost-effective tool to combat global warming. Are the offsets merely a fleeting balm for a guilty conscience or are they a meaningful tradeoff? The money that finances the offsets is supposed to be used to subsidize activities, like reforestation and the production of renewable energy, that slow down atmospheric carbon dioxide buildup. But critics question just how much of the compensation ends up being spent as intended, considering that the companies and organizations selling the offsets are rarely monitored. Moreover, some doubts have been raised about the offsets' effectiveness, even if they are legitimately administered. Part of the problem is that their individual impacts are difficult to quantify. Could offsets actually encourage more environmentally destructive behavior than they supposedly counterbalance? Again, are they effective tools for mitigating global warming or token maneuvers to mask overindulgence? Only time—and better analysis—will tell.

The cap and trade of carbon emissions is an offset-type mechanism that has gained favor in the campaign to combat global warming. Devised with corporations in mind, the procedure entails putting a cap on greenhouse gas discharges. Within that framework, the federal government would auction off permits to companies, allowing them a certain amount of carbon dioxide emissions. Those businesses that exceeded their allowance would have to purchase extra credits from "cleaner" companies who had a surplus. Could the same approach be applied to individuals? Some British scientists think so. They envision an arrangement in which everyone would receive an allowance of CO2 emitted from their household appliances and vehicles. Those who went beyond their allowance would have to buy extra shares from those who had effectively conserved. Is such a system practical? Would its fiscal restraints on energy usage be universally accepted in the United States? Skeptics abound.

Questions also persist about the efficacy of industry utilizing cap and trade. As a major tool in addressing climate change, it has the potential to end up as a glorified shell game in which "pollution hot spots" are permitted to persist. Any system that allows some companies to continue to pollute whole hog could be susceptible to exploitation if not scrupulously monitored.

Regardless of cap and trade's fate, the growing impact of accelerated climate change makes the enactment of some version of a carbon tax both necessary and inevitable in our country. Just how imminent depends on our political leaders' degree of determination to implement the levy, as well as their skill in selling the idea to the American people. Again, the unanswered question is whether the tax will be instituted before carbon emissions proliferate to levels that signal irreversible climate decline.

CHAPTER TWENTY-FOUR

—

THE UPSIDE

A ND NOW FOR THE POSITIVE SIDE of the ledger. There are signs that at least some Americans are becoming more disposed to scaling back their conspicuous consumption-oriented lifestyle. Many opinion polls have found that if given a choice, a majority of us would prefer more time off with our families than a pay hike on the job. Other surveys suggest that may of us are disillusioned with the frenzied materialism of the Christmas holidays and yearn for a more spiritually oriented celebration.[1]

Then there is that recent poll by University of Cambridge researchers. To repeat, it found Danes to be the happiest people in Europe. Why? The Danes had the most close-knit and widest networks of family, friends, and acquaintances of any European nationality. Danes also reported the greatest trust in their public officials as well as a strong sense of self-fulfillment in their jobs. Monetary wealth and material consumption were not identified as major determinants of contentment.[2] Over time, other nationalities can't help but notice.

In a 2007 Zogby poll commissioned by the U.S. Conference of Mayors, a majority of Americans said their communities should make environmentally friendly and energy-efficient changes, regardless of whether that meant significantly altering their lifestyles.[3] The poll suggested that an important opportunity existed for the mayors (and higher officials), if they were bold enough to seize it. Respondents seemed convinced that "going green" would enrich the local economy and create numerous jobs, even where fiscal stagnation had been endemic. Furthermore, nearly half of those polled said they would be amenable to paying higher taxes provided the proceeds were used to finance environmentally friendly improvements in their respective communities. Maybe they meant it, maybe not. But if that predisposition doesn't present an opening for an outspoken progressive political leader to exploit with seemingly minimal career risk, I don't know what does.

Ample evidence of the positive impact of monetary disincentives surfaced when gasoline temporarily surged above $4 a gallon in the United States late in 2008. Virtually overnight, many Americans modified their driving habits by reducing vehicular travel, opting for public transit, bicycles, walking, or shifting to more fuel-efficient cars, all environmentally beneficial changes. What could be a more convincing demonstration that fiscal pressure is the language the free enterprise system understands best?

A bright note overseas is the successful installation of solar-energy-generating units in scattered rural hamlets throughout India and other developing nations. The addition has revolutionized lives by providing daily access to electricity for the first time, and it offers a preview of the environmentally benign progress that would occur if this "clean" technology could make further inroads.

In the concerted effort to address climate change and poverty, the transfer of technology to the less fortunate is essential. Yet some major companies in the industrialized nations have complained that making such transfers would mean the loss of proprietary rights. The companies need to put things in perspective. Humanitarian concerns must ultimately trump monopolistic exploitation of trade secrets in an ever more interconnected international community. Otherwise, instability will spread inexorably across the planet.

Humanity's inherent imperfection sometimes seems an insurmountable impediment to sharing technology, adopting a conservation ethic, and experiencing sustainable prosperity. But let us not write off the human race just because progress has been painfully slow. Human beings are a resilient lot, especially when their backs are up against the proverbial ecological wall. Moreover, it does seem that in numerous instances, they are finally getting better at learning from their mistakes.

We undoubtedly have the cognitive capacity to adopt the necessary environmental reforms, but do we have the temperament to do so on a consistent basis? There are indications that we do, provided we are fully informed. During George W. Bush's tenure, governors of more than half of our states and mayors of 142 cities, distressed at the growing body of incriminating circumstantial evidence and federal vacillation, began instituting mandatory measures to cut back on polluting greenhouse gases.

A number of coastal states—including Alaska, California, Oregon, Washington, and Maryland—sought to adapt to climate change with housing setbacks, landfills, zoning relocation, and the strengthening of seawalls.[4] Incentives were also introduced at the state and local level in the form of free parking and express lanes for hybrid cars, grants to pay closing costs on homes purchased in the vicinity of work, and cash rebates for solar installations, energy-efficient appliances, and low-flow toilets. All of that constituted a major first step away from a fossil-fuel-dependent society towards an environmentally sustainable one.

It should also be noted that greenhouse gas reduction became a bipartisan affair at the grassroots level, even if it did not in Washington, D.C. Republican Governors Arnold Schwarzenegger of California and

Charlie Crist of Florida were in the vanguard of those who defied the intransigence of George W. Bush, the titular head of their party at the time. We thus had a diverse crew of officials at the state and local levels adopting the emission-reduction strategies necessary for our nation to remain a thriving democracy and world leader.

As referenced earlier in this book, Japan and parts of Europe, through substantial national government subsidies, led the way as Washington lagged in providing adequate fiscal incentives for renewable energy development during the Bush years. The task of drawing even with our allies and eventually surpassing them was left to Bush's successors, starting with Barack Obama. Early in 2009, the United States actually did supplant Germany as the world's leading producer of wind energy, no thanks to Bush, but ironically due in large part to commercial activity in his home state of Texas.[5]

Important elements of the private sector also began facing up to the modern-day environmental challenge. A host of individual businesses and industry trade organizations joined a climate registry established in 2008 by 39 states, five Canadian provinces, two Mexican states and three Native American tribes. All members of the registry had to report their greenhouse gas emissions annually as a first step towards creating a comprehensive regulatory regime to decrease heat-trapping pollutants in the atmosphere.

In addition, some enlightened companies with household names voluntarily began launching environmental initiatives. For example, General Electric, DuPont, and a number of other blue chip corporations linked up with environmental groups in 2006 to form the U.S. Climate Action Partnership. Together, they started lobbying for carbon dioxide emission reductions of 10 to 30 percent over a 15-year period and for an additional decrease by 2050.[6] A further positive contribution was made by the 400 or so companies that specialized in developing filters and other carbon-mitigation projects of use to major industrial polluters.[7] In the corporate world, energy efficiency is becoming universally regarded as a revenue-producer.

On a much smaller scale, seafood restaurants engaged in the periodic removal of dangerously depleted fish as selections on their menus. The motivation may have been purely pragmatic, but with biodiversity in the balance, why quibble over a lack of altruism? Every little bit of conservation helps.

Private investment in clean energy technologies amounted to $8.6 billion in 2006, a 69 percent increase over 2005. DuPont excelled in this respect. In 2007, the company streamlined its production processes to reduce greenhouse gas emissions by 72 percent below 1991 levels and recorded $3 billion in savings by doing so, even as the listless Bush administration looked on.

Another optimistic trend: as referenced earlier, an increasing number of participants in the private sector have come to understand that technology offers a pathway to continued prosperity when it is able to mimic nature. Conversely, just as heartening is their realization that technology is ultimately doomed to disappoint when designed to conquer nature.

Seeing the Light

Americans on an individual basis have gingerly begun to take modest steps towards an environmentally sustainable lifestyle. A 2008 Stanford University poll found that seven out of ten respondents had replaced some of their incandescent lighting with ultra-energy-efficient fluorescent bulbs. Hybrid vehicles, especially the Toyota Prius, were no longer curiosities on the road, although its proliferation was more likely due to higher gasoline prices than to pangs of conscience over environmental degradation.

While the mainstream media's general indifference towards the need for change was bad news, the good news was that an environmental activist message was permeating the public consciousness through niche publications. This is not to suggest that such publications were more "moral," just that they were constantly seeking to differentiate themselves in a crowded field; and to accomplish that, they sometimes resorted to environmental advocacy journalism. Thus, many lifestyle magazines donned a "green" mantle. Even some widely circulated periodicals—such as Vanity Fair, Newsweek, Time, and Sports Illustrated—produced environment-themed issues. Blogs and websites operated by environmental organizations and grassroots groups multiplied on the Internet, the mode of communication rapidly and relentlessly displacing much of the print media. Typical was EcoMom Alliance, which as of 2008 boasted 9,000 members across the country. Founded by an enterprising woman named Kimberly Danek Pinkson, the alliance advocated a lifestyle that amounted to much more than just buying energy-efficient light bulbs. Pinkson's outfit preached car pooling, the use of non-toxic products, buying from local farmers, utilizing carbon offsets, and a host of other measures to reduce adverse human impacts on the biosphere and integrate conservation into daily life.

So far, the closest we have come to a "conservation messiah" has been former Vice President Al Gore. In his reincarnation as a Nobel Prize winner and high-profile environmental advocate, he has attracted an international audience with his appeals for a worldwide campaign to curb global warming. Political leaders ignore this growing public sentiment at their peril.

Another hopeful sign is that virtually every institution of higher learning throughout our nation has added or is considering adding courses in environmental studies to their curriculums.[8] Such academic exposure has certainly been a significant factor in the keener environmental sensitivity younger generations display when compared to their elders. Financial pressures, exacerbated by the 2008 recession, forced some colleges to reduce their environmental academic programs; but the programs—and the moral obligation to offer them—were too well entrenched for the hard times to cause anything more than a temporary setback.[9] Moreover, outside the formal curriculum, environmental values were being introduced into the classroom at the middle school and high school level by such organizations as the non-profit Colorado Springs-based Green Education Foundation. The Foundation was able to reach more than a million students across the nation with a national public awareness campaign conveying the virtues of waste reduction.[10] Some unsympathetic parents complained that their kids were being brainwashed. If that were the case, it was brainwashing desperately needed to enhance the odds of a better quality of life in the years ahead.

Classroom indoctrination is a welcome tool of enlightenment, but what happens when students leave academia and enter the rough and tumble outside world? If they make a mess of nature, do they have what it takes to make amends and apply what they learned in school? Assuming they have the motivation and access to the required resources, the outcome may well depend on how far the deterioration has progressed. What is encouraging is that there are often ample opportunities for at least partial atonement.

The prime example can be found in central Florida. To facilitate commercial traffic, Congress long ago ordered the U.S. Army Corps of Engineers to transform the once-meandering Kissimmee River into a 53-mile-long, straight-as-an-arrow channel. Much was ventured in the enterprise, pitifully little was gained, and ultimately a tremendous amount was lost in terms of wildlife habitat, flood control, and water quality. A contrite Congress authorized the Corps to engage in a 12-year, $578 million effort to reclaim 40 miles of original river channel, 39 square miles of valuable floodplain wildlife habitat, and 27,000 acres of wetlands.

The Corps' restoration program soon reaped dividends with the return of a host of indigenous species. That was remarkable, considering that more than 90 percent of the waterfowl had vanished from the area following the conversion of the river into little more than a glorified, 30-foot-deep ditch.[11] The water quality of the Kissimmee River flowing into Lake Okeechobee also improved—an important development because the lake constitutes a significant source of hydration for South Florida, including the majestic Everglades, which as earlier noted is the continental United States' only semi-tropical wilderness and has been at risk of being drained by encroaching urbanization. It just might be that in this instance, humanity will ultimately make the appropriate restitution to nature on a

Kissimmee River—Straightening out a river

grand scale.

Kissimmee may constitute the top of the line in positive ecological engineering to restore nature's grandeur, but more modest acts of redemption have been taking place across the country. Among the most notable have been projects to remove levees in order to reclaim wetlands and natural flood plains in Louisiana, Oregon, and Illinois.[12]

Future Quest

The status quo remains a significant obstacle to progress where people tend to focus on today and let tomorrow take care of itself. But at least in the United States, the general public has gradually become more conscious of long-term environmental threats, even if they have done relatively little to avert them. Fewer individuals are unaware of ecological deterioration, even when it proceeds at a snail's pace. (Awareness amounts to progress as long as it doesn't serve as a prolonged excuse for inaction.) Conservation is more in vogue, even if its expression can be selective and at times cosmetic, as in the case of the widespread ceremonial observation of "Earth Hour." In the early evening of March 29, 2008, many cities around the world agreed to shut off the lights of their buildings for 60 minutes to symbolize support of energy conservation. Environmental sensitivity was on display in what was officially to become an annual event. Hopefully, that global intensity will eventually spread to the other 364 days of the year.

Community gardens, which defray some of the enormous energy costs of importing food from faraway places, have been proliferating in our country as well as abroad. Pending Congressional legislation would provide tax breaks to city dwellers who cover their roofs with natural insulation in the form of vegetation.[13] An innovative extension of this effort has emerged in the United States. Local community organizers and individuals are gaining permission to plant fruit trees in city parks and other urban public property and subsequently sharing the harvest with people in the neighborhood, often from low income strata.[14]

In the private sector, the Palo Alto, California-based Bon Appetit national restaurant chain, displayed its civic conscience by setting aside a day (September 30, 2008) for an "eat local" theme in its 400 cafés across the land. Corporate management required that at least 20 percent of the fare served at each outlet be derived from sources within a 150-mile radius to demonstrate the energy savings and high nutritional quality associated with locally grown food.[15]

Have grassroots trends like these created a climate for some enterprising (and gutsy) politician to render large-scale environmental justice to future generations? The moment of truth is fast approaching. Even President George W. Bush's painfully sluggish response team began late in his second term to react, albeit in limited fashion, to the challenge of reducing dependency on fossil fuel. His team presided over passage of energy legislation that would phase out the availability of incandescent light bulbs and replace them with the compact fluorescents that win awards for efficiency, if not beauty.

Between 1980 and 2008, the German government had a much more ambitious "green" energy program than we did. Europeans have also been more aggressive than we have when it comes to auto-efficiency standards, having raised their requirement to 49 miles per gallon. (It is only a matter of time before Americans chuck their 27-plus mpg and follow suit.) Officials in Berlin enacted laws requiring their country to shut down its centuries-old, polluting hard-coal industry by 2018 and fill the void primarily with renewable energy sources such as wind and solar. Indeed, during much of the 21st century's first decade, governments throughout Europe and the leaders in Japan and China moved much more aggressively than the United States in subsidizing the development and distribution of a full range of renewable energy alternatives.

Our overseas friends' superior enterprise could be traced not just to a lack of ideological bias that American conservatives directed against "left wing favored" renewables. Major factors were a greater population density and a more modest natural-resource base. Our allies across the Atlantic were also influenced by such studies as the well-documented work of the European Renewable Energy Council (EREC) and the environmental group, Greenpeace.[16] That 210-page EREC report detailed how renewable energy could meet all of the world's energy demands by 2090. The EREC conclusion may be debatable, but one thing is indisputable: the transition away from a dependency on finite polluting fossil fuel will require trillions of dollars in government subsidies and private investment. Since that transition is inevitable, humanity has no rational choice but to confront the daunting numbers, and it has begun to do so.

There is another cause for optimism. Most people instinctively favor preservation of wilderness for wilderness' sake, a preference that is undermined only by struggles for daily survival in the face of abject poverty. Hence, if we can dramatically mitigate poverty, there is an excellent chance that what is left of the unspoiled natural world will be spared for us—and future generations.

Successful Copycats

Clearly, we can manipulate nature to our advantage if we are able to act in symmetry with the basic functions of natural systems, whereas we are ultimately bound to suffer grievously if we cannot. There is no question that the human race has the capacity to co-exist harmoniously with the environment. As was previously noted, the use of solar panels to heat water and generate electricity, whether in an American suburb or a rural Indian village, exemplifies a successful synergy. Brazilian rubber-tapping operations that harvest their product in a sustainable manner in the Amazon jungle, and African safaris that deploy cameras rather than rifles against wildlife are instances of environmentally sustainable commercial ventures.

There are numerous other examples of successful environmental accommodation. Well-thought-out zoning laws draw an appropriate balance between development and preservation. Harvesting timber through selective thinning, rather than through clearcutting, preserves invaluable old-growth stands and avoids soil erosion. Integrated pest management meshes with nature in a manner that enhances agricultural productivity while minimizing highly toxic pesticide use that can reduce soil fertility and wipe out beneficial species as well as targeted ones. Restoring coastal marshes (even if they don't always end up with their original rich, biological texture) serves to reinstate nature's buffers against hurricanes and tidal waves.

Good Samaritans

There may be a mindless beast in all of us, but not all of us are mindless beasts, and therein resides another cause for hope in retaining what remains of the Earth's incredibly bountiful biodiversity. Throughout history, many individuals have made valiant efforts to save threatened species from extinction. No one was a greater advocate for the survival of lower life forms' survival than Dr. Albert Schweitzer, the Nobel Prize winning philosopher. In the first half of the 20th century, he urged mankind to revere the life of every living creature as much as was conceivably possible. Noting that human beings were cognitively superior organisms, he considered eradication of lower life forms a perversion of that supremacy— and he practiced what he preached.

Today, animal activists and organizations solely dedicated to safeguarding species and threatened habitats abound throughout the world, and within the crusaders' ranks, some individuals stand out. Jane Goodall won international acclaim for her campaign to save chimpanzees in the African wild. She then proceeded to broaden her horizons. In 1991, she established the "Roots and Shoots" program in which tens of thousands of youngsters in 114 countries were signed up to interact through the Internet and launch local projects to clean up and preserve the environment. Some other daring preservationist advocates are less well-known. For example, two Lebanese women, 57-year-old Mona Khalil and 48-year-old Habiba Syed, braved cannon shells to rescue green turtle hatchlings on a Mediterranean beach in the midst of artillery exchanges between the Israelis and Hezbollah guerillas in August 2006.

The ultimate outcome of these organizations' and individuals' campaigns to save what remains of the Earth's biodiversity is uncertain.

Dead Sea—A peace maker

But never has the effort been so well organized and international in scope, thereby evoking cautious optimism, provided major inroads are made in rolling back global poverty.

Magic Formulas

The universality of environmental concerns has demonstrated the potential to bring about cooperation where enmity and violence have long held sway. For instance, water will be the ultimate peacekeeper in the arid Middle East. If not, everyone in the end is destined to lose. Edgy collaboration already exists to some extent between Israelis and the populations in neighboring Arab states.

An example of what lies ahead: Jordan has won the cooperation of Israelis and Palestinians to transfer water from the Red Sea to replenish a fast-dwindling Dead Sea. Jordanian (and to a lesser extent Israeli) tourism depends on such a transfer, as does a desalinization plant that provides Amman with precious water for drinking and irrigation.

Humanity has been war-prone from the start, but climate change and other globally interconnected environmental challenges could just as easily alter the pattern as perpetuate it. Shouldn't conflict subside when it dawns on mankind that international détente is essential to the perpetuation of life itself? After all, what sets human beings apart from other earthly organisms is the use of rational thought to reign in instinctive violent impulses.

In the industrial world, the voluntary simplicity lifestyle described earlier in the book has begun to attract converts weary of the rat race. Their growing numbers increase the prospect of a more judicious interaction with nature in the years ahead.

A few features of voluntary simplicity have already been incorporated into the mainstream of our society. Recycling is no longer an anomaly (although it seems to be practiced much more religiously in some communities than in others). New Urbanism is beginning to take root, hopefully marking the beginning of the end of sprawl and its plethora of environmental negatives. The revolutionary paradigm can be found in scattered locations around the country, especially in Florida where the concept of modern self-contained, energy-efficient communities was shaped by the University of Miami's pioneering School of Architecture.

Obama

The move to set our country on an environmentally sustainable course has been percolating from the ground up. But the pace of that progress can never match the speed generated by decisive leadership at the top. Nor can the grassroots confer the same degree of permanency as an edict from on high. That is why our destiny will greatly depend on

the emergence of leaders with the ability to rally the country to meet the
awesome environmental challenges of the 21st century. It will take great
courage for a president to push ahead with a controversial agenda of
systematically restructuring our economy to no longer rely on obsessive
material acquisition and planned obsolescence. It becomes even a tougher
task if it occurs in the midst of seemingly more immediate high-profile
problems—a severe recession, widespread unemployment, terrorist-related
national security threats, military conflicts, and a health care system badly
in need of reform.

A return to frugality not evidenced in our nation since World War II
will need to occur. Some initially wrenching choices will have to be made in
order to live within nature's constraints and our own means. The transition
can be achieved if the leader is skillful enough to convincingly communicate
that such lifestyle changes—along with fulfillment of a custodial obligation
to keep the planet biologically viable—are the only sure paths to enduring
prosperity. Beyond that, he (or she) must possess sufficient perseverance
and political acumen to navigate initially controversial reforms past a
sometimes-balky Congress and skeptical general public.

It helps the cause if some sort of scarcity forces Americans to
reassess any spendthrift habits they might have. The fiscal meltdown in
the United States (and globally) in 2009 was a case in point. Although
it created temporary widespread hardship, it also compelled many
consumption-oriented, debt-ridden Americans to trim the fat off their
lifestyle, an unlikely metamorphosis in more prosperous times.

Enter the new American president, Barack Obama. Clearly, the
moment was ripe for a president with his astute intellect, bountiful
charisma, extraordinary oratory skills, and progressive vision to set in
motion the dramatic change that the challenging times demanded.

In contrast to his predecessor, Obama recognized that sovereign
self-interest alone could not carry the day in a modern world where the
fate of all nations had become intertwined. Soon after being elected to the
presidency, Obama enumerated a list of major challenges facing humanity,
ranging from environmental degradation and nuclear weapon proliferation
to international terrorism and age-old regional conflicts. He then went
on to say that they were "challenges that no single nation, no matter how
powerful, can confront alone. The United States must lead the way. But our
best chance to solve these unprecedented problems comes from acting in
concert with other nations… Let us not allow whatever differences we have
with other nations to stop us from coming together around those solutions
that are essential to our survival and success."[17]

Not only Americans were impressed. Many around the world were
enthralled by the bold words of this young president, and obviously, so was

Obama—The challenge of change

the panel that awarded him the Nobel Peace Prize only nine months into his term.

Gripped by fiscal crisis, our nation was in a mood for change, and Obama had a forward-looking set of political appointees and a Congress controlled by his own party to help carry out his visionary agenda. Just as importantly, he demonstrated a keen awareness that time was running out on our chances to slow climate change and halt the degradation of the Earth's biosphere. This realization was made clear in his presidential campaign when he laid out a plan to gradually replace carbon-polluting fossil fuel with clean, renewable energy and "green" our economy in general. New jobs would be created and environmental protection strengthened through a single transformational energy policy.

Prospects for Obama's grand design were enhanced by the public's conviction that high gasoline prices had nowhere to go but up. That widespread belief motivated people out of pragmatism, if not conscience, to edge towards more conservation-oriented behavior.

Nonetheless, disengaging from a firmly entrenched status quo has always entailed painful adjustments. If Obama were to hold steady to his ambitious, albeit controversial reforms, he would run the risk of being an unpopular one-term president who would have to settle for vindication from future historians. Even if Obama were to achieve a two-term presidency during which he won large-scale public support for a leaner lifestyle, the societal evolution he envisaged would be too all-encompassing to culminate on his watch. That would not detract from his record of accomplishment, since he would have established a new direction and cleared the most difficult hurdles, thereby paving the way for his successors to complete the task.

Obama is guaranteed a unique place in American history as the nation's first African-American president, and the Afghanistan military campaign will be the cover page of his administration. But when the historical dust clears, his overall performance will be judged by whether his stirring appeals to the national conscience, combined with the public's growing concern about an environmentally stressed planet, lead to widespread acceptance—and practice—of a sustainable lifestyle as the norm.

Reflection

What centuries so often fraught with failure have taught us (if we deign to listen) is that to come to terms with nature, we must first come to terms with ourselves. That means a willingness to confront our destructive impulses and minimize them as best we can, a process which gives rise to the humble realization that we are a part of—rather than apart from—a sphere greater than our own and should act accordingly.

   In a world replete with diverse cultures, moral relativity has a place, which significantly narrows the applicability of moral absolutism. That having been said, there are ecologically-related moral constants that clearly transcend all societies, religions, races, and ethnicities—a respect for the natural world and a custodial obligation that if properly brought to bear will ensure the preservation of a viable, productive environment for generations to come.

THE END

ADDENDUM

—

GULF SPILL

AN EFFECTIVE STRATEGY for making environmental regulation politically palatable in a democratic capitalistic system is to demonstrate that its financial benefits surpass any short-term dividends from a laissez-faire approach. There is no more graphic illustration of this than BP's massive Deepwater Horizon oil rig blowout on April 20, 2010, which is likely to adversely impact the Gulf of Mexico ecosystem for decades to come.

In the aftermath of this horrendous spill that claimed 11 lives, the beleaguered advocates of offshore oil drilling defended the extraction process by making much of deep sea petroleum's importance to the economy and national security.

The truth is that what they were selling us was a short term fix. Use of the oil gushing out of the ocean's depths is a one time proposition. Exhaust the supply from that source, and the jobs and revenue vanish.

By contrast, if the renewable natural resources (i.e. fisheries, tourist beaches, hurricane-mitigating wetlands) are treated in a manner that allows them to regenerate, they will provide the region with permanent employment, perpetual cost savings, and an endless stream of substantial revenue.

As for national security, we can always obtain oil and gas from other places than the Gulf should an emergency arise. If the region's natural resources were to sustain long term damage from the negligent drill operators, however, the ensuing Gulf Coast societal instability would be a destabilizing influence on our nation's security.

Even in its earliest stages, the Deepwater Horizon spill was an excellent example of how disastrous the consequences of regulatory failure could be. On May 14, 2010, the New York Times recounted how industry-friendly federal government bureaucrats suppressed scientists' warnings about ecological threats posed by the BP rig and granted permission to drill without requiring an environmental impact statement and various mandated permits.

Meanwhile, the much criticized energy industry tried to burnish its image by creating the false impression of an ecological paradise in the waters beneath working rigs, and was aided and abetted by some in the news media. Indeed, in the wake of the BP Gulf spill, a major television network, along with the New York Times, tried to balance the bad news by noting that oil rigs in the Gulf of Mexico acted as artificial reefs sheltering healthy fish populations.

These news organizations were guilty of a glaring omission. Abandoned oil rigs and platforms fit the media's idyllic description; active drilling facilities—not so much. Operational rigs routinely discharge pollutants into the sea, primarily in the form of drilling muds, cuttings, deck drainage, and petroleum residues. The drilling muds contain—among other nasty things—arsenic, lead, and mercury, ingredients that even in minute amounts can negatively impact fish. Should these fish end up on the dinner table, their bio-accumulated toxicity would pose a health threat to consumers.

Scientists have actually found that fish in the proximity of working rigs in the Gulf possess especially high concentrations of mercury (which is a particular menace to pregnant women). They also discovered that chronic exposure to less than one part per billion of the trace hydro-carbons released into the water column in a rig's normal operation can disrupt filter feeding and cause genetic damage and fatalities in fish eggs.

It should be noted that the fish hanging out near the surface in the vicinity of active rigs are not the only ones in jeopardy. According to the U.S. Department of Energy, marine organisms (including corals) on the ocean floor around the platforms can be smothered by the cumulative buildup of discharged drill cuttings or succumb from direct contact with the toxicity of the waste materials.

To those enthralled with the idea of expanding fish habitat in the Gulf by creating artificial reefs, why put fish through the punishing, sometimes fatal ordeal of ingesting toxic residues while waiting for the operational rigs to run their course? Simply sink a bunch of pilings into the sea and be done with it!

Although oil and natural gas are realistically a significant part of our energy mix for the immediate future, the BP Gulf blowout dictated that all offshore drilling be put on hold until the cause of the catastrophe was identified and reliable preventive measures were put in place. Once that occurred, previous functional offshore rigs could resume operation. Ideally, no new leases would be issued until all existing ones on land and sea had been checked out. Hopefully in the interim, the transition to alternative sources of energy, including wind, solar, and biomass, would accelerate, lessening the need for further drilling.

In the midst of all of this was the glaring human tragedy of the Louisiana coastal dwellers. The oil industry saddled them with the moral dilemma of having to sacrifice their environment and well-being of future generations or risk losing their livelihood.

The BP spill only magnified the ecological damage the oil industry had been inflicting for decades on Louisianans. Yet residents were able to remain in a state of denial because of the corporate contribution to the local economy and the incremental pace of the environmental degradation. Long before the BP blowout, the petroleum industry was wreaking havoc, not by spills as much as by dredging and carving shipping canals through the marshes. This precipitated salt water intrusion which killed the grasses and led to the land destabilizing and sinking into the sea. Louisiana has lost an average of 24 square miles of its coast every year in this manner. At such a rate, one-third of its remaining wetlands will be gone by 2050, and all will vanish within two centuries. Not a pretty picture for a state that has relied on its wetlands to act as a buffer against the periodic hurricanes roaring off the Gulf of Mexico.

It doesn't have to be this way. An aforementioned crash program to develop clean, renewable energy alternatives to the Gulf Coast's offshore oil-based economy offers ultimate salvation. As for those Louisianans reluctant to gradually disengage from reliance on oil industry wages, it should be noted that the supposed economic bonanza that petroleum companies bestow on the state is vastly overblown. Despite all the oil money, Louisiana ranks 40th out of 50 states in per capita income.

But isn't a shift to solar, wind, biomass, and other renewable energy sources (using conservation and natural gas as bridges) farfetched? Skeptics should be apprised that by 2010, renewable energy already comprised 10 percent of the nation's energy production and was increasing faster than nuclear power, which contributed approximately the same share to our energy mix.

As was previously mentioned in this book, researchers at the University of California at Berkley see brighter days ahead for clean energy, having concluded that an investment in renewables creates ten times more jobs than putting the same amount of money into fossil fuels. Reference has also been made to respected scientists, who have outlined a plausible scenario in which solar could provide 50 percent of the nation's energy by the year 2050.

Salvation won't arrive overnight. But if government policies at all levels provide tax incentives and subsidies to establish a robust alternative energy industry in the state, Louisianans will eventually be able to shed their petroleum shackles and accompanying painful toxic legacy to future generations.

NOTES
—

INTRODUCTION
1.   "Oceana: Too Few Fish," *FAO's State of World Fisheries and Aquaculture*, 5/26/08.
2.   John Kusler & B.L. Bedford, Association of State Wetland Managers, *Ecological Applications*, 1996.
3.   James Titus, U. S. Environmental Protection Agency.
4.   *Environmental News Service*, 10/13/06.
5.   *Manchester Guardian*, 6/06/08.
6.   *English Government Economics Service*, 2006.

CHAPTER ONE: TAMPERING WITH NATURE
1.   *New York Times*, p.A6, 3/20/09.
2.   U.S. Geological Survey 2007 Open File Report, p.1169.
3.   *Le Monde*, 9/21/06.
4.   Woodrow Wilson International Center Symposium, 8/2/06.
5.   Constanza, "Ramsar Convention Wetlands," *World Resources Institute*, 12/21/00.
6.   Jungle soil derives its nutrients from the roots of native plants. Remove the plants and the thin soil quickly erodes, leaving a wasteland and loads of extinct species in its wake, as the settlers soon learned.
7.   *Pew Charitable Trust Study*, 10/30/08.
8.   Attempts have been made to revive the wolf population in the Western United States with a smattering of success. But we still haven't learned our lesson. The animal remains reviled by many in that part of the country, and some wolf-haters are always looking for opportunities—legal and illegal—to set back the recovery program.
9.   *New York Times*, 1/11/08.
10.   Edward Flattau, 8/15/92.

CHAPTER THREE: RESPECT FOR GOD'S WORK
1.   Edward Flattau, 4/26/00.
2.   *Washington Post*, 5/24/81.
3.   *Reuters*, 3/10/07 and *Journal of Natural Products*, 3/23/07.
4.   *American Chemical Society's Journal of Natural Products*, 9/25/09.
5.   Dr. Eric Chivian and Dr. Aaron Bernstein, "Sustaining Life, How Human Health Depends on Biodiversity," *Harvard Medical School's Center for Health and the Global Environment, Oxford University Press*, 2008.

CHAPTER FOUR: ABUSE OF FELLOW HUMANS
1.   John Vidal, *Manchester Guardian*, 2/20/09.
2.   *Boston Globe*, pg. 1, 8/19/07.
3.   *Los Angeles Times*, 10/8/06.
4.   *Journal of American Medical Association*, 5/17/08.
5.   *Washington Post*, pg. 1, 6/12/08.
6.   *OMB Watch*, 5/1/07.
7.   Those countries would benefit from providing the raw materials and low-cost labor necessary to meet our insatiable demands for finished goods.
8.   A notable exception was a Southern California single, unemployed mother who used in vitro fertilization to give birth to octuplets in February 2009, on top of the six young children she already had. Her behavior raised serious bioethical and economic questions that triggered a negative public reaction. The adverse environmental ramifications of such large broods were also serious matters but were conspicuously absent in media coverage, probably more out of ignorance than design.
9.   *London Telegraph*, 7/25/08.
10.   "Saving Water: From Field to Fork-Curbing Losses and Wastage in the Food Chain," *UN Food and Agriculture Organization*, 5/14/08.
11.   "Environmental Food Crisis", *UNEP Report*, 2/17/09.
12.   Center for Environment and Population, 9/06.
13.   "World Overpopulation Awareness, Sustainability: Carrying Capacity and Consumption," 3/31/08.
14.   Alan Durning, "How Much is Enough," W.W. Norton, 1992.
15.   Poll conducted by Deloitte, Spring 2008.
16.   "The Cost of Climate Change," Tufts University study commissioned by the Natural Resources Defense Council, May 2008.
17.   "Nairobi," *Environmental News Service*, 3/19/09.
18.   "The Economics of 350: The Benefit and Costs of Climate Stabilization," *Economics for Equity and Environment*, October 2009.

CHAPTER FOUR: CORPORATE INTEREST
1.   In a 2006 interview, Dr. Elias Zerhouni, director of the National Institute of Health, warned that the practice of medicine in this country was financially unsustainable, and if bankruptcy were to be avoided, prevention would have to supplant treatment of expensive diseases whenever possible.
2.   EPA, "The Benefits and Costs of the Clean Air Act," 1970-1990.
3.   "Hidden Costs of Energy: Unpriced Consequences of Energy Production and Use," *National Research Council Report,* 10/19/09.
4.   *New York Times*, p.A16, 10/20/09.
5.   "Oceans Under the Gun," *Environment America Research and*

Policy Center, October 2009.

6.   United Nations Environmental Programme, sponsor of report by the Economics of Ecosystems and Biodiversity Commission, 11/16/09.

7.   United Nations Environment Programme press release, 10/14/09.

8.   "Economists and Climate Change," *New York University Law School's Institute for Policy Integrity*, November 2009.

9.   Congressional Research Service, 10/4/04.

10.   *Green Scissors Report*, 2001.

11.   The private sector demonstrated in 2009 that it still wielded considerable influence. In a World Water Forum held in Istanbul and attended by officials from 150 countries, a Ministerial Declaration was issued that defined water as a human need rather than a human right. Twenty nations, mostly from the developing world, signed a counter-declaration stating that access to potable water and decent sanitation was a basic human right, and its implementation should be of paramount importance. Given the cost of rescuing the 900 million people without clean drinking water and the 2.5 billion souls lacking adequate sanitation facilities, there was no mad scramble to join the 20 conscientious objectors. Unfortunately, we were one of the many nations not prepared to go beyond asserting water was a "need," which was just a euphemistic way of saying "no money, no honey." As has so often been the case, mercenary concerns were a constraint on the brotherhood of man. (Environmental News Service, Istanbul, 3/27/09).

12.   Under protest from the Democrats, Bush reluctantly withdrew the nomination.

13.   *London Daily Mail*, 9/13/07.

CHAPTER FIVE: MORAL ABSOLUTISM

1.   *AVSC Working Paper*, No. 13, 10/01.

2.   Guttmacher Institute, 10/07.

3.   *IPS*, 11/30/07.

4.   *Reuters*, 10/30/07.

CHAPTER SIX: MILITARIZATION

1.   *World Almanac*, p.149, 2007,.

2.   *National Priorities Project*, 4/6/07.

3.   World Bank data.

4.   National Priorities Project 1/9/10.

5.   "A Climate of Conflict," published by International Alert, 11/4/07.

6.   "From Conflict to Peace Building–The Role of Natural Resources and the Environment," *United Nations Environmental Programme*, 2/20/09.

7.   Andrew Pendleton, "Truly Inconvenient–Tackling Poverty and

Climate Change at Once," *Christian Aid*, 11/4/07.
8.   Lester Brown, "Plan B 3.0," W.W. Norton, 2008.
9.   WorldWatch Institute update, 2/13/08.
10.   United Nations Environmental Programme press release, 9/5/08.
11.   American Cancer Society.
12.   *San Francisco Chronicle*, 7/20/07.
13.   *Associated Press*, 7/16/07.
14.   *Manchester Guardian*, 2/21/08.
15.   *New York Times,* pg. A11, 8/21/09.

CHAPTER SEVEN: RESPECT FOR THE LAW
1.   *New York Times*, 9/22/06.
2.   *USA Today*, p.11, 5/8/07.
3.   Frank Bandiera, American Psychosomatic Society Meeting, University of Miami School of Medicine, et al, 2009.
4.   Ibid.
5.   *Washington Post*, 11/17/06.
6.   Edward Flattau, 12/19/81.

CHAPTER NINE: ALL THINGS EQUAL
1.   It took a while for all of these groups to realize they were among the most vulnerable to industrial pollution and ought to be in the front lines of the environmental movement.
2.   NWF press release, 7/10/09.
3.   Edward Flattau, 4/09/05.
4.   *Parade Magazine*, 7/29/07.
5.   MSPCA at Northeastern University, 1997.
6.   Alan Guttmacher Institute.
7.   World Health Organization and Guttmacher Institute, Lancet, 10/12/07.
8.   National Survey of Family Growth, *USA Today*, 3/27/08.
9.   Center for Disease Control, 7/20/09.
10.   British Medical Journal, August 2007.
11.   *Feminist Wire*, 7/5/07.
12.   This ideological myopia was thankfully dispensed with by Barack Obama.
13.   *Millennium Development Goals Report*, 2007.
14.   Some scientists contend that has already occurred. The international think tank, Global Footprint Network, maintains that people are using up the Earth's resources at one-and-a-half times the rate these resources can be replaced. *Agence France-Presse*, November 24, 2009.
15.   State of the World Population 2009, United Nations Population Fund.

16.   Oscar Wilde.
17.   All modern-day presidents, up to and including Barack Obama, presided over opulent inauguration-day programs; but Bush's participation was particularly grating, given his particularly miserly policies towards the impoverished at home and abroad.

CHAPTER TEN: POLITICAL COURAGE AND COWARDICE
1.   *New York Times*, 10/17/09.
2.   "Temporary" is the operative word here because unchecked power in the hands of inherently flawed human beings, no matter how benevolently applied, can turn bad in a hurry.
3.   *New York Times*, p.D3, 4/15/08.
4.   Todd Woody, *Grist*, 1/6/10.
5.   *Associated Press*, 7/7/07.
6.   *New York Times*, p.18, 4/23/07.
7.   *Washington Post*, 8/21/08.
8.   *Los Angeles Times*, 3/12/08.
9.   Edward Flattau, 2/5/76.
10.   David Helvarg, "The War Against the Greens," Sierra Club Books, 1994.

CHAPTER ELEVEN: MORE UPSTARTS
1.   Only after the European economy finally rose from the World War Two ashes in the 1980s did widespread environmental sensitivity begin to kick in.
2.   Pacific Environment, San Francisco, 3/2/09.
3.   *IPS*, 11/30/07.
4.   *Associated Press*, 4/7/08.

CHAPTER TWELVE: BRAINWASHING
1.   *Energy Citations Database*, Doc. 5414976.
2.   All the more reason to have accompanied the misleading ads with a clarifying addendum that would have put the public on notice, and possibly saved the American automobile companies from themselves.
3.   *International Herald Tribune*, p.1, 7/22/08.
4.   "Products, Packaging and US Greenhouse Gas Emissions," Product Policy Institute, September 2009.
5.   Ben Bolch and Harold Lyons, "Apocalypse Not," Cato Institute, 1993.
6.   "Ecology in the 20th Century," Yale University Press, 1989.

CHAPTER THIRTEEN: TOOLS OF THE TRADE
1.   Democratic minority staff report of House Committee on

Government Reform, 6/21/02.
2.   *Journal of NCI.* Vol. 86, No.24, 12/21/94.
3.   *National Cancer Institute, Trends Progress Report,* 2005 update.
4.   Environmental Protection Agency's Inspector General's Report,
7/24/08, *Associated Press,* 7/25/08.
5.   *BuzzFlash,* 8/19/04.
6.   DNC memo, 3/1/06.
7.   Alliance to Stop the War on the Poor press release, 7/29/08.
8.   Harvard School of Public Health, publication, Acquire Immune
Deficiency Syndrome publication, Vol.49, No.4, 12/08.
9.   A recent study added dementia to the list of adverse health effects.
10.   Investigation by Rep. Henry Waxman's, D-Calif., House Committee
on Oversight and Government Reform, September 25, 2007.
11.   *Christian Science Monitor,* 11/24/08.

CHAPTER FOURTEEN: DEFENDING THE INDEFENSIBLE
1.   *American Smokers Journal,* Fall, 1994.
2.   *New York Times,* 9/14/93.

CHAPTER FIFTEEN: PERFIDIOUS MYTHS
1.   Joint Center for Political and Economic Studies poll, 9/30/09.
2.   *Black Agenda Report,* October 3-8, 2007 issue.
3.   *USA Today,* p.1 7/20/08.

CHAPTER SIXTEEN: RAMPANT HUBRIS
1.   Luke 12:15.
2.   Psalm 8.
3.   World Health Organization.
4.   Pekka Haavisto, UNEP's Iraq Task Force Chairman, June 2005.
5.   *Reuters,* 8/24/08.
6.   Opinion Research Business poll, 8/12/07.
7.   FAFO Institute, 2004.
8.   Where would humanity be without sorghum? The nutritional
needs of more than 500 million people in 98 countries are filled by this
nondescript cereal plant, whose unique genetic makeup enables it to thrive
in arid regions where other crops would perish. [*Science Magazine,* 1/30/09,
Vol.323, p.573]
9.   *Orion Magazine,* p.31, January/February 2008.
10.   Jeanne McDermatt, *Smithsonian Magazine,* December, 1984; Ed
Wagner, *Associated Press,* May, 1989.
11.   *Washington Post,* p.A3, 5/1/08.
12.   *Climate Wire,* 6/02/08.
13.   OECD data, 2007.

14.   OECD, 2007, data based on latest recorded year—2005; the U.S. number is derived from EPA Municipal Solid Waste Generation facts and figures for 2007.
15.   "Sustainability: Carrying Capacity and Consumption," 3/31/08.

CHAPTER SEVENTEEN: AFFIRMATION—AND BREACH—OF TRUST
1.   *Wall Street Journal,* June 1997.
2.   *Washington Post,* 4/23/08.
3.   EPA document, 2/12/1982.
4.   *U.S. Public Health Service*, July 1999.
4.   *Journal of the National Cancer Institute*, Vol. 101, No.10. 5/20/ 09.
5.   M.A. Palmer, E.S. Bernhardt et al, "Mountain top Mining Consequences", *Science Magazine*, Vol. 327, January 8, 2010, P.148.
6.   *Associated Press*, 2/5/08.
7.   In April of 2010, President Obama, Bush's more environmentally sensitive successor, instituted strict guidelines designed to severely curtail if not eliminate altogether mountain top mining. Perhaps some of Appalachia's mountains and sparkling clear streams will survive after all.
8.   NRDC press release, 10/23/07.
9.   Centers For Disease Control.
10.   *Washington Post*, 4/23/08.

CHAPTER EIGHTEEN: IDEOLOGY, DEVALUED INTENTIONS, AND GOOD DEEDS
1.   Some 2900 municipalities in the United States have a smoking ban in public areas. American Non-Smokers Rights Foundation, 7/1/08.
2.   Susan Freinkel, "Why I Still Believe in the Zoo", *On Earth*, Spring 2008, p.21.
3.   Association of Zoos and Aquariums, 12/18/07.
4.   "Encyclical," *Charity and Truth*, 7/09/09.
5.   *UNEP Year Book*, 2009.
6.   *New York Times*, 3/21/09.
7.   "Green Guilt Survey, Rechargeable Battery Recycling Corporation," *USA Today*, 5/8/08.
8.   *New York Times*, 5/10/08.
9.   *National Geographic, Greendex,* 2008.
10.   In National Geographic's 2009 Greendex, the United States performed slightly better, but improvement appeared due to recessionary pressures rather than attitudinal change, and Americans still brought up the rear in the survey.

CHAPTER NINETEEN: THE GOOD
1. *Independent*, 1/31/2008.
2. *National Geographic News*, 1/29/08.
3. *Japan Times*, 8/25/08.
4. "State of the World, 2008," Worldwatch Institute, p.42.
5. "State of the World, 2008," Worldwatch Institute, p.40.
6. United Nations Environmental Programme press release, 5/28/08.

CHAPTER TWENTY: THE BAD
1. Fall 2000.

CHAPTER TWENTY-ONE: THE UGLY
1. Cambridge Reports.
2. Greenberg Quinlan Rosner Research, 7/24/08.
3. U.S. Energy Information Administration, 9/24/08.
4. *Environmental News Service*, 5/13/09.
5. Brookhaven National Research Center, 12/16/07.

CHAPTER TWENTY-TWO: FORMULA FOR SUCCESS
1. USDA data, 2002.
2. *Reuters*, 10/22/08].
3. "Coastal Capital: Belize," World Resources Institute, 11/13/08.
4. DPT Environ. *New York Times*, 12/27/08.
5. *Science*, p.752, 2/8/08.
6. Rachel Kurowski, *Associated Press*, 9/19/09.
7. Residential Conservation Trust, 2009.
8. *Greenwire*, 4/9/09.
9. *Reuters*, 11/18/09.
10. Even the most successful transition will probably take several generations.
11. *Washington Post*, p.A1, 6/12/08.
12. Prof. Jon A. Krosnick, Stanford University, *USA Today*, 8/14/08.
13. *USA Today*, p.7d, 8/13/09.
14. Bob Inglis and Arthur B. Laffer, *New York Times* op-ed, 12/28/08.

CHAPTER TWENTY-THREE: FIGHTING THE DOUBTS
1. *Science Daily*, 1/10/02.
2. Endangered Species Handbook, Animal Welfare Institute, 2005.

CHAPTER TWENTY-FOUR: THE UPSIDE
1. The recession of 2008 did indeed force record-breaking numbers of Americans—whether out of a spiritual epiphany, or more likely, fiscal expediency—to back away from modern-day Christmas's compulsive

commercialism, much to the chagrin of retailers.

2.   *University of Cambridge News*, 3/13/08.
3.   *Environmental News Service*, 1/24/08.
4.   Pew Center on Global Climate Change.
5.   Our preeminence looks fleeting at the moment, given China's rapid expansion in that energy sector where it is already the world's leading manufacturer of windmills.
6.   *Washington Post*, 1/15/09.
7.   *USA Today*, 2/25/08.
8.   *Washington Post*, 6/22/08.
9.   *National Wildlife Federation Campus Ecology Survey*, 2008.
10.   *USA Today*, 1/27/09.
11.   South Florida Water Management District, 4/3/08.
12.   Cornelia Dean, *New York Times*, June 20, 2009.
13.   Office of Sen. Maria Cantwell, D-Wash., 7/11/08.
14.   *USA Today*, p. 4A, 3/9/10; *Neighborhoodfruit.com*.
15.   Bon Appetit Management Co. press release, 9/11/08. Whole Foods, a high-end grocery chain, has instituted a system in which products grown locally are labeled as such. Small family farms have been increasingly creating new business by exploiting environmental sensibilities through the marketing of locally grown agricultural products to surrounding communities. And these enterprises received a publicity boost when President Barack Obama moved to set up a farmer's market just outside the White House. Stalls were stocked with fresh foods picked from the presidential garden as well as from the fields of local farmers.
16.   *Reuters*, Planet Ark, 10/28/08.
17.   Obama weekly radio address, 4/11/09.

ILLUSTRATIONS

—

Page 34: "A limestone karst on Nauru Island as a result of the over-mining of phosphate." 4/3/07. U.S. Department of Energy's Atmospheric Radiation Measurement Program. Photo in the public domain.

Page 59: "Aerial view of Kivalina, Alaska, USA." 1999. U.S. Army Corps of Engineers. Photo in the public domain.

Page 77: "President George W. Bush addresses the class of 2007 at this

years Academy's commencement." 5/23/07. United States Coast Guard.
Photo in the public domain.

Page 82: "Marsh Iraqi Woman Manuevers Boat in Abu Sholan." 5/19/03.
Damir Sagol. All rights reserved.

Page 84: "Gorillas in Uganda and Rwanda." 3/16/08. Hjalmar Gislason.
This work is licensed under the Creative Commons Attribution 3.0 United
States License. To view a copy of this license, visit http://creativecommons.
org/licenses/by/3.0/us/ or send a letter to Creative Commons, 171 Second
Street, Suite 300, San Francisco, California, 94105, USA.

Page 104: "Flipper dolphin show at the Miami Seaquarium, Miami,
Florida." 4/16/09. Lisa Jacobs. This work is licensed under the Creative
Commons Attribution-No Derivative Works 3.0 United States License. To
view a copy of this license, visit http://creativecommons.org/licenses/by-
nd/3.0/us/ or send a letter to Creative Commons, 171 Second Street, Suite
300, San Francisco, California, 94105, USA.

Page 121: "Mayor Bloomberg." 4/21/09. Center For American Progress.
Photo By: Ralph Alswang. This work is licensed under the Creative
Commons Attribution-No Derivative Works 3.0 United States License. To
view a copy of this license, visit http://creativecommons.org/licenses/by-
nd/3.0/us/ or send a letter to Creative Commons, 171 Second Street, Suite
300, San Francisco, California, 94105, USA.

Page 130: "Mexico City Aerial View." 7/19/07. David Claassen. All rights
reserved.

Page 133: "Lake Baikal." 7/22/08. Sergey Gabdurakhamanov. This work
is licensed under the Creative Commons Attribution 3.0 United States
License. To view a copy of this license, visit http://creativecommons.org/
licenses/by/3.0/us/ or send a letter to Creative Commons, 171 Second Street,
Suite 300, San Francisco, California, 94105, USA.

Page 147: "Scenes from an operation of the Crook Lumber company of
Groveland, California." 8/7/08. Steve Ryan. This work is licensed under
the Creative Commons Attribution-Share Alike 3.0 United States License.
To view a copy of this license, visit http://creativecommons.org/licenses/by-
sa/3.0/us/ or send a letter to Creative Commons, 171 Second Street, Suite
300, San Francisco, California, 94105, USA.

Page 160: "Mountain-top removal mining." 10/12/08. The Sierra Club.

Page 169: "Brooks Range Mountains, Arctic National Wildlife Refuge. 4/5/05. United States Fish and Wildlife Service. Photo in the public domain.

Page 177: "Traffic jam on the highway during rush hour." 12/17/08. Olivier Blondeau.

Page 199: "President Reagan speaking at a rally for Senator Durenberger. 2/8/82. National Archives: Ronald Reagan Library. Photo in the public domain.

Page 207: "Sarah Palin in Savannah, Georgia, Dec 1, 2008 campaigning for the re-election of Saxy Chambliss." 12/1/08. Bruce Tuten.

Page 208: "Al Gore." 8/14/08. Center For American Progress.

Page 217: "Vatican Cityscape." 12/20/07. S. Greg Panosian.

Page 238: "Members of the Louisiana National Guard set up a road block in the upper 9th Ward of New Orleans as water in the industrial canal starts to overtop the levees and pour into the city." 9/1/08. Chuck Simmins.

Page 270: "Kissimmee River canal section." 6/1/95. U.S. Army Corps of Engineers. Photo in the public domain.